DEVELOPMENT
ECONOMICS
THROUGH THE DECADES

DEVELOPMENT ECONOMICS
THROUGH THE DECADES

A CRITICAL LOOK AT 30 YEARS OF THE WORLD DEVELOPMENT REPORT

SHAHID YUSUF

with Angus Deaton, Kemal Derviş,
William Easterly, Takatoshi Ito,
and Joseph E. Stiglitz

THE WORLD BANK
Washington, D.C.

ISBN: 978-0-8213-7255-5
eISBN: 978-0-8213-7756-7
DOI: 10.1596/978-0-8213-7255-5

Library of Congress Cataloging-in-Publication Data

Yusuf, Shahid, 1949-
Development economics through the decades : a critical look at thirty years of the world development report / by Shahid Yusuf.
    p. cm.
    Includes bibliographical references and index.
    ISBN 978-0-8213-7255-5—ISBN 978-0-8213-7756-7 (electronic)
    1. Development economics. I. Title.
HD82.Y87 2008
338.9—dc22

2008044500

CONTENTS

Foreword   *ix*
Acknowledgments   *xi*
Contributors   *xiii*

1. A Star Is Born   **1**

A Postbellum World   2
Development Becomes a Discipline and a Crusade   4
A Discipline in the Making   6
A War on Poverty and the Making of the
    World Development Report   15

2. Freeing the World of Poverty   **19**

An Innovative Report   20
No More Trickle Down   21
Adjustment Gains the Upper Hand   23
Imagine That There Is No State   32
Contesting Poverty and Inequality under Globalization   34
From Getting Prices Right to Getting Institutions Right   39

The Green Agenda and Agriculture 41
Searching for Growth, Finding Poverty 44
Achievement and Questions 47

3. **How Much Farther Can We See?** 51

Growth through Perspiration 53
From Machines to Institutions 56
Inspired Growth 63
Resource Balances and Capital Flows 67
The Role of the State 72
Reducing Poverty 75
Aid and Growth 80
A *WDR* Policy Scorecard 84

4. **Where To Now?** 89

Putting Knowledge to Work 94
Warming Climate, Scarce Water 95
The Geography of Human Habitation 98
Resilient Complex Societies 100
An Equal Marriage of Politics and Economics 102

Commentaries

The *World Development Report* at Thirty: A Birthday
Tribute or a Funeral Elegy? 105
by Angus Deaton

The World Bank and the Evolving Political Economy of
Development 115
by Kemal Derviş

The Indomitable in Pursuit of the Inexplicable: The *World
Development Reports'* Failure to Comprehend Economic
Growth Despite Determined Attempts, 1978–2008 121
by William Easterly

The Evolution of Development Economics and
East Asia's Contribution   131
by Takatoshi Ito

The *World Development Report:* Development
Theory and Policy   139
by Joseph E. Stiglitz

Appendix A   List of *World Development Reports,*
1978–2008   153

Appendix B   Citations of *World Development Reports* in
Peer-Reviewed Articles, 1990–2005   155

References   157
Index   183

Figures

1.1 Growth Rates of Developing and Developed
Countries, 1961–74   10
1.2 Growth Rates of Six Developing Countries, 1956–71   11
1.3 Average Growth Rates of Five Industrial Countries,
1871–1970   13
1.4 Per Capita Average Growth Rates of Five Industrial
Countries, 1871–1970   13
1.5 Growth Rates of Developing Countries, 1972–90   14
3.1 Net Foreign Direct Investment in South Asia and
Sub-Saharan Africa, 2000–06   68
4.1 Per Capita GDP Growth of the United States, 1870–2003 91
4.2 Per Capita GDP Growth of Korea, 1960–2003   91
C.1 The Transition to a High-Growth Path   137

Tables

2.1 Total Rain-Fed and Irrigated Land in 12 Agriculture-
Dependent Countries with High Population Growth Rates,
2000 and 2050   43

3.1 Net Foreign Direct Investment in South Asia and
Sub-Saharan Africa, 2000–06   68

3.2 Average Investment of Slow-Growing South Asian and
Sub-Saharan Africa Countries and India, 1990–2006   85

FOREWORD

The 30th anniversary of the *World Development Report* (*WDR*) is an auspicious event for the World Bank. The report has served as one of the principal and most widely read vehicles for encapsulating the Bank's knowledge of and policy recommendations on key development issues. The very earliest *WDRs* concisely summarized the Bank's views on national and sectoral development priorities with reference to the evolving global context. Since 1980, the reports have acquired a thematic focus and have provided the reader with an overview of current thinking on specific topics complemented with a wide-ranging synthesis of practical experience, all of which is anchored to the Bank's core concerns of sustainable growth and poverty alleviation.

The essay by Shahid Yusuf, himself a former director of a *World Development Report*, takes an erudite, measured, and dispassionate look over 30 years of thinking on development through the prism of the *WDR*. The essay traces the genesis of the report and accounts for its success, explains why particular topics were addressed, sums up the main messages, and distills the themes that recur in report after report. It asks whether the *WDRs* have not just illuminated a topic but also contributed to the science of policy making by delineating choices and showing clearly how specific actions can lead to predictable outcomes. The essay appropriately acknowledges the huge advances in our understanding of development made possible by empirical research; however, it also rightly notes that the forging of effective policies to promote sustainable growth, reduce poverty, contain inequality, and achieve macrostability, which are the principal objectives of the Bank's member countries, remains a complex task—in fact something of an art—with few precise and reliable rules. The stock of tested policy tools is small, and it grows slowly. Although we can all agree that institutions matter, creating and embedding new institutions remains a forbiddingly difficult exercise. And although knowledge is viewed as the principal driver of growth, policy struggles to find ways to accelerate the generation, transfer, and assimilation of knowledge.

In the final section of the essay, Yusuf discusses the future role of the *WDR* and points to some of the challenges that beckon. The list of development issues deserving the kind of illuminating and constructive attention *WDRs* can provide is a long one, and I can see the *WDRs* continuing to contribute meaningfully to the fund of knowledge and practice on development. I also expect that the reports will continue to evolve in content and focus, as they have done in the past, as the global context changes.

This essay and the crisp insightful commentaries by distinguished contributors not only provide us with fascinating perspectives on the past three decades of the *WDR* and on development economics, they also offer valuable suggestions on the orientation of *WDRs* to come.

Justin Lin
Sr. Vice President and Chief Economist
The World Bank

Acknowledgments

I thank François Bourguignon for inviting me to prepare this essay and Justin Yifu Lin, Santiago Pombo Bejarano, Stephen McGroarty, and Carlos Rossel for their encouragement and support. I am also grateful to Cindy Fisher for managing the editorial production of the book under an extraordinarily tight deadline, and to Denise Bergeron for her expert coordination of the printing process.

The draft benefited greatly from the suggestions provided by Shanta Devarajan, Francisco Ferreira, Alan Gelb, Roumeen Islam, Emmanuel Jimenez, Martin Ravallion, Ritva Reinikka, and Vinod Thomas. Any remaining errors—of omission and commission—are mine.

The assistance and comments I received from Lopamudra Chakraborti and Kaoru Nabeshima were of immense help in writing this piece. I am most grateful to both.

And finally, writing this book would have been inconceivable without the enabling home environment provided by Natasha, Zain, and Nadia, who have tolerated oceans of paper and book after book.

Contributors

Angus Deaton is Dwight D. Eisenhower Professor of Economics and International Affairs at Princeton's Woodrow Wilson School and Department of Economics. He has previously held appointments at the Universities of Bristol and Cambridge in England. In 2006, he chaired a panel charged with the evaluation of World Bank research over the previous decade. He is a Fellow of the British Academy, of the Econometric Society, and of the American Academy of Arts and Sciences. He earned bachelor's and master's degrees and a Ph.D. from the University of Cambridge, and he holds honorary degrees from the University of Rome, University College London, and the University of St. Andrews. He will serve as President of the American Economic Association in 2009.

Kemal Derviş is head of the United Nations Development Programme. He is also the Chair of the UN Development Group, a committee consisting of the heads of all UN funds, programs, and departments working on development issues around the world. Derviş was a member of the Turkish Parliament from 2002 to 2005 and was Minister for Economic Affairs and the Treasury from 2001 to 2002. From 1977 to 2001 he held various positions at the World Bank, including Vice President for the Middle East and North Africa Region and Vice President for the Poverty Reduction and Economic Management Unit. He earned his bachelor's and master's degrees in economics from the London School of Economics and his Ph.D. from Princeton University.

William Easterly is Professor of Economics (a joint apppointment with Africa House) at New York University, and Co-Director of NYU's Development Research Institute. He is a Research Associate of the National Bureau of Economic Research and a nonresident Fellow of the Center for Global Development in Washington D.C. He spent sixteen years as a Research Economist at the World Bank. He is the author of *The White Man's Burden: How the West's Efforts to Aid the Rest Have Done So Much Ill and So Little Good* and *The Elusive Quest for Growth: Economists' Adventures and Misadventures in the Tropics*. In 2008, *Foreign Policy* magazine named him one of the world's Top 100 Public Intellectuals. He holds a Ph.D. in economics from Massachusetts Institute of Technology.

Takatoshi Ito is Professor at the Graduate School of Economics, University of Tokyo. He has taught extensively both in the United States and Japan, including at the University of Minnesota, Hitotsubashi University, and Harvard University. Ito served as Senior Advisor in the Research Department at the International Monetary Fund and as Deputy Vice Minister for International Affairs in Japan's Ministry of Finance. He was President of the Japanese Economic Association in 2004 and was a member of the Prime Minister's Council of Economic and Fiscal Policy from October 2006 to October 2008. He is the author of many books, including *The Japanese Economy*, *The Political Economy of the Japanese Monetary Policy*, and *Financial Policy and Central Banking in Japan*.

Joseph E. Stiglitz is University Professor at Columbia University, Chair of Columbia University's Committee on Global Thought, and Co-founder and President of the Initiative for Policy Dialogue. Stiglitz was awarded the Nobel Memorial Prize in Economics in 2001 for his analyses of markets with asymmetric information and was a member of the Intergovernmental Panel on Climate Change that was awarded the Nobel Peace Prize in 2007. He served as chairman of President Clinton's Council of Economic Advisers and was Senior Vice President and Chief Economist of the World Bank. His latest book, *The Three Trillion Dollar War*, coauthored with Linda J. Bilmes, was published in 2008.

1

A STAR IS BORN

This essay is on development economics, viewed through a lens created by the World Bank in 1978. That was the year when the first *World Development Report* (WDR) was released. The slender report proved to be an instant success and attracted widespread attention. Almost overnight and quite unexpectedly, a brand crystallized, a reputation was forged, a worldwide readership was created, and expectations were generated. A second *WDR* appeared a year later and then a third. The prestige of the publication grew, and among members of the international development community it quickly achieved iconic status. Imitators followed, and the bandwagon launched more than three decades ago is crowded with reports, all inspired by the *WDR*. If imitation is the sincerest form of flattery, then the *World Development Report* has certainly received more than any serial publication in the annals of development. Other reports have carved out niches for themselves and have built their own brand names,[1] but the *WDR* remains

---

1. Among them, I would include the United Nation's *Human Development Report*, the Asian Development Bank's *Asian Development Outlook*, the United Nations Conference on Trade's *World Investment Report*, the Inter-American Development Bank's *Economic and Social Progress Report*, and the United Nations Industrial Development Organization's *Industrial Development Report*.

the towering oak in the forest that has sprouted on all sides. It provides a unique perspective on the evolution of thinking, policy making, and practice in the field of development. It tracks the waxing and waning of policy concerns and the cycling of policy fashions as perceived by the World Bank. And the WDR reveals the beliefs and ideological leanings of the Bank's management and principal shareholders—beliefs that filter perceptions of development, that modulate policy advice, and that overtly or subliminally shape the operational activities of the Bank.

The WDR has become such a fixture that it is easy to forget the circumstances under which it was born and the Bank's motivation for producing such a report at that time. In the first chapter of this essay, I provide a brief background on the circumstances of newly independent developing countries and summarize some of the main strands of the emerging field of development economics. This backdrop to the genesis of the *World Development Report* accounts for the orientation of the earlier reports. The thinking on development in the 1960s and 1970s also provides a baseline from which to view the evolution that has occurred since. From the coverage in chapter 2, I isolate a number of key issues common to several or all of the WDRs, and I examine these issues individually at greater length in chapter 3.[2] The discussion in chapter 3, which builds on the material in the WDRs, presents some views about how far development thinking and, relatedly, policy making have advanced relative to 30 years ago. It asks whether promoting growth, building institutions, tackling inequality and poverty, making aid effective, and defining the role of the state have been rendered more tractable policywise by the knowledge encapsulated in the WDRs. Chapter 4 looks ahead and points to some of the big challenges that the Bank might explore through future WDRs and the value it can add through the knowledge acquired from its cross-country operations and research.

A Postbellum World

In the middle of the 20th century, the world economy was struggling to find its feet after a hugely destructive conflict that had followed on the heels of

---

2. See appendix A for a listing of all 30 WDRs and their directors.

the severest economic depression in memory.[3] The Great Depression had eroded faith in the ability of markets to equilibrate supply and demand and to sustain economic activities at a high enough level of employment in the industrial countries. Fears of secular stagnation from a closing of the economic frontier, from flagging innovation, and from declining population growth came to be debated (Fogel 2005; Hansen 1939). There was greater receptivity to Keynesianism, and the Depression certainly did nothing to undermine the attractions of socialism.[4] The war effort elaborated and entrenched planning and controls everywhere, vastly expanding the role of the state. An increasingly self-confident Soviet Union, which was able to draw much of Eastern Europe into its orbit, and the coming of a communist regime in China in 1949 lent additional support to the case for detailed planning undergirded by state ownership of substantial segments of the economy. This recovery, particularly in Europe and later also in China and Japan, proceeded under strong state tutelage. The hand of the state plucked most of the economic strings, and state entities were responsible for half or more of total production in mixed economies and up to 90 percent in communist countries. Much to the surprise of the pessimists, post–World War II reconstruction progressed smoothly, and the rebound in economic activity was remarkably swift, with communist countries showing production gains as significant if not greater than those of the predominantly capitalist economies. The great industrial resurgence, which gathered momentum in the 1950s, was state directed, disciplined by targets, and frequently led by the public sector. It tended to be autarchic or quasi-mercantilist and was buttressed by a multitude of import restrictions. The retreat from the first globalization, which began in 1914,[5] entered a new phase as capitalist and socialist economies

---

3. When one looks at the Great Depression using time-series data on per capita income growth, it is remarkable how quickly even the most damaging shocks fade out. The great influenza epidemic is another example, and very likely the most recent shocks will also be smoothed over fairly rapidly.

4. However, the reflationary measures introduced from 1933 by President Franklin D. Roosevelt through the New Deal were rooted in his effort to help the "forgotten man"—the "one-third of the nation ill housed, ill clad, ill nourished." John Maynard Keynes's ideas did not motivate the first New Deal. In fact, after their first meeting in 1934, Roosevelt was impressed by Keynes but baffled by his economics (Cord 2007, Stein 1969).

5. Scattered evidence of global integration as a result of advances in shipbuilding and the growth of trade begins accumulating from the 15th century onward (on "archaic" globalization, see Bayly 2002). One scholar maintains that the Roman Empire was a major globalizing force because it expanded markets; imposed peace; and integrated culture, technologies, and ideas (Hitchner 2008).

and newly independent colonies embraced inward-looking growth policies (Findlay and O'Rourke 2008).

Development Becomes a Discipline and a Crusade

Decolonization, which largely created the universe of developing countries, started in the late 1940s, with Indonesia becoming the first country to claim independence in 1945 (and to secure full independence four tumultuous years later), followed by India and Pakistan, which gained independence in 1947 (Low 1993). In the majority of cases, it was a hurried process. The colonial powers had not the resources,[6] nor the patience, nor the foresight to carve out viable states with due attention to history, ethnic composition, and economic potential[7] or to attend to the precise and well-conceived delineation of boundaries that would ensure a fair division of resources and minimize the disruption of regional economic and trading relations. In several instances, local insurgencies in colonies and battle fatigue on the home front precipitated hasty withdrawals.[8] Most new states came into existence with backward, frequently impoverished, predominantly agrarian economies; the bare bones of a physical infrastructure; and minimal

However, the first round of globalization, as scholars generally perceive it, occurred between 1880 and 1914 and is searchingly examined by O'Rourke and Williamson (2001) and Osterhammel and Petersson (2005). A many-sided examination of globalization is provided by the contributors to Ritzer (2007).

6. Ferguson (2002, chapter 6) traces the dismantling of the British Empire back to the huge costs of the World War I in terms of matériel and lives. American opposition to Britain maintaining its empire after the World War II sealed the empire's fate. Clarke (2008) and Zakaria (2008) are of the view that financial and other commitments during and immediately after the World War II drove the final nail into the coffin of imperial power.

7. Alesina, Easterly, and Matuszeski (2006: 2) state that, "former colonizers, newly independent nations, or post war agreement among winners regarding borders have often created monstrosities in which ethnic or religious or linguistic groups were thrown together without any respect for people's aspirations. Eighty percent of African borders follow latitudinal or longitudinal lines, and many scholars believe that such artificial borders ... are at the roots of Africa's economic tragedy." Judt (1996: 56) makes similar observations regarding the countries of Eastern Europe "born from the collapse of empires ... a process that is still incomplete.... This is the great misfortune of the eastern half of Europe: that its division into states came late and all at once." The ways new states came into being and the strategic interests of the great powers in the second half of the 20th century have also shaped the governance of these states and caused the flaring of civil wars that have smoldered for years, especially in Africa. (Hironaka 2005).

8. The hurried dismantling of the British Raj in India, the "shameful flight," and the mayhem that followed is a story well told by Wolpert (2006). According to Hill and others (2008), the population losses in the Punjab amounted to between 2.3 million and 3.2 million from deaths and unrecorded migration.

organizational and technical skills. Some were scarred by the conflicts and uprooting of populations that preceded independence. For the most part, they were almost devoid of the institutions that are part and parcel of functioning market economies. There were exceptions, such as India, but they were few. Even in India, the industrial base was pitifully narrow,[9] the infrastructure was threadbare, the stock of modern technical skills was exceedingly limited, and the administrative and legal institutions were just adequate for a largely agrarian economy. The division of the subcontinent into two countries—one of them Pakistan—added to administrative costs and complexities and further undercut even these limited capabilities.

Newly created countries, unlike the established states of industrial Europe, were wholly unprepared for the poorly understood task of development. But their emergent leaders—nascent elites and fledgling governments—frequently sought to legitimize their power and improve the welfare of the people by immediately embracing ambitious economic goals. By borrowing from their former colonial masters and by observing the prowess of the Soviet Union, they variously adapted three major precepts of development.[10] Foremost was the need (a) to maximize economic growth, (b) to do so by dint of rapid industrialization,[11] and (c) to emphasize the production of capital goods because the autarchic frame of mind

---

9. Being a part of colonial empires promoted countries' participation in trade and the global integration of Africa and Asia, but it also slowed or stifled industrialization (most notably in India) and created institutions and economic systems favoring natural resource–based activities. Lucas (2003) in commenting on Niall Ferguson, observes that the per capita incomes of regions subject to British colonial rule stagnated. See also Mitchener and Weidenmier (2008) on the effects of colonial rule on Indian industry, and Chaudhury (1995) on the decline of the Bengali economy in the 18th century. Galor and Mountford (2008) add that though trade promoted specialization and induced the accumulation of human capital and the deepening of skills in industrializing economies, in nonindustrial economies the gains from trade stimulated population growth, which by arresting the increase in per capita incomes contributed to the Great Divergence.

10. About the consequences of World War II for planning and welfare in Europe, Judt (1996: 25), notes, "Everywhere the organization of society for war paved the way for a presumption that in peacetime there would be comparably high levels of state involvement in everything from social welfare to economic planning. This presumption in favor of centralized economic and social organization, shared to a greater or lesser degree by all major political groupings in every major European community, was a crucial factor in facilitating postwar reconstruction, domestic and international alike." Some of those who later put on the garb of freedom fighters were earlier seduced by Fabian socialism during a sojourn in the United Kingdom. Jawaharlal Nehru, for example, became wedded to the statist model after he was drawn to a pragmatic Fabianism in the 1930s (Smith 1959).

11. Policy makers in developing countries were searching for a second industrial revolution, and to them development was synonymous with industrialization (Ranis 2004b).

assigned primacy to heavy industry (Allen 2001; Bideleux 1985; Ellman 1979). After all, the reasoning went, producing anything required steel and machinery. The shortest route to industrialization for most states was through planning by newly empowered ministries, with the implementation being left to freshly minted public enterprises. For these embryonic industrial engines to have a chance to achieve industrial traction, they had to be protected from import competition.[12] Meeting foreign exchange needs often called for subsidies in various forms to promote exports of manufactures, when the exports of primary products generated insufficient foreign revenue.[13]

Rapid growth through industrialization that was planned and partially— or wholly—executed by government agencies and buffered by import and exchange controls was the model of development that the new nations adapted from the industrial West and from the then-resurgent communist bloc.[14] Late-starting economies tailored the mix depending on leadership, ideology, composition of elites, comparative advantages, and organizational and institutional realities. Inevitably, the borrowing from the West and from the Soviet bloc was a haphazard process, as was its translation into practice across the developing world. But under the circumstances and given the state of knowledge, it could hardly have been otherwise.

A Discipline in the Making

What was the contribution of development economics to this approach? A rereading of the sparse literature from a half century back,[15] reminds

---

12. Every country, whether developed or developing, has used infant-industry protection at some point; hence, the approach adopted in the 1950s and 1960s followed accepted practice (Ranis 2004b).

13. The volatility of raw material prices and the downward trend in these prices overall put a brake on development in the 19th and 20th centuries (J. G. Williamson 2008).

14. Latin American countries adopted a protectionist regime in the late 19th century to raise revenue from tariffs and duties and to develop local industry. However, tariff rates were in the 20 to 40 percent range, few nontariff barriers existed, and—at least until the early 20th century—many Latin American countries were fairly tightly linked to the global economy and sustained large imports (Rubio 2006).

15. Meier (2005: 53) observed that the first edition (published in 1948) of Paul Samuelson's introductory textbook on economics had only three passing references to issues pertaining to development. Meier goes on to note that quantitative analysis was in short supply because the experience

one that countries could choose the path being traced by the socialist economies or they could opt for a variant of the mixed capitalist model, with a greater or lesser dose of planning. The geopolitics of that time left scant room for bold departures and innovative new paradigms.[16] Inevitably, given the youthfulness of the discipline, development economics was empirically thin, and the articulation of theories was at an early stage.[17] In pursuit of growth—which was the Holy Grail then, as it arguably is now—capital was the kingpin, and the conceptual apparatus underlying much of the reasoning was loosely related to the Harrod-Domar model. The fulcrum provided by this model was the capital-output ratio. How much growth a country derives from each incremental unit of capital is a function of this conversion factor. An economy's growth hinged, therefore, on capital accumulation and the efficiency with which such accumulation was combined with labor to produce goods and services.[18] With most developing countries viewed as having elastic supplies of labor in rural areas available at subsistence wages for expanding industrial production—a notion certified by the Lewis model, as well as the Ranis and Fei models—capital emerged as the principal determinant of growth.[19] Under conditions of autarchy, countries that saved more and judiciously accumulated industrial capital grew faster—in Walt

with development was much too scanty to allow economists to come to analytical grips with the subject matter (Meier 2005: 78).

16. Yugoslavia, with its self-managed enterprises, exploited its strategic location between the Western and Soviet blocs to experiment with some exotic ideas; on the whole, however, few countries strayed far from the dominant models.

17. By the 1960s, Simon Kuznets's (1966) work was providing the foundations for the empirical research on modern economic growth (see also Fogel 2000).

18. Domar (1946) and Harrod (1939) put the spotlight on capital, and more refined modeling by Cass (1965), M. Frankel (1962), and Solow (1956) later maintained the centrality of this factor.

19. Arthur Lewis's point of departure was the classical tradition, but he saw the developing economy moving from a dualistic framework to the stage of modern economic growth focused on the urban industrial sector (Ranis 2004a). Rozenzweig (1988) has questioned whether the elastic supply of labor Lewis envisioned is empirically valid and showed that even in thickly populated economies, labor supply curves were upward sloping. Many observers believe that Chinese industry will reap the advantages of an elastic supply or workers from the rural sector, but since about 2003, employers in coastal cities have complained of labor shortages and are having to pay steadily higher wages. The upward tilt acquired by the supply curve even though a large pool of workers remains employed in agriculture, is the outcome of a several factors: the numbers of the most eligible young workers are shrinking rapidly after two decades of emigration, those left behind are older and more reluctant to emigrate, many more young people are going to secondary schools or seeking tertiary education, the labor market is segmented, and expectations have changed with a concomitant upward drift in the reservation wage (Cai and Wang 2008; "China: Labor Shortages" 2008).

Whitman Rostow's deathless phrase, they "took off." If they persevered year after year, these countries were expected to achieve the nirvana of self-sustaining growth.

This idea came in a number of flavors. Rosenstein-Rodan (1943) and Gerschenkron (1962) argued for a Big Push[20] or a Great Spurt[21] of investment-led growth that would enable an economy to loosen multiple constraints, realize scale economies, and generate the needed demand. Leibenstein (1957) put forward the notion of a "critical minimum effort" that economies needed to make to escape from what Nelson (1956) called the "low-level equilibrium trap." The related conceptualization of balanced growth by Nurkse (1959) visualized a mutually supporting advance across a broad range of sectors, through a coordinated investment strategy that would propel the economy out of the rut of poverty. Hirschman (1958) countered with a plea for unbalanced growth, maintaining that leading sectors should emerge that would stimulate the rest of the economy, with the help of profitable forward and backward links. All parties subscribed to the need for industrialization and the gradual shifting of the economy's center of gravity from agriculture to the industrial sector. Most of the participants were partial to the notion of export-elasticity pessimism first voiced by Prebisch (1962) and Singer (1950). They tacitly or otherwise acknowledged that, because the terms of trade for primary products were declining, longer-term growth could not be hitched to the export of primary commodities alone. Countries had to develop the manufacturing sector to meet domestic demand and, where possible, generate revenues from exports to earn enough foreign exchange.

Although the primacy of investment and of industrialization was widely accepted, one school opted for import-substituting industrialization behind high barriers to trade, and another school began championing

---

20. The Big Push was justified then, as it is now by Jeff Sachs and others, with reference to relatively inflexible complementarities. For countries to move to a higher-growth path, all constraints that could become binding needed to be eased more or less simultaneously, which required investment in many different areas (C. Jones 2008; Murphy, Schleifer, and Vishny 1989; Sachs 2005). This explanation echoes the notion put forward by Kremer (1993) that in complex systems the failure or nonperformance of even very minor components (the "O-ring") can precipitate the failure of the entire system. Jones (2007) differentiates his analysis from that of Kremer by noting that the latter arrives at large changes in incomes by assuming strong scale economies.

21. In Gerschenkron's (1962) schema, economic backwardness could be turned to the advantage of late-starting economies by means of institutional innovations that enabled them to surmount barriers and to exploit the potential inherent in catching up (see also Mathews 2005).

the advantages of nurturing export-oriented industrialization once a few countries showed what could be achieved.[22] Both sides embraced—or at least acquiesced—to a dirigiste approach to development, complete with five-year plans and an array of tax incentives, subsidies, exchange rate policies, tariffs, and directed credit, to help new industries germinate and grow a generation of public and private entrepreneurs.

Although many developing countries struggled to accumulate enough capital through domestic savings, economists invented theories to explain savings (or consumption) behavior and tried (somewhat ineffectually) to identify instruments for enhancing saving propensities so as to close the gap between a desired investment rate and the rate of domestic savings. It soon became apparent that growth would be constrained not only by the scarcity of domestic capital but also by the paucity of foreign exchange to finance purchases of capital goods and other needed intermediate and consumption goods. The two-gap model, which formalized and linked the domestic and foreign resource needs, in a sense closed this circle of development thinking.[23]

Throughout the 1960s, development economics helped to dignify and to impart greater apparent rigor to the efforts of planners and policy makers of all stripes throughout the developing world. In virtually every planning ministry (and countless World Bank country reports), the stated objective was to raise growth rates—preferably to 7 percent per year, so as to double gross domestic product (GDP) in 10 years—by dint of industrialization and to do so by using a combination of measures that promoted domestic resource mobilization and foreign exchange earnings or, alternatively, in the case of relatively closed economies such as China, by minimizing reliance on imports and reducing the need for foreign exchange.

Looking back over the period from the mid 1950s to the early 1970s, one notes that the pace of growth quickened in many developing (and

---

22. Latin American countries were among those to pursue import-substituting industrialization most vigorously, perhaps because of a long tradition of protectionism. From the middle of the 19th century, Latin American governments had begun relying on tariffs to generate revenues and protect special interests. The raising of import barriers after the World War I to develop industry was a natural outgrowth of past policies (Coatsworth and Williamson 2002).

23. Hollis Chenery, the World Bank's chief economist from 1972 to 1982, was one of the architects of the two-gap model and was responsible for embedding it into mainstream discourse. See Chenery and Bruno (1962).

Figure 1.1: Growth Rates of Developing and Developed Countries, 1961–74

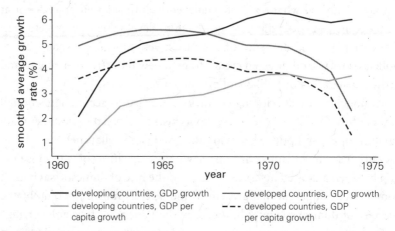

Source: World Development Indicators database.

developed) countries, all of which were starting from very low bases (see figure 1.1). After some initial floundering, a frequently messy sorting out of leadership issues (as the torch was transferred from a first to a second generation of political bosses), and a measure of success at achieving a semblance of national identity, countries such as Brazil, Ghana, Kenya, Malaysia, Pakistan, and the Philippines, as well as many others, began registering respectable growth rates as new manufacturing industries came on stream and as the performance of the agricultural sector improved (see figure 1.2). Much of this growth was the result of catching up, in the same way as European countries were closing the gap with the United States, except that developing countries recently exiting from colonial tutelage had a lot more ground to cover. Even adding a little industry and expanding the scope of commercial agriculture made a large difference to their performance. It did not matter that the five-year plans were often little more than formulaic statements of intention and that the policy makers were inexperienced and generally innocent of technical skills. As long as the broad objectives were reasonably clear, the government was moderately committed to achieving them, and the policy measures were coherent (or innocuous) by the standards of those times, economies expanded. The only direction was up. The economies that did not grow were victims of extreme predation by dictatorial regimes; civil unrest,

Figure 1.2: Growth Rates of Six Developing Countries, 1956–71

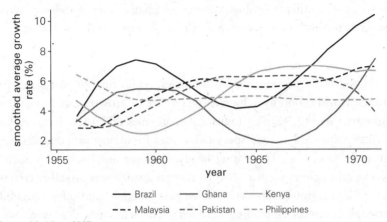

Source: Maddison 2007.

which stifled economic activity; or extraordinary incompetence on the part of inexperienced and rapacious ruling elites.[24]

It is impossible to say whether the concepts, techniques, tools, and metaphors of the development economics of those two decades made any difference. If they did, it was very much on the margin. The "science" of planning was a "god that failed."[25] The input-output (I-O) techniques using flimsy data that were pressed into use to lend glamour and a measure of exactitude to planning, at best, did no harm.[26] At worst, they created a corset of targets, controls, and regulations, which slowly began stifling economies where planning was king, as in the Soviet Union and its satellite states, but also in countries such as India, which endured a "Hindu rate of growth" for almost 40 years.

24. Some "stationary bandits" or leaders who established dictatorial regimes achieved success, but they were the exceptions (Olson 2000). Bates (2008: 20) describes them as specialists in violence and proposes that such specialists maintained political order or behaved in a predatory manner depending on the level of public revenues, the rate of discount, and the gains from predation.

25. This failure is reminiscent of that expressed against communism by the contributors to Crossman's (1950) famous book.

26. In fact, the Bank was in the forefront of the I-O and social accounting matrix programming exercises. It built some of the largest I-O models in the 1970s and contributed to the writing of the software such as GAMS (General Algebraic Modeling System) to run these models (see Kendrick 2003). As Stern and Ferreira (1997: 556) remark, "At one point it seemed as if the solutions to the problems of the world were perceived as lying in ever more disaggregated linear programming models."

Despite the muddle-headed trade and exchange rate policies, the millions wasted on (heavy) industrial white elephants,[27] the inability of most countries to raise domestic savings and investment to the levels reached by the Soviets and the Chinese, and the endemic corruption, this initial stage of development is remembered as a golden age for the industrial world and for newly developing countries. At no time in past centuries had the world economy achieved such a rate of growth, and at no time in the past had the leading industrial economies and a few industrializing ones expanded at such spectacular rates for almost two decades (see figures 1.3 and 1.4). These were heady times for development economics, even though its contribution to this prosperity was arguably trivial. I-O models, turnpike models, "golden rule" models, and other dynamic optimizing models employing mathematical techniques that were borrowed from the engineering sciences[28] and topology celebrated the high growth rates and attributed these rates to advances in economic thinking (see, for instance, Bardhan 1970; Kendrick 1981; Kendrick and Stoutjesdijk 1978; Phelps 1966). Greater access to computers, coupled with progress in econometrics and in software, brought with it a flood of simulation results, which appeared to light the way forward.[29]

The worth of this modeling and simulation is now debatable. Although the Harrod-Domar model lies at the root of the AK models, the current development literature has little use for turnpikes or golden rules or I-O-based planning. Neither does it have use for the large econometric models that attempted to represent the workings of economies, although computable general equilibrium models remain in use.[30] The findings of the empirical literature from that era were equally ephemeral.

---

27. A *white elephant* is a project generating negative social surplus. The survival of this exotic species is ascribed by Robinson and Torvik (2002) to its utility in facilitating exchanges between politicians and voters. Politicians who can credibly commit to build patently indefensible projects are better able to convince their supporters that they have the capacity to follow through with promised rewards.

28. Hollis Chenery's (1950) Harvard PhD dissertation under Wassily Leontief on "The Engineering Bases of Economic Analysis" was one of the earliest contributions to this genre.

29. It is impossible to avoid the temptation to note that financial innovations such as derivatives, options, and swaps, whose near impenetrable complexity underlies the seriousness of the financial crisis of 2007 and 2008, owe their spread and progressive sophistication to computer power and to the many rocket scientists who have lent their skills to Wall Street.

30. Blanchard (2008) observes that dynamic stochastic general equilibrium models are widely used to forecast and to evaluate policy rules. As computers have become more powerful, the number of structural parameters of these models has steadily increased.

Figure 1.3: Average Growth Rates of Five Industrial Countries, 1871–1970

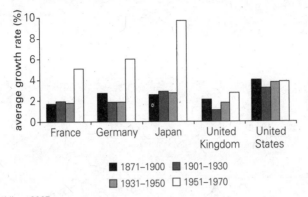

Source: Maddison 2007.

Figure 1.4: Per Capita Average Growth Rates of Five Industrial Countries, 1871–1970

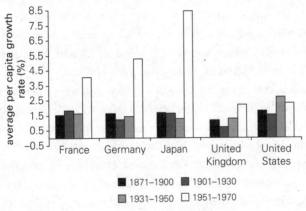

Source: Maddison 2007.

The long boom of the 1960s came to an end with a whimper in the early 1970s (see figure 1.5). Growth began slowing in many developing countries as policy induced distortions and inefficiencies took their toll. The shock inflicted by the oil crisis of 1973 was enough to precipitate a downturn by curtailing the demand for primary commodities and light manufactures from the industrial countries, which were hard hit, and by sharply raising the price of energy. As is apparent from figure 1.5, growth and development slowed in many countries and went into reverse in some.

Figure 1.5: Growth Rates of Developing Countries, 1972–90

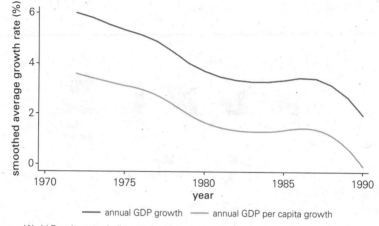

Source: World Development Indicators database.

Countries in Sub-Saharan Africa were affected the most, not just by economic hardships, but also by a parallel upsurge in political turbulence and civil conflicts, which were exacerbated (or caused) by the rivalries of the Great Powers locked in the lengthening Cold War.

The 1970s, coming on the heels of a golden age, were a period of mounting frustration tinged with helplessness (Marglin 1992). Seemingly unstoppable economic progress suddenly stalled in the industrial West and across most of the developing world (Ben-David and Papell 1997). Even the communist powerhouses, such as China, were enfeebled by political turmoil, which fanned economic uncertainty and severely undermined the effectiveness of the command system. The models and policies that had appeared so potent in the 1960s were found to be ineffectual once the momentum was broken, and countries—hitherto buoyed by virtuous spirals—began to drift into vicious cycles (Krueger 1993). Mounting economic pressures were worsened by the unraveling of the often provisional political arrangements, which had been stitched together by a generation of leaders who came to power following decolonization. By the 1970s, this generation was fading fast, and in the absence of tested political institutions, accepted modes of political succession, and rules for sharing of power and wealth among the heterogeneous groups, many of the new nations became battlegrounds for rivalries between factions, between elites, and between ethnic groups and tribes.[31] Inevitably, economic management weakened; economic activity suffered as risks multiplied; and in the face of rising populations, the world-wide poverty headcount increased from 1.9 billion in 1970 to 2.2 billion in 1980 and to 2.4 billion in 1990 (Bourguignon and Morrison 2002).

A War on Poverty and the Making of the *World Development Report*

In his state of the union message in January 1964, President Lyndon B. Johnson had declared a war on poverty in the United States. In time, the necessity for waging such a conflict worldwide against an unseen enemy by harnessing the firepower of social programs seeped through osmosis into the World Bank (Kapur, Lewis, and Webb 1997). The opening shot was fired in 1973 by Robert McNamara, then president of the World Bank, at a speech delivered during the Bank's Annual Meetings held in Nairobi. Although the war on poverty had been ongoing in the United States for a decade, the economic profession had little to offer by way of solutions for industrial or developing countries. McNamara (1973: 10) warned that "growth is not equitably reaching the poor. And the poor are not significantly contributing to growth." He added further that "800 million individuals—40 percent of a total of 2 billion—survive on incomes estimated (in U.S. purchasing power) of 30 cents per day. They are suffering poverty in the absolute sense." At the close of his speech, McNamara called for an eradication of absolute poverty by the end of the 20th century, and he indicated that essential to accomplishing this goal would be an increase in the productivity of small-scale agriculture. There was no dearth of research, but nothing remotely resembling the sought after silver bullet was forthcoming.[32]

---

31. Ethnic conflicts and the degree of ethnic fractionalization of societies are associated with political turmoil and weak economic performance (see Alesina and La Ferrara 2004; Caselli and Coleman 2006). However, Bates (2008) cannot find a systematic relationship linking ethnicity with political disorder. Nor can he find a relationship between civil wars in Africa and a country's endowment of natural resources, which were also viewed as a source of instability. Brunnschweiler and Bulte (2008) also fail to reproduce a relationship running from resource endowment to slow growth and conflict, because so much hangs on how resource endowment is measured and how endogeneity issues are tackled. If the discounted value of expected resource rents is used, the effect of resource wealth on income growth is positive. "Resource dependence appears as a symptom rather than a cause of underdevelopment," they write (Brunnschweiler and Bulte 2008: 617).

32. Following McNamara's speech, the Bank issued a book titled *Redistribution with Growth* (Chenery and others 1974, not to be confused with Chenery's earlier paper), which attempted to

International aid and development programs lacked sound and tested instruments, and they lacked country role models. The conditions were ripe for a world development report to reinvigorate thinking on objectives, policies, and implementation.

The economic environment of the 1970s offered the World Bank, under a dynamic president, the opportunity to assume a leadership role and to craft a widely shared understanding of how growth could be resumed by stimulating a fresh round of thinking and development policies, how it could be made to benefit the poorest segments of societies, and what a desirable scale of development would entail by way of resource transfers from industrial to developing countries. The intense interest aroused by a paper on global trends and the prospects for developing countries issued in 1974 by Hollis Chenery, the Bank's chief economist, encouraged McNamara to pursue the idea of an annual publication that took the pulse of the international economy, that stimulated the search for answers, and that synthesized the "truth" as it was revealed. Such a book could become a vehicle for the Bank to lead, to propagate its ideas, to mobilize official development assistance, and to win adherence for a renewed push to develop. Hence, in 1977, McNamara entrusted Chenery with the task of preparing a flagship report.[33] A team comprising the Bank's best and brightest was assigned the task of assessing the state of the world economy and, in broad strokes, indicating the essentials of a strategy for growth that was equitably shared.

The first *World Development Report*—a slim volume with just 68 pages of text—appeared in August 1978. In McNamara's words, the purpose of the *WDR* was to provide "a comprehensive assessment of the global development issues" (World Bank 1978: iii). It was a vehicle for dealing "with a number of fundamental problems confronting developing countries and explo[ring] their relationship to the underlying trends in the international economy." McNamara saw the Bank as ideally suited to undertake such an assessment because of "its broad-based membership,

show how growth could be achieved with equity, particularly by emphasizing rural development through multiple channels, including institutional reform, better water management, access to credit, public services, and extension.

33. It was around this time (1977) that the Brandt Commission was created.

its long experience, and its daily involvement with the development problems of its members."[34]

With the publication of the first of an annual series, the Bank took it upon itself to try to filter and systematize the knowledge on development so as to enhance the operational utility of such knowledge. In producing the WDR, the Bank was not seeking intellectual leadership or attempting to break new ground in the development field. Instead, the WDR was seen as a vehicle for persuading the Bank's member governments to broadly unite behind a strategy and to cooperate in making it succeed.

The first WDR was published at a time of considerable despondency as to the future of development. Progress appeared to be stalling. The optimism and intellectual excitement of the 1950s and 1960s was on the wane. The modest rates of growth achieved were being swallowed up by increases in population. *The Limits to Growth*, published by the Club of Rome in 1972 (Meadows and others 1972), had added to the gathering gloom by warning that the world risked running out of resources.[35] With the development enterprise beginning to drift, a hunger arose for practical solutions that the somewhat sterile and increasingly formal literature on economic growth of the preceding decade was signally unable to satisfy. The WDR—because it came from the premier development institution, which could draw on a wealth of country-specific experience and comparative analytic expertise—promised to break the impasse. It catalogued the substantial economic gains that had been achieved by developing

---

34. The Bank's advantage lies in providing a global public good—knowledge about sound and tested development policies. It uses its access to information on policy initiatives worldwide and to data, as well as the latitude it enjoys, to screen and adapt theories with an operational content that were developed by others (Gilbert, Powell, and Vines 2000).

35. *The Limits to Growth* (Meadows and others 1972) was the child of advances in computing power and software languages, which permitted the simulation of complex systems (using first-order differential equations) with multiple feedback loops (Ayres 1999). Although it represented only a minor elaboration of Forrester's (1971) *World Dynamics*, the 1972 book caused a sensation by claiming, on the basis of a mechanical modeling of five key global variables (with no causal structure or economic content), that the world risked overshooting its carrying capacity. *The Limits to Growth* and the writings of Barry Commoner and Rachel Carson helped to generate an awareness of rising environmental costs and stirred the notion of sustainable development into the discourse during the 1980s. Twenty years after the original volume was published, Meadows, Randers and Meadows (1993) came out with an update called *Beyond the Limits*. In 2004, they published a 30-year update emphasizing once again that the world economy was threatened by collapse because it remained in an overshoot mode.

countries, thus reviving flagging spirits; it acknowledged the existence of major hurdles but offered sober hope that they could be overcome; and it proposed plausible ways of making that happen.

Today, a new report from an international agency enters a crowded field and must struggle to be heard. In 1978, the *WDR* was the lone star. It was an instant hit, even though its offerings were relatively meager because the shelf of economic knowledge was not well stocked. Each succeeding *WDR* has added more information on the state of development and the state of the global economy, has showcased new research findings, has presented examples of successful economic initiatives and institutions, has attempted to sharpen the edge of existing policy tools, and has proposed modest additions to the toolkit. Perhaps most important, the *WDR*s have attempted to direct the attention of decision makers to priorities and to gather opinion around the principal objectives of development. Reading the successive *WDR*s, one can sense the shifting of attention as times changed, crises erupted, the Cold War ended, poverty as the defining goal lost ground (temporarily) to adjustment in its many incarnations, and faith in one set of "solutions" to the problems of development was partially superseded by conviction in another set of "solutions." The pile of *WDR*s has kept mounting, and recent *WDR*s are three and sometimes four times the length of the earliest reports. The first contained no references; the most recent ones come with hundreds. And from the third *WDR* onward, the content is organized around a specific theme. The earlier reports came with an opening section that looked out onto the state of the world economy. After 1986, this section was hived off into a separate annual publication called the *Global Economic Prospects*. The recent reports are certainly weightier, but fewer readers venture beyond lengthy executive summaries.

In the chapter that follows, I examine the coverage of the *WDR*s and explain the priorities as reflected in the topics addressed by individual reports. The topics not only provide a window on the Bank's perception of what mattered or matters in the sphere of development at a particular time, but also give an indicator of the current fashions in development economics that are attracting a significant amount of attention from researchers.

2

Freeing the World of Poverty

It was inevitable, given the conceptual and empirical content of development economics in the mid 1970s, that the early *World Development Report*s (*WDR*s) painted with a broad brush. Raising growth rates and enhancing the capabilities of the poor were viewed as the primary objectives. Growth for low- and many middle-income countries was linked to the performance of the agricultural sector, which employed the majority of the workforce and provided a bare livelihood for most of the poor. Because poverty was and remains predominantly a rural phenomenon and grain yields have risen slowly (1.1 percent per year), proposals for curtailing rural poverty focusing on agricultural production, rural industry, trade of agricultural commodities, and migration to cities have recurred in report after report, even as the share of agriculture in the gross domestic product (GDP) has shrunk in virtually every country, even the poorest. Whether the content and efficacy of the policy recommendations have deepened significantly with the advances in analysis is a point I return to when discussing key themes in chapter 3.

In setting the stage, the first *WDR* pointed to the emerging role of industry as the leading sector. It also drew attention to trade as a source of demand and a channel for earning the bulk of vitally needed foreign exchange, because resource transfers through aid and private flows of capital were too small to satisfy potential demand at that time.

The first *WDR* touched on and the second further elaborated the changing sectoral composition of developing countries, which was affecting their ability to grow and to raise living standards. Hence, in the 1979 *WDR*, the emergence of the urban-industrial economy—which would be the source of most of the new and higher-value-adding jobs and most new exports—received attention.

An Innovative Report

Conceptually, neither of the first two *WDRs* broke any fresh ground. The policy suggestions were general and conventional. The first two reports presented mainstream thinking in an accessible manner, with three important additions, which might explain the mystique of these documents. First, they provided between one set of covers a narrative on development and the international context within which this narrative was unfolding. Such reports are commonplace today, but not in the 1970s. At that time, we were not inundated daily with facts and opinions on the global economy.

Second, the World Bank used its resources and its access to data to generate a decent statistical picture of development.[1] This was a considerable innovation. For the first time, many statements on the dynamics of development could be buttressed by facts. For the first time, readers were given a good sense of the magnitudes involved, and this insight was vital for determining the scale of problems and for calibrating policies. In effect, the *WDRs* helped to make development economics more numerate and altered the nature of discourse. Henceforth, arguments and counterarguments had to be backed by numbers, and the *World Development Indicators*, which were an annex to the earlier *WDRs*, fundamentally thickened the empirical content of development economics.

A third addition was the embedding of poverty into the discussion on development, making poverty alleviation an inextricable, if not prime, objective of development. From at least the time of McNamara's speech in

---

1. The review of the first *WDR* in the *Guardian* newspaper praised the "absolutely riveting set of new style statistics on world development."

Nairobi, poverty was a part of the lexicon of development, but the championing provided by WDRs pulled poverty to the very apex of the development effort. The idea of ridding the world of poverty began to acquire both urgency and a moral imperative that it had never possessed before.[2] Moreover, the World Bank made poverty tangible by offering numerical information on the extent and depth of poverty.[3] Poverty alleviation became a rallying cry for the Bank and for all those engaged in making development a meaningful objective. Vanquishing poverty gave the Bank a new focus and a credible mission, and it added moral underpinnings to the economic case for resource transfers from the rich to the developing nations. Moreover, growth economics, which was in danger of losing its purchase on reality, acquired a tangible purpose. With faster growth, a nation's domestic product would increase, and the incomes of the poor would be more likely to rise. Growth acquired a more human face.

No More Trickle Down

From the mid 1970s onward, poverty alleviation was much debated at the Bank, and the current of opinion began to run against the passive approach that assumes that as long as there is growth, it will eventually trickle down to the poor.[4] How rapidly and to what degree this process would occur was unknown.

The 1979 WDR enumerated pathways to increased agricultural productivity such as availability of credit, use of fertilizers, research into new varieties, extension, improved infrastructure, pricing policies, and—where feasible—land reform. The WDR pointed to star performers such as the Republic of Korea and Taiwan, China. The authors of the WDR expressed

---

2. The process was akin to the emergence and widespread acceptance of the inalienable "natural" rights of man by the late 20th century, a slow and tendrilous outcome of the divergence between God and politics in Western societies that Thomas Hobbes helped to induce and to widen.

3. The Bank's earlier efforts highlighted the inadequacy of the available data and led to the launch of the Living Standards Measurement Study in 1980. This study is now in its fourth phase extending through 2010.

4. Although per capita GDP is the standard economists' measure of well-being, growth in per capita income affects the quality of life measured by a variety of indicators with long and variable lags. The effects are by no means instantaneous. Furthermore, the Easterlin Paradox, validated by research in many countries, consistently shows that expressed happiness seems not to have risen as incomes have climbed in the industrial countries (A. Clark, Frijters, and Shields 2008; Easterlin 1998).

the wish that a prospering agriculture would partially quench the hunger for urban "bright lights," but if cities continued to grow, the WDR exhorted municipalities to strengthen their finances, provide mass transport, increase the housing stock and upgrade slums (as Jakarta was doing), and perfect a system for delivering services at low cost. With energy prices on the rise once again in the late 1970s, the WDR also added a pitch for energy efficiency and for alternative sources of energy. All of this advice was as sound then as it is now. Singapore appeared to be on the road to success, and we know that it traveled far. Other cities, such as Karachi, Lagos, and Manila, were struggling then and continue to struggle with problems that have multiplied.

The spadework associated with this WDR (conducted mainly by the Bank's operational staff) and the prior research for *Redistribution with Growth* (Chenery and others 1974) helped to stimulate thinking on measures that might accelerate the trickle-down process. From this research emerged an approach to meet the so-called basic needs of the poorest 40 percent of the population.[5] This notion was conceptually rather amorphous. It never won a sufficient following because it did not acquire theoretical foundations, and some suspected that it might become a device for reducing official development assistance (Ranis 2004b). But along with advances in the theory and measurements of human capital, the concept of basic needs mobilized strong support for education and health as ways of enhancing living conditions and improving the earning capacity of the poor (Ranis 2004b).

The persistence of poverty and the need for pro-poor policies to whittle down the number of people living below the poverty line were the themes of the 1980 WDR—the Bank's first report on poverty. Although growth was underscored, the report saw it as a necessary—not a sufficient—condition

---

5. The basic needs approach had its genesis in some work conducted at the International Labour Office (ILO 1976) and in the Bank's Policy Planning Department. In the Bank, those engaged in making basic needs more than just an empty box were Shahid Burki, Mahbub ul Haq, and Paul Streeten. The fruits of their labor were presented in Streeten and others (1982). Basic needs intersects with Amartya Sen's (1979) concept of human capabilities, which he first described in "Equality of What?" and subsequently elaborated in later publications and work done jointly with Martha Nussbaum. The United Nations Development Programme's first *Human Development Report* (UNDP 1990) pursued this theme and the implied targeted provision of services to the poor, under the overall direction of Mahbub ul Haq (who later joined the United Nations Development Programme) with inputs from Paul Streeten and Amartya Sen. In an interview with Nermeen Shaikh (2007), Amartya Sen describes his role and interaction with Mahbub ul Haq.

for reducing poverty, and the report stressed the importance of managing health, education, and population growth.[6] The 1984 *WDR* (World Bank 1984: 185) noted that because poverty can be worsened by rapid population growth, donors and developing countries must cooperate to slow population increase. But after recognizing that family planning policies needed to complement measures to provide education, health, and social security to the poor, the Bank decided not to pursue this issue.[7] Education and health were to acquire ever-greater prominence, but only after a hiatus that lasted almost a decade. During the balance of the 1980s, the attention to poverty and social services was overlain by other objectives associated with international "shocks," a changing of the guard in the Bank, and the strengthening of new ideological currents.

Adjustment Gains the Upper Hand

The 1970s were a decade of creeping disillusionment—not development. The frustration in the 1970s was made more acute by perceptions that had been jelling over the course of the 20th century: perceptions about the idea of progress, its seeming inevitability, and its diffusion throughout

---

6. Human capital seems to be firmly ensconced as a determinant of growth despite lingering doubts as to its explanatory power. But physical capital has not been dethroned. Even those who have made room for human capital in their models continue to show that physical capital is correlated with long-term growth in output per worker and with longer-term GDP growth (Bernanke and Gurkaynak 2001; Mankiw, Romer, and Weil 1992). And other research shows that domestic saving remains the key source of financing, even in open economies, foreign saving being a partial substitute induced to a degree by the incentives offered by local financing (Aghion, Comin, and Howitt 2006; for an update on the Feldstein-Horioka puzzle, see Coakley, Kulasi, and Smith 1988). The trouble with all of these findings for the policy maker looking a year or two ahead is that the long-term story of growth is at odds with the shorter-term story. Neither physical capital nor, for that matter, human capital can explain growth accelerations, and these accelerations have a distressing tendency to fizzle out (Rodrik 2007). In any case, increasing either in a short period of time is extremely difficult, and while reforms and regime changes can sometimes do the trick, the likelihood is quite uncertain (Hausmann, Pritchett, and Rodrik 2004; B. Jones and Olken 2005). Growth slowdowns are another matter. In Southeast Asian countries, savings have remained stable since the crisis of 1997 to 1998, but investment rates have dropped, and this decrease has not been offset by a lower incremental capital output ratio or a faster increase in total factor productivity (which would occur if declining investment reflected more efficient allocation and less irrational exuberance), with the result that growth rates have followed investment down (Eichengreen 2007).

7. At the first United Nations–sponsored international conference on population held in Bucharest in 1979, developing countries were cautious and a little skeptical about the recommendations from Western countries that they needed to control population growth. When the second conference was convened a decade later in Mexico City, developing countries were coming around to the view that the increase in population needed to be restrained, but by then the United States was focused on free markets as the elixir for development (see Rosenfield and Schwartz 2005).

the world. As DeLong (2000: 3–4) remarks, "If in the eighteenth century people began to think of the idea of progress and in the nineteenth there actually began to be visible progress, in the twentieth century we expected and today we expect progress. We find it hard to imagine what it would be like to live in a society not experiencing rapid material progress." For most developing countries, the 1980s turned out to be even harsher, although a small number dramatically improved their performance and began exerting a profound "demonstration effect." A second oil shock in 1979 and 1980 was a brake on growth,[8] but worse, it ushered in an era of stagflation and resource imbalances for many countries. Thus, achieving macroeconomic stability and resource equilibrium became a major preoccupation over-shadowing both growth and poverty alleviation.[9] Adjustment became the mantra of the decade. In the Bank, structural adjustment became the axis of development thinking and policy and the driver of operational activities.

McNamara's departure from the Bank in 1981 and his replacement by A. W. "Tom" Clausen, a former head of the Bank of America, moder-ated the World Bank's commitment to the dual objectives of growth and poverty alleviation. "The Bank," wrote Stern and Ferreira (1997: 560), "under A. W. Clausen as president, took a cautious line, changing the focus from macroeconomic concerns with the availability of foreign finance (so prominent under McNamara) to microeconomic advice on 'getting the prices right.' External causes were de-emphasized, and blame for the crisis was laid predominantly on domestic policy errors, notably the use of bor-rowed funds for consumption or for investment purposes that were badly directed, partly due to distorted prices." The 1980s were a decade when the earlier approach to development was being sidelined in view of the flag-ging performance of developing economies in the 1970s. Under the Bank's

---

8. Frustration with progress on the development front also arose from the smallness of aggregate aid flows, the resistance of military governments in countries such as Brazil and Chile to policy advice, the need to subordinate sound assistance practices to avert chaos in countries subject to often self-inflicted economic injuries and also to maintain Cold War–related alliances, and the readiness of countries with access to newly augmented supplies of petrodollars to follow their own wayward policies (Kapur, Lewis, and Webb 1997). The constraints that alliances imposed on donor countries continue to hamstring efforts to "advise" client countries or constrain a withdrawal of assistance, as examined by Root (2008).

9. Stern and Ferreira (1997: 545) write that, "under the new direction given to the research depart-ment from 1982 to 1987, the concern with the effects of adjustment on inequality and poverty does seem to have been deemphasized. This is apparent in the little attention dedicated to that concern in the WDRs of that time."

new management, market-based economics began to dominate, echoing a similar change in mindset among mainstream American academics.[10] In particular, the Bank's vice president for development economics, Anne Krueger, who replaced Hollis Chenery, was a staunch advocate of market solutions, and by prevailing over the views of her peers in the management group, she hitched the Bank's approach to development firmly to market forces.

Such thinking had been gaining ground, especially in the United States, for some time. Stagflation in Western countries and slow growth in developing economies through the 1970s induced skepticism of the state-led formulas, import-substituting industrialization (ISI), and the leading role of the public sector and of regulations governing trade, finance, industry, and the labor market.[11] Economists began looking to market forces and competitive pressures to restore growth and revive productivity.[12] Influential politicians found this message appealing, and a diminution of the regulatory state along with the partial dismantling of the public sector through privatization was championed by two of the most influential leaders of the 1980s: Ronald Reagan and Margaret Thatcher. Their political support changed the rules of the economic game and reinforced the ideological current urging reforms and greater openness. Kanbur

---

10. The efficiency of competitive markets, when they work, has a solid grounding in theory. By the 1970s, more and more empirical support had begun accumulating. Pricing, market competition, and free trade are like mothers' milk to economists. Everyone partakes of these factors, but the "hidden hand" is dearer to some than to others and the "magic of the marketplace" is more apparent in some times and at some places than in others. During the quarter century following World War II, the market received due respect in the mixed economies, but not unswerving commitment, and it was largely rooted out in the formal segments of the socialist economies. However, by the early 1970s, a neoclassical resurgence was noticeably apparent, especially in the United States. Among the believers, Béla Balassa's was one of the most respected voices, and his book, *The Structure of Protection in Developing Countries* (Balassa 1971), powerfully argued for the lowering and uniformity of trade barriers and for market pricing. Balassa began consulting for the Bank in 1966, and his views commanded respect, and under Anne Krueger, a more dogmatic neoclassicism gained the upper hand in the Bank. De Haan, Lundström, and Sturm (2006) approvingly survey the empirical evidence on the efficiency of market mechanisms.

11. Two pieces of research that did much to discredit the ISI approach by uncovering its costliness were by Little, Scitovsky, and Scott (1970) and by Bhagwati and Krueger (1973). Additional research buttressing this finding, commissioned by the World Bank, appeared in Michaely, Papageorgiou, and Choksi (1991).

12. Cole and others (2004) ascribe the slow growth of Latin American countries to the lagging rates of increase in total factor productivity. They maintain that the problem can be traced to the large size and inefficiency of the public sector and to trade and entry barriers that reduced competitive pressures on and technology acquisition by domestic industry.

(2005: 13) rightly notes that all of a sudden, in the early 1980s, a switch was thrown, and mainstream economics as practiced in the United States went "from a situation where the state could do no wrong to one where the state could do no right.... The pendulum swung too far the other way. That it began to swing the other way was due to experience. That it swung too far the other way was due to ideology."

External imbalances, financial crises, and inflation—which afflicted many countries, especially in Latin America—were linked to state mismanagement of finances and to the weakness of excessively sheltered financial systems, many of which were dominated by the publicly owned banks. In tackling the problem of resource imbalances, economists began emphasizing domestic resource equilibrium through reforms to increase revenue effort and a one-time augmentation of public resources through the sale of public entities. Tax and public sector reform and privatization, quite suddenly, became immensely popular with policy makers,[13] not the least because public sector deficits in some industrial countries made greater revenue effort a matter of urgency. Much scholarly energy went into designing optimal, decentralized tax systems that met revenue needs while minimizing disincentive effects and into devising optimal ways of auctioning and privatizing public enterprises.[14] This activity was matched

13. These changes encompass civil service reforms, decentralization, and reform of administration (see World Bank 2008a).

14. At that time, much research tried to show that the size of government spending, the size of the public sector, or the steepness of tax rates could slow growth. The Laffer curve captured the essence of this thinking, and although it garnered some empirical support, high levels of public spending in Botswana, the Nordic countries, and Singapore did not detract from their growth performance (Rodrik 2007: 39). Although privatization, especially of industrial enterprises, on balance improves performance and profitability, much depends on the incentives and competitive pressures emanating from the surrounding institutional environment. Creating institutions that will foster longer-term competition is a challenge for policy (Armstrong and Sappington 2006). The modest successes and variability of outcomes worldwide—and more specifically in Europe and in the former socialist economies, where privatization has occurred on a vast scale—is reviewed and assessed by Yusuf, Nabeshima, and Perkins (2005) and by the contributors to Köthenbürger, Sinn, and Whalley (2006) and to Ito and Krueger (2004). Needless to say, when it comes to public utilities, natural monopolies, and even the financial sector, the autonomy and technical expertise of regulatory agencies and the design of regulatory institutions strongly influence economic performance (Jalilian, Kirkpatrick, and Parker 2007). Moreover, as experience has repeatedly shown, the longer-term efficacy of the regulatory system in any area depends on the avoidance of politicization and industry capture of the regulators, the maintenance of high-quality management, and the progressive evolution of the institutions themselves so as to accommodate changing conditions and innovations (Kay 2002). The costly financial crises in developed and developing countries alike have repeatedly driven home these lessons, but legislators and regulators rarely learn and, at best, are prepared for a rerun of the last war and not for a conflict subject to new ground rules.

by equally intense efforts at creating regulatory structures to monitor and supervise newly privatized public utilities, natural monopolies, and banks. Theorizing and policy making triggered by political and economic exigencies in the United Kingdom, the United States, and a few other Western industrial countries quickly spilled over into the advice given to developing countries, with the World Bank leading the charge.

To balance internal adjustment through the reform of public finances and a deepening of the financial sector, development economists also pursued external adjustment, with increasing reliance on market forces. Greater exchange rate flexibility and a more open trading environment gained favor. The wrenching experience with devaluations in the 1970s and the constraints exchange rate fixity imposed on domestic monetary policies paved the way for a broad acceptance of varying degrees of flexibility achieved through a variety of more or less transparent mechanisms for pegging and floating, which were—and are—endlessly debated.[15]

Freer trade—already promoted by the Kennedy and Tokyo Rounds and the creation of the General Agreement on Tariffs and Trade—was boosted by the ambitious Uruguay Round launched in 1986. With countries anxiously seeking pathways to higher growth, a multilateral lowering of trade barriers offered a ray of hope, and the circumstances induced a mutual give and take that has been conspicuously missing from the negotiations associated with the Doha Round, which started in 2002.[16]

The case for openness—for developing countries wedded to protection—was buttressed by the experience of the East Asian "tiger economies,"

15. In many countries where inflation was a persistent concern, the enthusiasm for exchange rate flexibility was curbed by the need for nominal anchors for prices. The importance attached to stabilization also arose from the fear that inflation would smother growth. Following the oil shocks in the 1970s and because of weak macroeconomic management (with some governments attempting to bolster their public finances through inflation taxes), inflation surged, rising to hyperinflationary levels in a few countries. Earlier it appeared that efforts to stabilize might have been too aggressive. When Bruno and Easterly (1998) assessed the costs of inflation in terms of sacrificed growth, they found that only fairly high rates took a toll—in the 40 percent range or higher. More recently, Khan and Senhadji (2001) showed that the safe threshold was in the 11 to 12 percent range. In any case, reducing inflation to the low single-digit levels, as countries were urged to do, did not improve growth performance (Temple 2000).

16. Blonigen (2008) gives three reasons why trade rounds have become longer: more countries are involved, the lower hanging fruit has been picked and only the more complex issues remain, and the political will of all parties has weakened.

which quickly became the role models for other developing countries.[17] These economies were portrayed as single-mindedly pursuing growth through the export of manufactures, relying mainly on market forces to guide the allocation of resources, and exploiting the advantages of greater openness to gain access to overseas markets and to ensure the competitiveness of their industries. Although the degree to which market forces were responsible for directing resource flows to areas of comparative advantage was far less than was assumed, and although most tiger economies nurtured industries behind trade barriers, the East Asian economies, by virtue of their successful growth performance, became the ones to emulate.[18] The message distilled from their experience was that market-guided industrialization within the milieu of a relatively open economy could result in rapid growth if industries were able to compete in export markets.

Thus, economic stagnation in the 1970s and the interrelated oil, financial, and adjustment crises of the early 1980s, which engulfed developed and developing countries alike, prepared the ground for globalization and changes in the role of the state.

The early 1980s were a period of economic distress, with many countries suffering from severe imbalances. It was inevitable, therefore, that the theme of the 1981 *WDR* was adjustment or structural adjustment, as interpreted by the Bank.[19] Structural adjustment was decomposed into two types of policies. Macroeconomic policies stabilized the economy with the help of demand-reducing fiscal policies and resource-switching

---

17. The East Asian tiger economies were more predisposed to seek foreign markets because their domestic markets were small, whereas firms in several of the Latin American economies had relatively large and secure domestic markets (Etzkowitz and Brisolla 1999). Although Korea aggressively sought to expand exports, and the government doled out favors to the *chaebol* (large conglomerates) on the basis of their export performance, national interest and national pride made Koreans highly protectionist with respect to imports not directly feeding their export industries. This effect conforms with the findings of Mayda and Rodrik (2001) about what makes some people and countries more protectionist.

18. The East Asian model diverged substantially from the institutions and policies sanctioned by the mainstream consensus (Amsden 1989; Chung 2007; Crafts 2004a). In fact, Rodrik's visiting "Martian observer" would have had to conclude that because of these discrepancies Japan, Korea, Singapore, and Taiwan, China, had so egregiously violated neoclassical strictures that they had no chance of developing (Rodrik 2007: 18).

19. The 1981 *WDR* was only one among many reports and documents produced by the Bank on the merits of structural adjustment. The Berg report on Africa (Berg 1981) was at least equally influential, and incessant verbal reinforcement in the Bank, led by Stanley Please among others, generated a fervor that bordered on the religious.

exchange rate policies, which channeled more of the economy's resources into exports. Stabilization policies were supposed to reduce domestic and external resource imbalances and curb inflation, thus creating, in principle, an environment more conducive to growth. The other side of adjustment entailed microeconomic engineering through the decontrol of prices, deregulation, privatization of state-owned enterprises, and the dismantling or pruning of public bureaucracies through public sector reforms. This aspect of structural adjustment was seen as vital to ridding the economy of many distorting regulatory encrustations, shrinking the state, and (most important) optimizing the allocation of resources by getting the prices right—one of the enduring mantras of the 1980s and emblematic of the notorious "Washington Consensus" (see chapter 3).

Structural adjustment had an international dimension as well, which was to encourage the recycling of funds from surplus to deficit countries. The 1981 WDR recommended that developing countries faced with adjustment problems be given the breathing space not only through increased resource transfers from overseas in the form of official development assistance, but also through borrowing from private sources and greater reliance on foreign direct investment. This approach helped some countries. Others built up debt obligations that plagued them in the future (Ferreira and Keely 2000).

The Bank yearned for states that adopted a low profile, stuck to providing only the essential public services, and were sparing in their policy interventions, but as described in the 1991 WDR, generally the strong states were the ones that succeeded in satisfactorily stabilizing their economies and introducing market-friendly reforms. In weaker states, potential losers among the elites, state sector employees, recipients of subsidies, and beneficiaries of price regulation were able to resist taking the bitter medicine that was packaged with the structural adjustment loans.

The 1991 WDR also drew favorable attention to the flexibility and export orientation of some countries, such as Korea, which were singled out for their resilience. The note of neoclassicism was to deepen and echo through reports issued into the 1990s, as the Bank was persuaded that creating macroeconomic stability, weeding out internal distortions, and subjecting resource allocation to market discipline were the keys to adjustment and growth.

The 1983 *WDR* went searching for efficiency; uncovered plenty of inefficient projects in the Côte d'Ivoire and Indonesia, for example; and decried the poor maintenance of public highways in Brazil, Nigeria, and elsewhere and, more generally, the waste of resources by public providers. The report embroidered on the theme that was to become a hallmark of the *WDR*s: urging a reliance on the market mechanism, replacing public monopolies (in urban transport, for example) by private firms, and sharply pruning and streamlining regulation. Pragmatism, flexibility, and consensus building were the attributes supposedly responsible for the performance of Brazil, Japan, and Korea in the 1970s, and these attributes fitted well with the basic message the Bank wanted to convey to developing countries: build a robust, market-driven economy in the image of the dynamic Western economies.

Two years later, the 1985 *WDR* returned to the unsettled issue of adjustment and its financing, noting the advantages of complementing project assistance to developing countries with structural adjustment loans that could finance the transitional costs of restructuring and policy reform. The report dwelled on how the resource transfer process was being mediated by newly formed aid consortia and by the ongoing rescheduling initiatives to provide breathing room for borrowers and some relief to lenders caught in the financial train wrecks caused by oil shocks. For the many developing countries that borrowed from commercial sources, the pain from the second oil shock was made more severe by an interest rate shock caused by the massive borrowing of the United States to finance its budget deficit. Looking for exemplars, the 1985 report praised Korea for productively investing the large amounts it borrowed through the early 1980s. It also praised Hong Kong, China; Malaysia; and Singapore for the growth of export-led electronics industries.

By 1986, with adjustment proceeding haltingly and financing gaps continuing to hamstring borrowing countries that were slow to reform, the *WDR* fixed its sights on trade in agriculture products. If developing countries could increase the exports of agricultural commodities, they would partially reduce the financing shortfall. They would lessen poverty in rural areas, and importing countries would gain from scaling down the costly barriers against sugar, oilseeds, and food grains. As is well known, many of the barriers—mainly agricultural subsidies in Organisation for Economic

Co-operation and Development countries—are still firmly in place, despite the Uruguay Round and efforts made to free the trade in agricultural products as a part of the faltering Doha Round. The estimates of gains for all sides presented in 1986 failed to convince policy makers confronting powerful political constituencies.[20]

The issue of financing development from domestic and external sources recurs in the 1987 and 1989 WDRs. The first looks more into the scope for raising capital flows from external sources, given the environment of the 1980s, and for using the flows effectively. The 1989 WDR concentrates on domestic financial development and regulation against the backdrop of the financial crises that were a worrisome feature of the decade and in light of the increasing mobility of capital that the WDRs encouraged by calling for an easing of capital controls.[21] The 1987 WDR complemented the story of financial resource availability and mobilization by analyzing public finances in developing countries with reference to adjustment needs, the demand for capital, and the beginnings of a trend toward fiscal decentralization.

The decade of the 1980s was bookended by two WDRs on poverty. In 1990, the Bank took another close look at what the crises, adjustments, shifts in policy orientation, and greater openness had done for poverty. Predictably, given the weak and variable growth performance of all but the East Asian countries, the poverty scorecard and trends in income distribution were disappointing for most countries. Latin America had lost a decade of development. Sub-Saharan Africa was sliding backward with per capita GDP declining overall. South Asia was little better.

The 1990 WDR reaffirmed the new conventional wisdom regarding the need for leveraging the market in order to stimulate growth by strengthening market institutions. The WDR also stressed the importance of social services for building human capital, which was the ticket to development

---

20. However, with rising food prices in 2007 and 2008, importing countries may be readier to bring down tariff and other barriers on agricultural imports, raising hope for liberalization of agricultural trade.

21. Whether a deepening of the financial sector contributed to growth or was endogenous to growth was still being debated in the 1980s. The case for causality running from finance to growth has been strengthened by an outpouring of research that has examined the role of finance in development across countries over the past several centuries and in recent decades. Rousseau (2002) provides a taste for the former, and Levine (2004) provides a review of the latter. However, as Ang (2008) notes in his survey, the ample cross-country evidence, because of the econometric issues involved, still does not clinch the case, and there remains a need for country-specific research to settle this matter.

for most developing countries that were rich in labor resources. Cautiously the WDR also promoted the notion that even poor countries would benefit from well-designed safety nets. One of the enduring legacies of the WDR was the US$1-a-day metric for measuring poverty.

Some saw the fall of the Berlin Wall as validating free market capitalism and international integration, which had been gaining ground in the 1980s. Many countries were well on their way toward implementing fiscal, financial, and trade reforms initiated in the 1980s. On the threshold of the 1990s, there was a readiness to believe that the potency of a set of policies keyed to the market system had been established. What later came to be known as the Washington Consensus had created the macroeconomic foundations for growth. Now the task before developing nations required detailed attention to the many interconnected sectoral and institutional components of the economy so as to resume desired rates of growth and simultaneously come to grips with the outstanding and neglected poverty agenda. In other words, the macroeconomic fundamentals had been broadly secured in many countries, the axial role of the market was widely accepted, countries were taking steps to "get the prices right" so that the price mechanism could better perform its allocative functions, and the tensions caused by the Cold War were being left behind. As Francis Fukuyama memorably put it, the events in 1989 appeared to herald the "end of history" and the dawn of an era when the market would rule (Fukuyama 1989).[22]

Imagine That There Is No State

However, this brave new world, which seemed so tantalizingly close, quickly began to recede. In most developing and transition countries, markets were woefully underequipped with institutions, and only the state could do the job of carpentering them. Hence, redefining the role of the state, identifying missing institutions, indicating how they contributed to the working of an economy, and proposing blueprints for these institutions became one of the objectives of the WDRs that began appearing in the 1990s.

---

22. It was also seen as an era of accelerating democratization, with the "third wave" gathering momentum (Huntington 1993).

Making the state into a good economic citizen that provides better services was thought to require reducing its size so as to trim public expenditures, narrowing its purview so as to limit its activities to those that were within its institutional capability and those that only the state could realistically provide, increasing administrative efficiency, and engaging the state in crafting the infrastructure for a competitive market environment. The 1997 WDR spelled out the division of labor between resurgent markets and a less obtrusive state that focused on appropriately scaled regulatory needs of efficient markets. Both the 1996 WDR and the 1997 WDR gave special attention to the transition economies and priority to a right-sizing of the state, but neither recommended a "night watchman state."[23] There were things only the state could do, but many, if not most, states had overreached, apparently stunting market growth. A strategic withdrawal and a credible commitment to a narrower role were desirable, clearing the way for the market and for the private sector. This approach was especially urgent in the transition economies. The Bank did not recommend a Big Bang–type divestment of public enterprises and the transfer of numerous responsibilities for services delivery onto the shoulders of private providers, but it encouraged countries to move quickly for fear that resistance to change might harden as the costs of transition wore down people's resolve.[24]

Although the divesture of state assets, the defining of regulatory responsibilities, and the nurturing of market institutions were the themes of both WDRs, the 1996 WDR also was preoccupied with fiscal hygiene, picking up on elements of the 1987 WDR, and stressing how a successful transition demanded an overhaul of public expenditures to make them consonant with the emerging market economy. Many activities needed to be cut back, and in other areas, expenditure had to be redirected. Subsidies, which were widespread, had to be trimmed or eliminated; entitlements needed to be reappraised and reduced. This fiscal makeover had to be coordinated with a new tax structure and effective budget management backstopped by treasury systems that monitored and controlled outlay. In

---

23. The expression was popularized by the libertarian literature on the minimalist state, and a frequently cited source is Nozick (1974). "Night watchman" assumes that the state slumbers most of the time, as would the average guard on night duty.

24. In fact, the WDRs argued for a degree of state activism to lay the groundwork for market institutions and to redefine education policies in anticipation of changing circumstances.

some countries, a degree of fiscal decentralization was desirable so as to generate revenues from subsectoral levies adequate for the revised expenditure responsibilities, to provide better services to local users, and to give market participants the right incentives.

In the 1990s, with nothing approximating a roadmap at hand, the WDRs boldly attempted to put down the markers for a dynamic market and for a disciplined, market-friendly state.

Contesting Poverty and Inequality under Globalization

The Bank turned 50 in 1995 to faint applause. Public protests against the Bretton Woods Institutions at the World Bank–International Monetary Fund Annual Meetings in Madrid dampened the celebratory mood. The protesters' slogan, "50 years is enough," forced the Bank's management to reappraise the Bank's development policies and to intensify its efforts to convince civil society of the Bank's relevance. In June 1995, James D. Wolfensohn succeeded Lewis Preston as president, and Wolfensohn responded to the warning by vigorously burnishing the Bank's image by building bridges to civil society organizations. Wolfensohn's desire to contain the influence of economists in the Bank and to seek inputs from other social sciences nudged the Bank to take a more expansive view of how development occurred. He was supported by two Nobel Prize winners—Amartya Sen and Douglas North—both renowned for their many-sided views of development and, in North's case, for work on institutions. A Democratic administration in the White House and the waning of the Cold War also tempered the ideological passions of the 1980s and revived the objectives that had been prominent in the earliest WDRs.

"A world free of poverty" became the Bank's mission statement; inclusive and sustainable development was adopted as the new strategy; and in the face of external pressures, civil society was embraced as the Bank's partner in development. The changing global context of the Bank's operations began surfacing in the WDRs that appeared from the late 1990s onward—reports that also carried, to varying degrees, the imprint of the Bank's chief economist from 1997 to 2000, Joseph Stiglitz. The 1998/99 WDR acknowledged the enormous significance of information and knowledge for development and of the unequal access to this knowledge—one of

Stiglitz's major contributions to economic theory. In a globalizing world, information, information technologies, the Internet, and institutions that were transforming the sharing of information had become as intrinsic to growth as physical capital, opening a whole new range of opportunities for developing countries and at the same time bringing them face to face with a fresh sheaf of policy issues. These issues included the pricing of information technology services, the manufacture of telecommunications equipment, physical investment in infrastructure, training in new skills, the building of innovation systems, and the protection of intellectual property, to name some of the most prominent.

The changing context of development as the world stepped into the 21st century was examined in detail by the 1999/2000 WDR. According to this report, the landscape of development was being reshaped by four major forces—globalization arising from flows of trade, capital, people and ideas; climate and environmental changes; localization stemming from the combined effects of fiscal and administrative decentralization; and rapid urbanization, which was creating increasingly autonomous concentrations of people and economic activity.

Against this canvas, the Bank's third WDR on poverty took up the theme of inclusive, pro-poor growth strategies that more fully harnessed the potential inherent in communities through active participation by community members. In addition, it attempted to magnify the effects of growth by reducing disparities in the distribution of assets. The 2000/2001 WDR maintained the Bank's cautious line on the role of the state, emphasizing instead the value of public-private partnerships and private initiatives to supply vital education, health, and infrastructure services. The state could bolster these activities through public regulation of pricing for such services, for instance, and by enforcing education standards. In the spirit of earlier reports, the WDR made the obligatory and gnomic remarks on how the state and society needed to work together. But the WDR pinned its hopes on private individuals finding their voices, their banding together to monitor the quality of services, and their combating disease through immunization campaigns and education. Time and again, it fastened on community-planned, community-managed, and community-implemented schemes as the way to succeed and on the contributions of private suppliers as the agents for easing bottlenecks of water and sanitation services, among others.

It was left to the 2004, 2006, and 2007 WDRs to add detail to the pro-poor, services-led, and redistributive and participatory development strategy reaffirmed by the 2000/2001 WDR, by the 1993 WDR on health, and by the 1994 WDR on infrastructure. By this time, the Bank had gone almost full circle through a forest of new research back to the views expressed in the earliest WDRs. Growth was necessary but not sufficient. It had to be supported by infrastructure and other services so as to build human capital, especially among the poor, and to lessen the inequity of assets and incomes. The difference was that catalyzing and leveraging community capital to encourage grassroots development was given much greater prominence, and a profusion of examples and findings buttressed the case for development with a more participatory and egalitarian face.

It is impossible to convey a sense for the smorgasbord of ideas collected from across the globe. Clearly, solving the problems of services delivery has attracted attention from many quarters. That the delivering of services remains bedeviled by problems means that we can expect another round of WDRs on this topic 30 years hence, if writing such reports remains fashionable. What we now know more clearly than we did in 1978 is that providing quality health and education services is a task of daunting complexity. To arrive at decent results calls for a melding of market incentives with regulatory checks and direct public provision, which can vary from case to case. There is no one solution, naturally—only broad guidelines with multiple embedded requirements. An example is decentralization, plus the autonomy and flexibility of providers that are disciplined by standards, quality and certification procedures, and competition and by mechanisms of accountability that are enforced by individuals, the community, and public agencies working individually or in tandem. Limited autonomy given to teachers in designing courses that students find to be relevant and in adopting pedagogical styles can be usefully reinforced by financial incentives to induce motivation.[25] Attempts can be made to raise

---

25. Mullainathan (2005: 63) ascribes teacher absenteeism, which is widespread in South Asia and Sub-Saharan Africa, to a lack of motivation because "teachers are often frustrated by the apathy of parents towards their children's education.... As teachers perceive it, their own efforts to keep the children at school are not reciprocated by the parents." Mullainathan frames a solution in terms that would make the average policy maker quail. He writes, "The problem of teacher attendance cannot be studied in isolation.... The impact of teacher incentive policies may vary dramatically with the context. In a context of limited resources where attendance is low, these policies may have only a small or moderate impact. On the other hand, if teacher incentives are coupled with other policies to increase both resources as a whole and student attendance, the impact might be much

teacher quality through more rigorous certification, except that this process could diminish the supply of teachers. But it would not reduce the variation in teacher quality (Hanushek and Rivkin 2006). Conditional cash transfers can encourage students to attend school. But that alone will not do the trick when the home or cultural environment is unfavorable. The amount of time parents devote to nurturing their children matters, and at least the research in the United States shows that it is the wealthier and better educated parents who give more time and attention to their children (Guryan, Hurst, and Kearney 2008). If this is the case also in developing countries, then the gulf between the home environment of the lower- and upper-income groups will be harder to close. School resources are yet another policy instrument that receives attention, but as Hanushek (2006: 902) observes, "even in the poorest areas of the world, it is difficult to identify a minimum threshold of resources where there are clear impacts on student outcomes."

Although "findings" are abundant, policy making on education, even in the United States, faces severe challenges: the high school dropout rate is increasing and graduation rates are inching downward, although the demand for skilled labor is rising and with it the earnings premium for skills (Altonji, Bharadwaj, and Lange 2008; Deming and Dynarski 2008; Heckman and LaFontaine 2008). Economic incentives appear to be overshadowed by other considerations, and thus far, the best research is failing to produce a reliable compass.

Picking up some of the threads from the 1995 WDR, the 2007 WDR notes that youth in developing countries need—in addition to grants and loans—mentoring, employment services, on-the-job training, and at times employee sponsorship to be effectively absorbed into the job market: a big challenge for training systems in developed countries and an almost impossible one in developing countries.

---

larger. The teachers would then no longer feel self-justified for their absence, and the incentives needed to get them to work may be much smaller." The limited research on financial incentives for teachers is mainly derived from the United States and comes to equivocal results (Hanushek and Rivkin 2006). The problem of teacher apathy and low attendance appears more acute when it emerges that teachers are already relatively more expensive (in terms of salaries) in poor countries than in ones that are better off (Banerjee and Duflo 2004). Even if the problems of teacher and student absenteeism are solved, low-income countries do not necessarily derive the above-normal gains from education that one would expect in view of the shortages. In fact, the return to an extra year of education is no higher in poorer countries (Banerjee and Duflo 2004). Of course, we can cherry-pick the results that we like and that conform to our priors and criticize those that do not, which is common enough, but all econometricians live in glass houses, and sadly, all results have a soft and vulnerable underside.

Competition from private schools and health providers is an important spur to competition, and the main source of growth in supply for lower-income groups is access to privately supplied services, with some assistance from vouchers and targeted subsidies. Where public agencies or community bodies have the administrative capacities, contractual arrangements that set fees can help deliver quality services, appropriately distributed.

The WDRs recognize that setting, collecting, and regulating user charges for energy, sanitation, and water is never easy, because a consistently effective, autonomous, and apolitical body is hard to create. And even when user charges generate a flow of revenue, many projects need a diversity of sources of financing to break even. All of these challenges are illuminated by a wealth of examples on financing services, with commentary on how well individual initiatives have performed.

The three WDRs on poverty have impressively summarized the evidence at different points in time and have helped to make poverty the focus of national and global attention. Each decadal WDR has documented our deepening understanding of poverty and the multistranded efforts to drive poverty back. The earliest WDRs expressed the Bank's belief that growth must be supplemented with active measures to redistribute the benefits achieved for poverty to be decisively repulsed. The 1980, 1990, and 2000/2001 WDRs have successively elaborated on the scope for direct intervention and the forms it can take within the framework of a market economy. Other WDRs have described how human and community or social capital can attempt to accelerate the reduction of poverty. Increasingly, the WDRs have underlined the potential for decentralized community-led, community-financed, and community-monitored schemes and the desirability of public-private partnerships. A belief in the utility of direct actions has been fused with the view that such actions should enhance the supply of certain essential services that together will enlarge the economic potential of the poorest. The latest WDRs hew to the storyline of the earliest reports and echo sophisticated notions about basic needs and capabilities that first surfaced in the 1970s. However, they substantially embellish the proposals from three decades ago, and supporting the current views is the full weight of recent research on the microeconomics of services delivery.

What the research cannot establish is the scope for lowering poverty levels using services as the lever in the absence of robust growth, although with growth the effect of services can be enhanced. Nor has it been easy to find more than a small handful of examples of countries that have maintained or achieved a more equal distribution of income. Try as we might, there is no escaping the growth imperative. Better policies can reinforce the effects of growth on poverty, but when growth is weak, services cannot easily be financed, nor are they likely to contribute more than marginally to the overall reduction in poverty. However, in the majority of cases, growth has not improved the distribution of income. In fact, in most high-performing East Asian economies, the incomes have become more skewed. So the WDRs, since the beginning of the decade, have oscillated between topics related more to poverty alleviation and topics slanted mainly toward growth. Whether the reports address one theme or the other, the orientation is toward the microlevel issues that keep the private sector firmly in their sights and that offer suggestions on coping with narrowly defined problem situations.

From Getting Prices Right to Getting Institutions Right

The microeconomics of growth in the 2002 and 2006 WDRs places a heavy emphasis on institutions that affect market functioning and the entry, innovativeness, and growth of firms. The disappointing experience with implementing structural adjustment programs in the 1980s and the weak response of growth to the market (institution) building policies deployed during the period convinced the Bank that governance, rent seeking, and regulatory policies were critical bottlenecks to growth. The dead hand of even a shrunken state could continue stifling the economy. Hence, the WDRs directed their firepower at four target areas. First was the governance of regulatory bodies that affected the functioning of numerous private providers of everything from financial to infrastructure to health services. The transparency, accountability, and independence of these bodies needed to be improved, and their administrative and policy-making capacities strengthened. The WDRs loosened salvo after salvo at the recalcitrant issue of governance, as defined by the Bank.[26] The

---

26. The 1983 WDR was the first to draw attention to the quality of government. Its importance was further underlined by a report titled *Governance and Development* (World Bank 1992) and

second target was information gaps and asymmetries—the cause of market failures and countless economic ills. Fixing institutions or removing impediments to the free flow of information through market and media channels were matters of urgency.

The third target was a concern over barriers to the entry and functioning of firms, created in part by regulations that curtailed competition. Nick Stern, the Bank's chief economist from 2000 to 2003, was instrumental in making the assessment of the investment climate in member countries an integral part of the Bank's economic analysis of countries. His conception of the determinants of this climate was sweeping and required detailed, locally conducted surveys of firms. These surveys complement and go beyond the Doing Business data that the Bank has been collecting since 2004. To make the investment climate more supportive of growth required filing down the transaction costs arising from formal rules of entry, such as registration. It includes a rating of customs procedures, labor laws, visits to workplaces by inspectors, rent-seeking behavior of officials, and many more indicators. As with the Doing Business indicators, the Bank sees some merit to having entry regulations, so it has not called for a wholesale elimination (which would be logical) of such rules. But it is convinced that lowering costs, simplifying procedures, and shortening the time needed to fulfill them; making internal labor markets more flexible; and creating greater transparency would be good for competition and for growth. Whether or not this short-term advantage translates into longer-term gains in terms of lower life-cycle transaction costs and higher growth has been downplayed to make the diagnosis easier and to arrive at simpler decision rules (Arrunada 2007). It is no surprise that some empirical findings point to a relationship running from a lowering of short-term transaction costs to improved productivity in the short term. But these are early days, and we know from bitter experience that short-term accelerations have a distressing tendency to tail off.[27]

was elaborated in the 1997 *WDR*, as well as in a report by the Bank that identified the corrosive effects of corruption and stressed that combating corruption should be part and parcel of the effort to reform governance (World Bank 1997). On issues pertaining to the definition of *governance* and on indicators, see Kaufmann and Kraay (2008). Quibria (2006) notes that some of the successful East Asian economies cannot claim high standards of governance, and he fails to find much by way of a positive association between good governance and growth. A recent survey of worldwide governance indicators by Iqbal and Shah (2008) concludes that they fail on most fundamental considerations: the lack of a conceptual framework and the use of flawed and biased primary indicators.

27. The research on the investment climate reported in the 2005 *WDR* uses cross-country and single-country evidence to link an assortment of factors to explain changes in investment rates

A fourth concern is enforcement of property rights, of contracts, and of rules that affect market functioning. Efficient markets need effective mechanisms to make these rights, or rules stick through formal legal or administrative means or informal community- or group-related ones.

The 2002 and 2005 WDRs forcefully argue that institutions matter and that there is a need for institutional diversity. In addition, the 2002 WDR also stresses the importance of complementary institutions. Both WDRs stress the case for certain kinds of regulatory institutions and particular types of remedial measures aimed at governance and transaction costs. As with public services that augment human capital and its employability, the "getting institutions right" theme continues the effort to circumscribe the role of the state and to make markets and private entities do the jobs the state has attempted to do, supposedly at considerable cost to society.

The Green Agenda and Agriculture

In the late 1980s, the Bank came under pressure from environmental groups in Germany, the United Kingdom, and the United States to take cognizance of and factor in the environmental spillovers from development. By the

---

and in productivity. For instance, it uses property rights, licensing procedures, tariff reforms, and reforms of regulation and of the legal system to establish the gains from a better investment climate. The net is cast widely, and whatever is caught is classified as a fish. The notion that greasing the channels through which investment flows will enlarge the flow is plausible. The eclectic selection of evidentiary material and the absence of robust, econometrically reliable results running from a limited and uniform set of explanatory investment climate variables to growth raise questions. If a set of interventions does not reliably feed through into growth and if estimation is beset by the usual medley of problems, then do we have a dependable policy tool? Investment climate surveys somewhat akin to the narrower Doing Business approach run into similar problems of determining how to make comparisons across countries, how to interpret and explain responses of firms, and how to gauge the adequacy and appropriateness of regulations. Firms frequently report a shortage of skills but will do little to remedy the problem through in-house training or by use of public training facilities. They will complain about the lack of access to credit on terms they deem acceptable; however, this response crops up in economies with flourishing businesses and in stagnating economies. In rich countries and poor, start-ups and small businesses rely mainly on their own resources, so determining whether the shoe is really pinching from these surveys is hard. It is the same with regulation. All businesses want less red tape, and this cry is heard in successful economies such as China and lagging ones in Sub-Saharan Africa. If one assumes that a sound regulatory framework to manage business development is desirable and that circumstances vary from country to country, there is no reliable rule to tell us when regulation is excessive and how much room there is for scaling back the time costs without compromising the system. Current comparisons are much too coarse grained and apply crude rules of thumb when the heterogeneity among countries would argue against such approaches. Making policy with reference to cross-country Investment Climate Assessments borders on rank empiricism and casts overboard theory and analysis, which supposedly underlie policy making. The approach runs the risk of becoming mechanical, ahistorical, and detached from context.

end of the 1980s, the Bank had created a new department for this purpose and introduced environmental reviews for all projects supplemented by environmental assessments where indicated (Marcus 2002: F134). In 1992, the *WDR* put forth the Bank's views on how growth could be made environmentally friendly. In accordance with the conventional wisdom at that time, the Bank stayed very much in the middle of the road. It supported conservation of resources and control of pollution with the help of pricing, regulation, and technology. It looked to advances in science and technology to diversify sources of energy and to increase the efficiency with which other resources were used. And the Bank turned to institutions such as titling to protect land, forest, and water resources and international agreements to safeguard the global commons.

Eleven years later, the 2003 *WDR* returned to this very same terrain. It had fresh observations and information on many of the topic areas of the 1992 *WDR* because so much more was known. However, with the Bank enthusiastically committed to the theme of institution and community development and grassroots initiatives, it was inevitable that this *WDR* was especially vocal on institutions for protecting rights over resources such as water, institutions for coastal and river basin management, and international institutions to share environmental abatement costs. Likewise, the *WDR* pursued sustainable development at the local level, exploring the role of communities, nongovernmental organizations, informal village networks, and associations in the broad and even distribution of the benefits.[28]

The first *WDR* talked of measures to raise agricultural productivity and observed that technological advances, now accelerated by biotechnologies and made more urgent by impending climate change, are a potent force. They will need to complement other factors. The 1978 *WDR* briefly

---

28. Local participation is attractive in theory but is an uncertain mechanism for delivering results. Thirty years ago, self-managed units in the former Yugoslavia looked better on paper than in terms of execution and outcomes. Similarly, achieving the kind of participation that leads to better services is often an uphill task. This challenge has been shown by three experiments with village-level participation to improve education services in India. Even though many villagers signed up for the programs, the effect on teacher effort or on student learning was negligible, thus suggesting that the act of participation is only a first step. How to make such programs produce results is little understood (Banerjee and others 2008). Mansuri and Rao (2004) further add that community participation in the World Bank's projects does not tend to improve outcomes. It is only with careful design, strong government commitment, the avoidance of capture by elites, and a long time horizon that a better targeting of the poor and better results can be achieved.

touched on institutions, which occupy far more space in the 2008 *WDR*. The 2008 report embraces the agricultural innovation system, mechanisms for promoting technology transfer, market coordination, and many other issues, including, of course, community-based development. Thirty years ago, sustainability was not yet on the horizon; now there is rich experience in specifying and monitoring rules, in mobilizing resources, and in disseminating technology. This theme was in tune with the *WDR*s written after 2000: the melody was the familiar one, but the high notes struck were institutions, inclusiveness, and sustainability.

The 2008 *WDR* also comes at a time when record-high prices for grain and edible oils and worries about the implications of global warming for the low-income countries with large rural populations are bringing hunger and food security to the center of policy debates. Sharp peaks in food prices have occurred in the past, most markedly between 1977 and 1980 and again in 1986, 1994, and 1998, but after each surge, supply responded to bring prices down, and such an adjustment is likely this time around as well. However, the extreme drought in Australia (which has dramatically cut the rice crop) and uncertainties about future rainfall in other parts of the world are making people less sanguine about the longer-term prospects. For many low-income countries in Africa, the situation is rendered precarious by sharply declining cultivable acreage per inhabitant (see table 2.1). Rapid population growth is one factor. Low and variable rainfall and

Table 2.1: Total Rain-Fed and Irrigated Land in 12 Agriculture-Dependent Countries with High Population Growth Rates, 2000 and 2050

	Land distribution (hectares/inhabitant)	
Country	2000	2050
Afghanistan	0.28	0.07
Benin	1.38	0.45
Burkina Faso	1.83	0.53
Burundi	0.19	0.05
Chad	4.37	1.14
Congo, Dem. Rep. of	3.75	1.06
Ethiopia	0.59	0.24
Madagascar	2.08	0.77
Mali	2.35	0.65
Niger	0.98	0.23
Somalia	0.57	0.19
Uganda	0.57	0.11

Source: Alexandratos 2005: table 3.

desertification are two additional factors that will further exacerbate the already dire circumstances (Alexandratos 2005; UNDP 2007).

Quite unexpectedly, the 2008 *WDR* picked a theme perfectly in keeping for a world once again worrying over food security in the face of rising food prices.[29] The 1978 *WDR* had sought to arrange a marriage of growth and poverty reduction through the intermediation of smallholder agriculture. Despite the passage of time and substantial reductions in the share of the population falling below the poverty line, most of the poor are still in the rural areas (three-quarters of those living on less than a dollar a day). Realizing the Bank's dream of a world without poverty still requires measures to raise incomes in the rural areas across the world, to increase migration to urban centers, and to provide employment for the newcomers; national and community-level resource management efforts to ensure the sustainability of growth; and a host of techniques (many low tech) that will raise agricultural productivity.

Searching for Growth, Finding Poverty

This chapter completes a look back over the 30 reports that have catalogued the World Bank's "passions and interests"[30] in the sphere of development. All of them engage the issues of growth, poverty reduction, and development more generally, but that is a loose way of encircling the content of the reports. There is, as the above sketch indicates, no easy way of categorizing the reports so as to bring out the logic underlying the choice of topics and the progression from one topic to the next. I have tried to relate the topics to external circumstances to which the Bank was responding, to changing currents of thinking on development, and to the views of the Bank's management. Essentially, the first few reports were mapping the terrain of development, identifying the sectoral sources of growth, arriving at some baseline measures of poverty, and experimenting with ways of tackling poverty once growth was achieved. Through a stretch of the 1980s, the Bank's energies were devoted to inducing countries to adjust and to make

---

29. The 2008 *WDR* referred to a likely reversal in the downward trend in food prices; however, it did not foresee the sharp increase that occurred in 2008 (World Bank 2007: 8).

30. This expression was first delineated and discussed by Adam Smith and then adopted by Albert Hirschman (1997) as the title of a quirky and intriguing book, which is definitely not on the reading lists of those whose horizons extend from randomization to endogeneity.

the transition to a market-based system that scaled down the role of the state in a globalizing environment. Thereafter, from the mid 1990s, once James Wolfensohn became president, the *WDRs* became increasingly pre-occupied with growth and poverty, analyzing them from microeconomic, institutional, and sectoral perspectives.

The three big shifts between the earlier and later reports were from state-directed to market-guided development, from structural to sectoral issues, and from macroeconomic concerns to microeconomic ones. This summary glosses over details, but it approximately renders the significant changes in orientation.

These shifts are informative in several ways. They capture the big ideo-logical move from state-dominated economies whose inefficiencies were progressively revealed, to economic systems in which the state worked with and through markets. The collapse of communism in Europe was the decisive turning point. At the earlier stage of development, structural characteristics of the economy affected growth, macroeconomic stability, and adjustment. Financial and fiscal systems were weak, the public sector bulked large, and in many low-income countries, most of the popula-tion was in the rural areas, and agricultural performance and population growth exerted a major influence on the growth of per capita GDP. Devel-opment in the 1980s and early 1990s and the reform outcomes dimmed the appeal of structural policies, especially in Latin America.

By the 1990s, inflation and the worst of the resource imbalances were under control, and macroeconomic management was better codified. But growth had not revived, and both the poverty headcount and income dis-tributions had worsened throughout parts of the developing world. So the emphasis shifted to the micro issues. The fascination with microlevel anal-ysis tracked the prevailing fashions in academia. These approaches favor the framing and testing of narrow hypotheses and are greatly preoccupied with the minutiae of economic plumbing. They assume that if we can gain a better understanding of every bend and twist of the pipes that are already there and a sense for the ones that are missing, it will become easier to comprehend and to manage economic forces.[31]

---

31. Meier (2005: 183) has rightly underlined the penchant of development economists to "think small," preferring what one might call the "homeopathic" approach to problem solving by slicing the problem ever more finely. He writes that "much of the evolution of development economics has

Placing the 30th *WDR* alongside the first reveals glaring differences. The 2008 *WDR* is 318 pages in length, with references; it is tightly thematic; and it is shorn off the overview of the world economy that was a feature of the first nine *WDR*s. It is a more technical document, with 1,150 references and 1,100 footnotes. It is festooned with boxed information,[32] with some boxes straddling two closely argued and information-packed pages. It is immensely more informative, providing the reader with reams of cross-country experience and details on developments and policies—reflecting the outpouring of research on agriculture and related fields, not to mention the sheer wealth of information one can now marshal with a few keystrokes, thanks to the Internet. The 2008 *WDR* is far more numerate and dressed up with colorful charts and tables, reflecting advances in data gathering, computing power, and printing technology, as well as a relative decline in the costs of printing using four colors. Most notably, the 2008 *WDR* no longer contains the *World Development Indicators*. These indicators have proven to be so valuable to all those associated with the business of development that they now have a life of their own and are issued annually in a volume that rivals the *WDR* in size and sales. In keeping with the march of technology, the *World Development Indicators* are available on a CD-ROM and on the Web.

When the 1978 *WDR* was written, 70 percent of the population (and the most of the poor) in the developing world lived in rural areas. It was fitting, therefore, that the first *WDR* assigned substantial importance to the role of the agricultural economy. But the 1978 *WDR* also attempted to encompass development in the larger sense. It was concerned with the forest more than with the trees. Its ambition was pitched at a different level: to strike the high notes of development strategy as perceived in those times. Now a much lengthier report devotes many more tightly argued pages to ·

been based on the reductionist model of analysis—analyzing the problem in smaller and smaller constituent parts—going down from the aggregate economy to particular sectors, to firms, and to households." He continues, "In concentrating on microeconomics, economists [are] failing to focus on development as a dynamic process with attention to the interrelation of the parts" (Meier 2005: 185). The trend is to go ever deeper into the minutiae of economic decision making by trying to probe the mind of the decision maker as a saver, investor, or criminal. New subfields are springing up, such as cognitive and neurological economics, that are trying to find more scientific ways of determining how individuals make choices. Experimental economics has taken on a greater prominence, and the gaming perspective is now intrinsic to the teaching of economics.

32. This feature first appeared in the 1980 *WDR*, and its use has become rampant since, spreading in a viral fashion to other annuals and encouraging grazing instead of reading.

a small and shrinking part of the forest and takes the reader from one tree to the next. It is much more of a specialists' WDR, with a 25-page overview for the general reader. The 1978 WDR could, in those distant times, be read quickly and profitably by anyone with an interest in development issues. The circle of serious readers is likely to be smaller now because the content is far more specialized and more voluminous, and its density has risen manifold. The economic salience of agriculture is significantly lower than it was in the mid 1970s. Agriculture now contributes on average just 20 percent of the GDP in low-income countries and 8 percent in middle-income countries. Exports of agriculture commodities in 2004 composed less than 7 percent of total world exports (FAO 2006). More than half of the world is urbanized, and economic growth will be derived mainly from urban activities; agriculture itself is becoming coextensive with industry.

The 30th WDR does not provide a compact assessment of the state of development. It takes a narrower cut and seeks to go deeper, leaving it to other reports to satisfy the readership wanting a bird's-eye view and a sense for what the broad policy directions ought to be. Many will argue that the thematic and weightier WDR adds greater value, and cumulatively the WDRs are uncovering layer by layer the inner workings of development and making them easier to manage. That may be true. However, the fact remains that only the diligent student will read the WDR from cover to cover, and the vast majority of even the selected readership with an interest in the topic of the WDR will not go beyond the usually well-crafted summaries.

Achievement and Questions

WDRs are expensive to produce, and as the report enters its fourth decade, it is worth asking whether the Bank's research funds and some of its elite human capital are being used most fruitfully and whether the distilling of the received wisdom on development and the careful teasing out of policies have actually codified and simplified the task of development. Policy makers with all 30 WDRs in their libraries can access an enormous amount of information on past and current economic theory and practice. They have at their disposal a wealth of research done within and outside the Bank.[33]

---

33. Whether they are worth consulting is a separate matter. Past research in economics dates very rapidly, and the shelf life of even the most exhaustive survey is short. The citation tally for the

In principle, all of this information should make development a lot less demanding. Sustaining high rates of growth and reducing poverty should be a science with clear logical rules because powerful and tested theories are at hand, thanks to the painstaking efforts of a reputable international agency. But are sustainable growth and poverty reduction a far simpler proposition for a policy maker today than they were when the first *WDR* was published? Are we seeing evidence of this trend from the demonstrated performance of low- and middle-income countries? Are we closer to the day when the policy maker can simply wind up the economy as if it were a mechanical clock and then expect it to run smoothly, with just the occasional adjustment, some oiling, minor repairs, the periodic cleaning?

Precise answers to these questions are inconceivable. The detailed weighing of theory, policy, and evidence—even if attempted—would be monumental, unreadable, and like all of economics, ultimately inconclusive.[34] I will not attempt to do this in a short essay. However, at a more general level, I will stand on the shoulders of the *WDRs*—or, more appropriately, the shoulders of the contributors to the *WDRs*—and examine six key themes that some or all of the WDRs have sought to elucidate directly and indirectly. My purpose is to gauge how far the research has moved toward more effective and reliable policies

- on achieving and sustaining rapid growth;
- on the necessary institutional conditions for building a dynamic market economy;
- on achieving resource balances with available supplies (what is the desirable equilibrium point and how might countries arrive at this point so as to maintain a medium term balance?);

WDRs in academic journals provides a revealing glimpse. Most *WDRs* receive 20 to 30 citations per year, with the number decreasing after about 8 to 10 years, although many more citations appear in books and other publications. See appendix B for details on citations. The 1993 *WDR* on health remains the most widely cited because it popularized an indicator for measuring and aggregating health conditions. This so-called DALY (for disability-adjusted life year) is a metric to gauge how much savings can be derived from each type of health intervention. Using this measure, the *WDR* showed that close to half of all DALYs lost in Sub-Saharan Africa could be traced to a small number of preventable infections—diseases such as diarrhea, measles, tuberculosis, and malaria. The DALY can be a useful yardstick; however, its very simplicity has tended to encourage mechanical analyses of the cost-effectiveness of different types of treatment and preventive measures, and these analyses frequently lead to a generic menu of policies with little differentiation to accommodate the circumstances of individual countries.

34. The contributors to Pardey and Smith (2004) nevertheless take a stab at evaluating the worth of economic research.

- on the role of the state in the changing development context;
- on the recipes for reducing poverty over the longer term; and
- on whether official development assistance is contributing to growth and poverty reduction in the receiving countries.

This list is not exhaustive, and it was not supposed to be; however, these are arguably themes that the *WDR*s have circled for 30 years, and they are central to the activity of development.

3

HOW MUCH FARTHER
CAN WE SEE?

The policy recipes being retailed in the 1970s had the advantages of simplicity and clarity: to grow, countries needed to raise the level of investment and to channel as much of the capital they could into industry. Capital accumulation that leveraged embodied technical progress and learning by doing was shown to produce results in capitalist economies such as Germany and Japan and in socialist economies such as the China and the Soviet Union. Rising investment also seemed to account for the performance of developing economies such as Brazil, Kenya, and Pakistan. By the early 1980s, the East Asian tiger economies added success at exporting manufactures to the list of recipes.

Conditions during the 1980s shifted the policy focus to adjustment supported by measures promoting reliance on market forces and openness. Starting in the 1990s, and in line with changing academic and popular perceptions in the advanced countries, the notion of an industrial Big Push fueled by capital and low-wage workers was gradually superseded by a far more ambitious and complex pro-poor approach to achieve growth. This approach recognizes the significance of many intersecting complementarities. In certain respects, it echoes the balanced-growth thinking of the 1950s. Capital is one ingredient, but rapidly ramping up capital spending is no longer a major objective. Instead, the approach emphasizes the following goals: (a) strengthening market institutions and improving the allocation of resources (a theme central to several WDRs), (b) whittling away the transaction costs of doing business, (c) following a multipronged strategy for augmenting human capital and its quality and for deepening technological capabilities so that more and more countries can realize the dream of smart growth based on inspiration, and (d) achieving desirable structural changes.

This approach seems to be a far cry from the old model of development that depended on a bucketful of perspiration: the input of labor and capital into the productive sectors.[1] It is a promising model supported by numerous microlevel findings that appear to validate specific details, but the big test of the model lies ahead in Sub-Saharan Africa and in South Asia. Can countries with low savings, low rates of capital accumulation, limited manufacturing capabilities, and ramshackle education systems achieve high growth by adopting the recipe emerging from the recent WDRs? After running 2 million regressions, Sala-i-Martin (1997, 2002: 19) confesses that "we have learned a lot about growth in the last few years. However, we still do not seem to understand why Africa turned to have such a dismal growth performance ... Understanding the underlying reasons for this gargantuan failure is the most important question the economics profession faces as we enter the new century."[2] It is not the only one. Why are the Russian Federation and Eastern Europe lagging behind East Asia in high-tech manufacturing and technological prowess? Can India maintain high rates of growth with a small manufacturing sector? What is the secret of innovativeness, and why is Europe's innovativeness so hard to increase? Why are Latin American countries marking time with growth rates of 4 and 5

---

1. The inspiration versus perspiration approaches were popularized by Krugman's (1994) article on the "Asian miracle."

2. The trouble with growth economics is that it looks mainly at the supply side and fixes its sights on the very long run: periods of 30 years or more. Short-term demand shocks that account for the perturbations that are the stuff of everyday policy concerns simply cannot be explained, which is unsatisfactory. Short-term fluctuations can have long-run echo effects because they influence investment decisions.

percent at best? And so on. There is no dearth of research and informed conjectures, but in several important areas, our understanding remains shallow, and there have been few significant gains on the policy front.

Growth through Perspiration

Currently, the two fastest-growing economies in the world, which have kept up this tempo for 10 years or more, are China and India. China's rate of investment is 43 percent and has been since the early 1990s. India's rate is almost 37 percent and could rise further if high growth is sustained. Other fast-expanding economies in East Asia, such as Singapore and Vietnam, also have notably elevated levels of investment, averaging 34 percent and 29 percent, respectively, during 1996 to 2000. In Sub-Saharan Africa, the acceleration in growth evident since 2001 to 2002 is directly related to demand shifts through increased spending on infrastructure, urban real estate, and resource development. It is also associated with rising prices of energy and mineral exports that have led to a boom in consumer spending.[3]

A reading of the experience of the fastest-growing economies would lead one to conclude that high and rising rates of capital accumulation are as significant as they were 30 and 50 years ago: they augment productive capacity; they introduce embodied technological change; they promote learning; they permit industries to realize scale economies and to diversify; and they facilitate infrastructure building and urban development, which further boosts productivity. In a world in which trade barriers are far lower and distances have been truncated by falling costs of transport,[4] countries that invest in capacity and become competitive

---

3. Nevertheless, gross domestic investment has increased relatively little, and earlier research by Devarajan, Easterly, and Pack (2001) fails to link faltering growth to low rates of investment in Sub-Saharan Africa. The growth surge in Sub-Saharan Africa is vulnerable to a decline in the prices of petroleum and raw materials and to decreasing flows of capital from overseas.

4. On this issue, see Hummels (2001). Unfortunately, Sub-Saharan Africa has benefited less than other parts of the world. The logistics cost of a typical import transaction amounts to US$2,000 in Africa and takes 58 days to complete as against US$1,130 and 33 days in East Asia (Eifert, Gelb, and Ramachandran 2008; see Portugal-Pérez and Wilson 2008 on the border and behind-the-border costs). It is interesting that Jacks and Pendakur (2008) find that the 50 percent drop in freight rates between 1870 and 1913 contributed minimally to the boom in trade during that period. With fossil fuel prices on an upward trend, one question that arises is whether the trade in certain kinds of goods will be affected and what will happen to the sprawling international value chains for manufactures and agricultural products. By mid 2008, the cost of shipping a 40-foot container from Shanghai to the U.S. East Coast had risen from US$3,000 in 2000 to US$8,000 ("High Seas, High Prices" 2008).

can command global markets for their products. Those left behind are the ones that have cut back on capital accumulation. Even though billions have been poured into infrastructure in developing countries, it remains an Achilles heel for most economies. The emphasis of the 1994 WDR was as appropriate then as it is now. A report on infrastructure in East Asia (Asian Development Bank 2005) estimated that countries in the region would need to invest close to US$200 billion annually over the next five years in new infrastructure to keep pace with growing demand and to maintain the existing facilities. Recent evidence of acute shortages of power in Indonesia, tightening power supplies in China as older coal-fired stations are closed, and infrastructure constraints more generally throughout South and Southeast Asia reinforces the point ("Indonesia: Power Problems" 2008; "International: Asian Infrastructure" 2008). The relatively high failure rate of such projects in the region and the limited funding available from private sources (5 percent) places the burden of responsibility on the public sector both (a) to improve the contractual and regulatory environment to attract more private capital and (b) to find the resources to make up for the difference. Meeting energy requirements will be one of the biggest challenges in view of global warming concerns and the tightening world market for hydrocarbons. Overall, the International Energy Administration projects that US$22 trillion will have to be invested in energy supply infrastructure between now and 2030 to meet rising demand, three-fourths of which will come from developing countries ("Developing Countries" 2008). If energy supplies become a binding constraint, one can expect slow progress or no progress on the poverty and redistribution front.

Now the story becomes complicated, because after decades of research, the mystery of how to raise investment through policy incentives remains mostly a secret. The 2005 WDR maintains that if the investment climate can be improved, the flow will increase, but the link between the investment climate and investment is uncertain. Other WDRs over the past decade have stayed away from the macroeconomic highway to growth. Conventional fiscal and financial instruments and exchange rates apparently have only a very limited effect on resource mobilization, investment, and growth, as Easterly (2005) shows. Very bad political circumstances can lead to macroeconomic policies that depress investment, total factor productivity (TFP), and growth.[5] This conclusion is supported by findings based on Bayesian "model-averaging" techniques that show that the imbalances and inflation arising from excessive government spending can affect growth (Durlauf, Kourtellos, and Tan 2008). However, macroeconomic policies of a middling sort do not influence macroeconomic performance. In fact, as Easterly (2005) and Tabellini (2004) both point out, when political institutions are controlled for, the effect of policy on growth is negligible.[6] Easterly (2005) views growth as a function of history and of shocks. The correlation between per capita incomes in 1960 and 1999 is 0.9, suggesting that a political economy milieu has long-lasting effects and is slow to change. The correlation in growth rates in successive periods for a large sample of countries is almost zero, reinforcing the point that, in the majority of cases, accelerations and decelerations arise from shocks rather than policies. These shocks, writes Rodrik (2007: 38–39), can be quite mild. "Small changes in the background environment can yield a significant increase in economic activity.... An attitudinal change on the part of the top political leadership ... often plays as large a role as the scope of policy reform itself."

If institutional factors do not stimulate resource mobilization and growth, the state can take the lead in mobilizing savings and enlarging public investment. From the Bank's standpoint, however, investment by public entities or underwritten by directed financial lending by either state-owned or state-controlled financial institutions is deemed risky or wasteful. Nevertheless, in China, Malaysia, and Singapore, the lion's share of investment was and is by public entities, and in the Republic of Korea and Taiwan, China, directed investment by public or quasi-public banks largely fueled industrialization.

---

5. Unfortunately, inefficient policies can persist longer than they should because they generate large benefits for small, influential groups and their costs are diffused in small per capita amounts over larger numbers of people (Dixit 1996: 4).

6. According to Feng (2003), political repression, uncertainty, and instability all impinge on growth. Democracy indirectly affects growth by introducing a predictable process of regime change. Thus, given the weaknesses of economic policies, growth in developing countries not surprisingly was slower during 1980 to 2000 than it was during 1960 to 1980, even though macroeconomic adjustment policies were being used more forcefully in the former period than in the latter. Growth rates of countries have differed widely between 1960 and 2000 irrespective of initial starting points, and past growth has proven to be a surprisingly weak predictor of future growth (Durlauf, Johnson, and Temple 2005).

The perceived difficulty of influencing investment through market incentives and conventional policy instruments has increased the importance attached to TFP, and the preferred path to growth now leads through the garden of "inspiration." Researchers are coming to the view that over the long haul, TFP is what counts, and TFP grows as a result of technological advances that improve fixed capital through improvements in the quality of human capital and through disembodied progress that floats down like the proverbial manna from heaven (Durlauf, Kourtellos, and Tan 2008; Lipsey and Carlaw 2004; Tabellini 2004; World Bank 2008a).[7] In mature, industrial, high-income economies with stable or declining rates of investment and very low rates of growth of labor supplies, TFP, however constructed, is visibly the main driver. Raising productivity with the help of institutions and knowledge deepening is becoming the favored approach to growth in middle-income countries as well.

From Machines to Institutions

In light of the false starts and failures in the 1960s and 1970s in much of the developing world (as indicated in several *WDRs* during the 1980s and early 1990s) and with macropolicies not holding out much hope, having turned away from public investment in industrial and directly productive activities, the Bank, in keeping with the current thinking, is looking to institutions and services to help generate sustained growth by boosting TFP. Investment is assumed to be weak or not sufficiently productive because market and nonmarket institutions that promote entrepreneurship and efficiently induce and allocate private investment are missing or frail or slow to mature. Financial systems remain shallow, and too few resources are mobilized and funneled into the right sectors. The risks for entrepreneurs rise above a tolerable level. Market signals are absent or distorted. A variety of supporting services that investors require are not forthcoming. Consequently, "animal spirits" are dampened and investment is suboptimal. The "institution gap–institution drought" story is rich in anecdote,

---

7. Craft's reestimation of what caused the spurt in the growth of the British economy from 1780 to 1860 tips the scales in favor of TFP. Of the 0.78 percent per year increase in labor productivity, 0.38 percent was because of TFP. Capital deepening plus TFP accounted for 0.68 percent of the total—not much, but 0.5 percent per year more than the increase from 1700 to 1780 (Crafts 2004b).

example, and sophisticated theorizing. It emphasizes property rights, the enforcement of contractual obligations, market failure and how it can be remedied, missing markets, the role and efficacy of regulation, and the effectiveness of enforcement mechanisms. In brief, the failings of growth are ascribed to weak or missing institutions, which results in lower than desirable levels of savings and investments, misdirection of investment, low returns from capital spending, and capital flight.[8]

When institutions are imported into the growth framework, the story is made richer and more believable, but the task of the policy maker is made no easier. The line running from institutions to outcomes is not straight at all. It can have several branches, as the experience of East Asia makes abundantly clear.[9] Unappealing political institutions can have good outcomes in terms of human capital development and poverty reduction.

Institutional shortcomings are blamed on stage of development, absence of complementary institutions, ignorance, bad policy, and immaturity of economic thinking (see for instance the 2002 WDR).[10] They are blamed on

---

8. The economics profession has demonstrated a special knack for finding new "failures" and "gaps" and also a remarkable facility for worrying about these for years without alighting on robust and widely applicable solutions. For example, market and coordination failures seemed to require intervention by the state or some institutional remedies, as did idea, object, and information gaps (Romer 1993). However, after government failures became uncomfortably visible in the 1970s, the discipline was forced to walk a fine line and propose smaller, indirect, and better-quality doses of state intervention and regulation. Government failures also discredited industrial targeting, the much dreaded "picking of winners." Instead, some in the profession are now proposing that governments work with industry to "discover" promising new production activities to diversify into and ensure that these activities are coordinated with other supplementary actions, broadly mimicking the not entirely unblemished Korean experience (Rodrik 2007). Rodrik (2004: 9) writes, "What is involved is … 'discovering' that a certain good, already well established in world markets, can be produced at home at low cost." Moreover, the height of tariff barriers appears to promote "self-discovery" of new exports because it minimizes competitive pressure. This process of discovery could lead to losses, just as picking winners can, but this possibility has been rationalized as a risk that is attendant on such decisions, whether the government makes them or a businessperson does. In fact, Rodrik (2004) maintains that a government that is not incurring sufficient losses is not taking enough risks. The advantage of balanced growth is being recycled to avoid "coordination problems" as when "profitable new industries can fail to develop unless upstream and downstream investments are coaxed simultaneously" (Rodrik 2004: 13). "Coaxed" can be a euphemism for the visible hand of the government providing subsidies, protection, or venture capital (Rodrik 2004: 11).

9. Among the variables most significantly related to growth, the East Asian dummy is at the forefront. This finding emerges from a Bayesian model-averaging exercise by Sala-i-Martin, Doppelhofer, and Miller (2004).

10. For improving transparency of the judicial system, institutions that maintain statistical databases with information on individualized clearance rates and times to disposition for judges have proven helpful (as in Colombia and Guatemala). Complementary institutions such as strong civil society groups and the media, acting as outside monitors, have often changed the behavior of judges and lawyers in developing countries (for example, Poder Ciudadano in Argentina and the CourtWatch

the stubborn resistance of most institutions to removal or modification. The work of La Porta, López-de-Silanes, and Schleifer (2007) on Anglo-Saxon and continental traditions of law and finance underscores the persistence of entrenched modes of doing things. Now, Acemoglu and Zilibotti (2001) are claiming that growth might be a prisoner of institutions that are linked to colonial conquests, resource endowments, and geographic location. If so, then drafting policies that bear on the making or unmaking of institutions becomes a formidable undertaking unless the meaning of institutions is trivialized to encompass the simple furniture of doing business—institutions for licensing and issuing permits, clearing customs, and so forth.

Instead of relying on fiscal and financial policies to promote investment, growth is now pursued through "institution building" carried out incrementally or in some unbalanced way or, alternatively, institution building that is coordinated along a broad front so that the entire structure is not imperiled by remaining gaps and flaws. The fly in this ointment—it is not a trivial one—is that, except in rather general terms, development economics (as revealed in the 2002 and 2004 *WDRs*, for example) has not come up with a well-articulated theory of institutions suitable for a world populated with heterogeneous economies that have checkered histories[11] and are at different stages of development.[12] An attempt to discern whether institutions lead

project established in 1992 in the Philippines by the National Citizens Movement for Free Elections and the Makati Business Club). In Brazil, for example, specialized courts—namely, small claims courts—have halved times to disposition and expanded access to justice. Similarly, the specialized commercial court established in Tanzania cut the average time to disposition from 22 months to 3 months. The presence of such institutions in competition with the formal judicial system is associated with reduced opportunities for corruption. Experience from New Zealand shows that specialized regulatory tribunals are needed to provide sufficient oversight for service providers, given the stage of technological development of the sectors within infrastructure and the reliance by governments on competition authorities to enforce their laws through the court system. Using grounds similar to those on which countries centralize their regulatory authority, groups of states have set up supranational regulatory organizations. For example, the Organization for Eastern Caribbean States created a regional regulator for telecommunications, and in 1995, the countries of the Southern African Development Community formed the Southern African Power Pool to coordinate national-level power production and regulation.

11. Nunn (2008) blames the slow growth of many African countries on the slave trade.

12. Institutions mean different things to different people, and most tend to lump all kinds of rules, regulations, customs, and organizations under the term *institution*. However, as Stiglitz (2000: 3) reminds us, "while it is easy to identify the outcomes of good institutions and to cite examples of institutions which work well and those which do not, it remains far from clear how to go about creating these good institutions. As a result the international community has increasingly resorted to exhortations for good governance in the public and private sector but without correspondingly clear prescriptions of how to achieve that goal in general." Easterly (2007a) challenges the top-down view of institution development. He maintains that expecting experts to determine the contextually

to growth using Bayesian model averaging (see Hoeting and others 1999) is unable to find a direct relationship, although indirect links through proximate determinants such as macroeconomic policies might well be operative. Durlauf, Kourtellos, and Tan (2008: 338) suggest that the reason others have found a relationship is that "they have often restricted the analysis to (competing) fundamental theories in isolation and used kitchen sink regressions for comparison."

The 2002 *WDR* offers an assortment of examples of institutions plucked from the four corners of the globe, but individually and collectively these institutions do not amount as yet to a workable framework for achieving sustained growth. Relative to Latin America, for example, and other regions, East Asia remains more regulated, with little change since the beginning of the decade, but it grows robustly. The uneven, long-drawn, and still incomplete efforts of China and India to remove market-unfriendly institutions and replace them with market-compatible institutions coupled with mechanisms for enforcement pose some serious questions. If these two countries can rack up rates of investment and growth that are the envy of the world under the most makeshift of institutional conditions, need other countries more attuned to the market strive after greater perfection? China was growing when it had few if any market institutions; as its institutional structure has strengthened, it has continued growing with investment serving as the principal driver without a clear relationship running from the specifics of institution building to growth.[13] Latin American countries aggressively reformed their policies and institutions in the 1980s and the 1990s but were not rewarded with growth (Rodrik 2007). Other high-performing countries in East Asia have seen their growth performance flag while their institutions have matured,

---

appropriate optimal institutions and policy makers to actually implement the recipes they propose is a stretch. Easterly (2007a: 4) thinks that such a view represents the "aid agencies' agenda for a second generation of institutional reforms." He points to research done by the Bank showing that land titling has had no effect on investment in agriculture in Africa and in farmers' access to credit. In Easterly's view, the only viable approach is the slow grassroots building of institutions through local effort. In a similar vein, Amsden (2007) maintains that each country must find its own path and that external tutoring is rarely helpful.

13. This is not to deny that China's growth over the past quarter century is undoubtedly the result of its distancing the economy from planning and gradually backing into a market system. But the contorted efforts to establish, for example, that the property rights conferred by the quasi-public ownership of township and village enterprises really did perform the same functions as market-based and legally enforced rights blurs the "institutions" thesis.

albeit slowly. However, all these economies have also witnessed a decline in investment and a partial withdrawal of the state from the forefront of economic decision making.

In attempting to learn from cross-country experience (in particular, the experience of the East Asian economies), WDRs published during the 1980s and early 1990s—particularly those on the institutional aspects of industrializing countries—were prone, in the interests of brevity, to simplify. Rarely discussed in any detail is the historical setting, the timing of the development process, and the changing pattern of constraints and incentives that shaped the behavior of market participants and created both a "policy logic" and a "market logic" (Zysman and Doherty 1995: 25). "In identifying policy, actions are in a sense added up, rather than seen as generating interaction that creates a particular dynamic. When distinctions are made (among countries and situations), they are descriptive and not analytic" (Zysman and Doherty 1995: 26). Except for the simplest ones, institutions are difficult to tailor, to embed, and to develop to a functional level. Carpentering institutions is not simply a matter of following rules, because there are no straightforward instructions. Moreover, the strength of institutions grows with time, adaptation, experience, voluntary adherence by those affected, and the efficacy as well as the perceived fairness and accessibility of the mechanisms for enforcement.

Do we need to get institutions "right" first before an economy will begin growing rapidly, and does getting them right mean rising to the level of best practice? This vexed question is a long way from being solved. "For every paper that endorses one kind of institution or policy," writes Dixit (2007: 137), "one finds another that makes precisely the opposite claim." He then gives examples of the claims and counterclaims for the role of institutions. That economic growth can create the pressure or preconditions for institutional development, which could then sustain growth, is perhaps easier to believe, given the experience of China, Korea, Singapore, and Vietnam—all countries where a number of supposedly key market institutions began taking shape mostly after growth had gathered momentum. This causality is demonstrated by Paldam and Gundlach (2008), who pit the growth-first argument against the one arguing for the primacy of institutions. As Paldam and Gundlach (2008: 66) observe, "the concept of institutions is *woolly*," and when Rodrik (2008) talks of "second-best institutions," it becomes even more amorphous. He maintains that trying to achieve first-best institutions so as to minimize transaction costs, which the World Bank preaches, ignores country characteristics and the potential interactions of some new institutions with other institutions elsewhere in the system. For example, Rodrik (2008: 4) writes that "an effort to strengthen judicial enforcement can easily do more harm than good in the presence of relational contracting." He adds that protection and entry barriers that generate rents for incumbents are desirable under some circumstances, because without them the incentives for entrepreneurs to take risks might be too weak. In other words, depending on the experts' reading of the situation, institutional changes can be delayed, watered down, or modified. No yardstick or blueprint exists in this second-best thinking, only good judgment and pragmatism, or what in East Asia is known as "development with Chinese characteristics." Anything goes, if it works (Rodrik 2007).[14] When this argument is combined with the long historical view of how institutions arose and their tenacious persistence, all verified with instrumental variables that (occasionally) strain credulity,[15] the institutional approach appears woollier still.

One approach in making institutional reform manageable is to narrow its scope, for example, by defining a number of simple rules that are assumed to be responsible for the "investment climate," and to trace a path to growth through a process that attempts to correct obstructive rules. The 2005 WDR reasons that every economy has a reservoir of entrepreneurs with latent initiatives, but that in many instances, these investors are unable to mobilize resources and are discouraged from setting up a business because of a multitude of land, financial, and labor market frictions and transaction costs, some arising from institutional constraints (Djankov and others 2002). By identifying as many of these deterrents as possible by administering questionnaires to market participants, the Bank

---

14. Or as Deng Xiaoping memorably phrased it at the Seventh Plenum of the Third Communist Youth League in 1962, "It doesn't matter whether the cat is yellow or black as long as it catches the mouse." This old saying from Sichuan province made a profound impression then and has acquired legendary status since (Ming 1994: 4–5).

15. See for example, Albouy (2008) and Bardhan (2005) on a paper by Acemoglu, Johnson, and Robinson (2001) that used mortality rates of European settlers to determine whether they decided to establish resource-extracting institutions (with long and negative echo effects) or to settle in the region.

has sought to provide policy makers with the means of smoothing some of the bumps in the pathway to growth.

That delays in obtaining licenses, acquiring land or loans, hiring and firing workers, and satisfying other administrative or regulatory requirements can depress investment; that corruption raises the costs for business; that rules governing land use, zoning, and labor retrenchment can become seriously obstructive are all plausible problems and can have practical remedies. The call to reduce transaction costs and to lower the hurdles to doing business is coextensive with the discourse on institution building because many of the hurdles to be removed would facilitate entry, market competition, and efficient functioning of a market economy. Some evidence presented in the 2005 *WDR* suggests that a better investment climate stimulates productivity. Indeed, it would be surprising if such ground clearing had no effect.

As with other institutions, however, the magnitude of the effects and their persistence remain open to questions. How much can patient improvement of an economy's plumbing raise the level of investment and the returns from each unit of investment? Can such efforts push growth rates from, say, the 3 to 4 percent norms to the sought-after 7 to 9 percent levels for economies still at an early catch-up stage and then keep them at those levels for two decades? Did Botswana, Chile, China, India, and Mauritius as well as the East Asian economies achieve growth mainly by mending the investment climate and taking the market institution–building route or through what Rodrik (2007: 38–39) denotes as "attitudinal changes" on the part of the leadership? Affirmative responses to the first two questions are hard to find. However, looking ahead one can take the view that in an integrated world economy, the cumulative effect of many relatively minor transaction costs and corruption can diminish the competitiveness of an economy and eat into its potential growth rate. The investment climate story has useful policy content—how much is hard to tell. It continues to underscore the primacy of investment for growth, and it points to previously unacknowledged problems that could reduce investment and the return on investment. Hence, it is a net addition to our understanding of the development process, and on balance it enlarges the scope for policy action. It does not promise higher or more stable growth.

Inspired Growth

The contribution of knowledge to growth is well known,[16] and Arthur Lewis emphasized mass education in his early writings (Lewis 2003; Tignor 2006: 71). It was highlighted for professional economists by Robert Solow in a landmark paper published in 1956.[17] Solow showed that growth was not just a matter of combining capital and labor but drew heavily both on advances in capabilities embodied in human capital and equipment and on those of a disembodied sort. It was only in the early 1990s, however, that knowledge was respectably integrated into growth economics, following the path-breaking work of Lucas (1988) and Romer (1989). They argued that people who are more skilled generate externalities and can raise the productivity of others; in other words, the social returns to education are greater than the private returns (Lange and Topel 2006). As a consequence, the TFP of the economy is increased. The 1998/99 WDR helped bring this argument into the policy mainstream. Efforts to raise investment in developing countries with fiscal and financial incentives were not seen to be bearing much fruit, and knowledge offered a worthy alternative means of raising the growth rate. Recall the Internet and information technology (IT) came into bloom in the 1990s, and they were seen as the harbingers of a new economy in which more of the growth impetus could be derived from intangible sources—in particular, advances in knowledge, new forms of organization, and new ways of doing business—and from a vast range of IT-based services requiring minimal inputs of physical capital.

Now that capital is being nudged imperceptibly into the background and growth is all about TFP, the foreground of growth economics is filling with variables serving as proxies for institutions or representing knowledge in one form or the other, such as human capital, research capital, research and development (R&D) spending, and IT spending. The 1998/99 WDR and the 2007 WDR, for example, sketch a future in which knowledge and human capital development could be the mainsprings of growth and poverty reduction.

---

16. Van Ark, Mahony, and Timmer (2008) estimate that Europe's slower pace of knowledge development explains the persisting and widening gap in productivity between Europe and the United States.

17. See Helpman (2004) and Warsh (2006) for lucid accounts of the role of technology and knowledge in growth.

Knowledge development is a capacious concept that is variously unpacked. The essential ingredient is human capital, measured by years of schooling; its quality; and the share of science, engineering, and math skills. It also includes spending on R&D and tertiary education in general, the outlay on IT capital, and the infrastructure of a national innovation system. Especially in the context of developing countries, knowledge development extends to institutions that promote the dissemination and trading of information, institutions that give rise to technology markets and address the problems of information asymmetry, and the "public good" nature of information.

The significance assigned to human capital is in tune with the Bank's objective of reducing poverty and income disparities.[18] Growth of per capita gross domestic product (GDP), associated with a rising stock of human capital, is a two-pronged approach to tackling poverty and income inequalities. With more human capital of better quality, countries, in theory, will find catching up to and closing productivity gaps easier and will thus make progress toward equalizing earnings.

The human capital–intensive, knowledge-based development strategy could be an avenue to shortening or skipping the stage of early and

---

18. Studies showing high private and social returns to primary and secondary education in low-income countries (Psacharopoulos and Patrinos 2002) and handsome returns also to health interventions such as immunization and better early childhood nutrition support the efficacy of policies that add to the human capital of the poor. Moreover, the returns to higher education appear to be perking upward as technology becomes more skill intensive (Boarini and Strauss 2007; Lutz, Cuaresma, and Sanderson 2008; Psacharopoulos 2006; Topel 1999), but these findings have not been fully validated by macrolevel research showing that human capital enhances growth performance. In fact, Benhabib and Spiegel (1994), Bils and Klenow (2000), and Pritchett (2001), do not find such a relationship. More recent studies are showing that the quality of secondary schooling affects growth (Hanushek and Woessmann 2007), and better data averaged over longer periods are beginning to reveal the desired relationships (Boarini and Strauss 2007; Lutz, Cuaresma, and Sanderson 2008). However, Pritchett (2006) is skeptical. He observes that growth of the leading Organisation for Economic Co-operation and Development countries has been stable over long periods even though schooling levels have increased massively. Schooling levels have also risen enormously in developing countries without this change showing up in the growth statistics. Pritchett (2006) sees no evidence that the evolution and dynamic of schooling affect growth, and he finds no evidence of excess social returns to schooling. He believes either that the relationship between quality and growth is picking up the effects of an omitted variable or that high test score results are correlated with a country's institutional quality. Pritchett concludes that the investment in education stems from its being a merit good and from the belief that it generates externalities whether or not the belief can be validated. The Commission on Growth and Development (2008), while supporting the case for investment in education and human capital, also equivocates about presenting evidence on the relationship between human capital and growth. And simulations done by Ashraf, Lester, and Weil (2008) suggest that improvements in health lead to minimal gains in per capita incomes. Their findings are vigorously challenged by Bleakley (2008), and the debate continues.

low-value-adding industrialization for some countries, based on their natural resource endowment.[19] Accumulating human capital does not, however, obviate the need to (a) increase rates of investment (as noted previously) and (b) build the physical infrastructure and, in most instances, the manufacturing capacity associated in the past with economic modernization and growth. In fact, the two are complements. The great upsurge of IT-based services; the large gains in the productivity of U.S. service providers in sectors such as finance, retailing, and logistics; and India's recent success in building a thriving export industry based on IT have encouraged some to think of growth options for developing countries that do not entail the time-consuming and capital-intensive creation of a manufacturing industry and its supporting infrastructure. In this model, a kind of "weightless" growth derives from human capital and entrepreneurship that gives rise to numerous small-scale and productive activities (Coyle 1998; Quah 1999). Such a model might be feasible for some smaller economies, such as an Ireland, a Mauritius, or a Singapore, but is unlikely to work for larger countries. Even in the cases of Mauritius and Singapore, the current prosperity is mainly the outcome of success at manufacturing, and only in the past decade has the contribution of services to growth become sizable. In Singapore, the investment in state-of-the-art infrastructure has been critical to success. Past experience with productivity growth in most services argues for caution, as pointed out by Baumol and Bowen (1966) and reaffirmed by Nordhaus (2008). Productivity in many services has grown slowly; value added can be low, which can worsen income inequality; and export prospects for many developing countries are limited. Thus far, neither advanced countries nor developing countries appear able to forsake manufacturing and to expect to prosper (Dasgupta and Singh 2005; Nicholas 2005).[20]

---

19. For example, countries can have different opportunity sets depending on whether they have abundant forestry resources or abundant mineral resources, according to Álvarez and Fuentes (2005).

20. Observing the vanishing of manufacturing activities in the United Kingdom, Sir John Rose (2008: 9), chief executive officer of Rolls Royce, reminds policy makers: "High value added manufacturing brings huge benefits. It penetrates the economy of the whole country rather than London or just the Southeast. It pays well but avoids bewildering distortions of income; it drives and enables a broad range of skills; it demands and supports a wide supply chain and it adds value and creates wealth."

The relative neglect of industrialization in the 2005 *WDR*[21] and the near-exclusive focus on services delivery, institutions, and building of human capital to rid the world of poverty are debatable. Building industrial capabilities and thus multiplying well-paid jobs in industry benefits from a lowering of entry barriers and transaction costs. It benefits from better governance and openness. But industrial capabilities increasingly require a mix of incentive policies aimed at the several components of the national innovation system; the provision of risk capital from the state to catalyze the formation of high-tech industrial cum services clusters (in particular, the coalescing of suppliers and the orchestrating of innovations) in key urban centers; and financing together with regulation to raise the quality of the urban, transport, and telecommunication infrastructures (Gómez-Ibáñez 2006; Hayami 2003; Sutton 2000). The 1998/99 *WDR* made a first pass at the national innovation system, the 1994 *WDR* tackled infrastructure, and the 2009 *WDR* examines spatial issues. However, these issues need to be yoked together with industrial development instead of being dealt with piecemeal.[22]

As previously noted, the most successful economies of the current decade are certainly leveraging knowledge capital as swiftly as they can; however, they are also accumulating physical capital and pouring it into industry at a feverish pace. China and India are deriving a significant share of their growth from TFP,[23] but capital is still the most important source of growth. Moreover, much of the gains in TFP are coming

---

21. The 2005 *WDR* conventionally views industrialization as a process of discovery and warns against targeting.

22. Unfortunately, empirical realities are unfolding in developing countries in a way at odds with the way economics would lead us to think that they should. Technology diffusion, increasing stocks of human capital, expanding domestic markets for goods and finance, and an integrating global economy should all lead to rising returns to physical capital and a coalescence of returns across firms. But as Banerjee and Duflo (2004: 10, 11) find otherwise. Returns demonstrate wide dispersion, and the average of the marginal rates of return is not very high—not much higher than the 9 percent or so that is the usual estimate for the average stock market return in the United States. Economics and common sense would lead us to believe that the return to education ought to be higher in developing countries than in developed countries because human capital is scarcer in the less developed parts of the world. Again, we would be wrong on both counts. To quote Banerjee and Duflo (2004: 12), "The returns to education ... range from 6.9 percent for the country with the lowest education level to 10.1 percent for the country with the highest education level. This is a small range. There is, therefore, no prima facie evidence that returns to education are much higher when education is lower, although the relationship is indeed negative."

23. From 1993 to 2004, the estimate for China is 4 percent and for India, 2.3 percent per annum (see Bosworth and Collins 2007). Other estimates, for example, by Kuijs (2006) are somewhat lower.

from the transfer of labor to the newly emerging or expanding cities—voracious users of capital—and technology embodied in (imported) production equipment (Bosworth and Collins 2007). Durlauf, Kourtellos, and Tan (2008: 344) conclude from their review of old and new models that the new growth theories account for less than 1 percent of the total variation in growth of income per capita. Physical capital accumulation accounts for 40 percent. This is the traditional model of development—with a larger role for market forces, but recognizably akin to the conventional wisdom of the 1970s. Whether policy making has been enriched by the research on knowledge and human capital is an open question.

Resource Balances and Capital Flows

The 1980s and a part of the 1990s were a time of domestic resource imbalances that were mirrored by current account deficits and mounting external debts. The Bank's response in the 1981, 1985, and later *WDRs* was to call for adjustment, which involved an increase in revenue effort by mobilizing financial resources through a deepening of the banking system, a strengthening of regulatory and governance-related institutions to enhance efficiency, and an easing of restraints on overseas capital flows.

The issues of resource equilibrium and adjustment have faded from the *WDRs* because of several developments. First, a perception exists that the capital intensity of growth is on a decline. Certainly middle-income countries are investing less, but they are also growing more slowly. Whether incremental capital-output ratios will trend downward in low-income countries remains to be established. Second, because of the expansion of trade from 2003 to 2007, many developing countries have been less pressed for resources.[24] The substantial increase in foreign direct investment (FDI) and in the flow of private portfolio capital to countries in South Asia and Sub-Saharan Africa has eased resource constraints in the two regions that were previously short of capital (table 3.1 and figure 3.1). This situation has reinforced debt-forgiveness deals that have attempted to reduce the burden of past accumulated external obligations on some of the poorest countries.

---

24. An associated—and surprising—factor is that investment rates in developing countries are not spiraling upward. The global pool of savings is large and growing, but profitable opportunities to invest those savings are not.

Table 3.1: Net Foreign Direct Investment in South Asia and Sub-Saharan Africa, 2000–06

Region	Net FDI (current US$ billion)						
	2000	2001	2002	2003	2004	2005	2006
South Asia	4.4	6.1	6.7	5.4	7.6	10.0	22.9
Sub-Saharan Africa	6.8	15.1	10.5	14.4	12.5	17.3	17.1

Source: World Development Indicators database.

Figure 3.1: Net foreign direct investment in South Asia and Sub-Saharan Africa, 2000–06

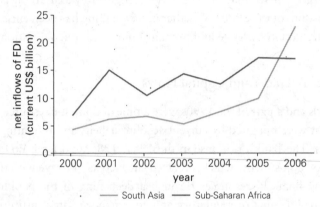

Source: World Development Indicators database.

Third, developing countries, including the economies of Sub-Saharan Africa, grew faster—at 5 to 6 percent annually on average from 2000 to 2007—helped in no small part by strengthening demand for their resource-based products. This phenomenon is relatively recent and may prove short-lived;[25] however, it is a welcome break after the doldrums of the 1970s on through the early 1990s and the brief spell of international panic that erupted when the East Asian crisis of 1997 and 1998 threatened to paralyze several icons of the developing world.

Fourth, techniques of adjustment and achieving resource balances are now a part of the common parlance (and the *WDRs* have assisted in making them so) and are being put into practice with varying degrees of success across the developing world. Some countries continue to perform

25. Should the resource-led boom resume once the world economy recovers its stride after 2008, the resource-rich countries of Sub-Saharan Africa will also have to show greater agility in sidestepping the "resource curse," which has dampened growth in the past.

below par mainly because of poor governance, but most are reaping the benefits from the adjustment efforts that gathered momentum in the 1990s. The medicine administered to troubled economies, which later came to be known as the "Washington Consensus" (and which appeared piecemeal in WDRs starting with the 1981 WDR), was surely painful because it curbed demand, affected governments' ability to finance a variety of activities, and opened economies to trade and capital flows. With the benefit of hindsight, however, it may have helped set the stage for greater macroeconomic stability in the industrializing countries during the past decade. The Washington Consensus comprised 10 reform items.[26] Some of them, when appropriately tailored, were sensible candidates for a reform package in the 1980s. Fiscal discipline, public expenditures that were growth promoting, a buoyant and broad-based tax system, secure property rights, and deregulation of some entry barriers administered the best medicine that economics could offer at that time to countries plagued with macroeconomic instability. More controversial were liberalization of interest rates, maintenance of competitive exchange rates, trade liberalization, opening of the capital account, and privatization. The controversy revolved around how these last were administered and their sequencing. Dogmatically applied, they could cause more harm than good, and critics of the Washington Consensus frequently complained more about the dogmatic one-size-fits-all approach of the World Bank, which appeared to mirror the agenda of major shareholders, than about the utility of the instruments.

For countries whose development policies relied on financial repression, rapid liberalization of interest rates was unwelcome advice. The political economy of exchange rate policy also generated resistance to change. With the benefit of hindsight, privatization has contributed to efficiency and profitability, but for many countries—especially the transition economies unprepared for a wholesale transfer of assets—the costs of some types of privatization were high and deeply resented. An opening of the capital account was widely resisted and associated with pressures from financial institutions in the United States. Again, with the benefit of hindsight and

---

26. See John Williamson (2003) for the original 10 policy guidelines and how they have morphed following intensive debates, which are puzzling in view of the limited and uncertain effects of policies on key target variables.

the distressing experience of the East Asian crisis of 1997 and 1998, we see that the dismantling of capital controls, after regulatory checks on the banking system and rules providing shareholder protection among others are in place, does more good than harm. A summary of the evidence by Jeffrey Frankel (2003/04) and papers by Gourinchas and Jeanne (2003) and Klein (2003) point to modest gains overall, more for middle-income countries with a mature infrastructure than for low-income ones.[27] Even a reappraisal of the effects of capital controls in Chile and Malaysia during 1997 and 1998 suggests that the two countries derived scant advantage, and in Malaysia, controls might have facilitated rent seeking (Corbo and Hernández 2006; Johnson and Mitton 2001; Johnson and others 2006; Prasad and Rajan 2007).

These outcomes leave trade liberalization, about which the consensus is that on average it promoted efficiency and growth, although the reallocation of resources once trade barriers come down imposes costs on those who stand to lose protection.[28] The case for protection as one strand of an industrial strategy to acquire comparative advantage remains unsettled.

The Washington Consensus became a lightning rod for criticism in the 1990s because the pain caused by undifferentiated doses of medicine administered to countries in distress outweighed the short-term gains. If anything, adjustment policies worsened poverty and income distribution. However, macrostability and openness that began accruing from 1995 to

---

27. As several of the leading economies endure one of the worst financial crises in a generation during 2008, a glance backward over past crises indicates that banking crises are correlated with greater capital mobility (Reinhart and Rogoff 2008) and with financial innovation that increases leverage (Bordo 2007). See Felton and Reinhart (2008) for a potpourri of interesting analytical and admirably brief articles on the recent crisis; and Eichengreen and Baldwin (2008) for a first of what will undoubtedly be many rounds of suggestions on how to resolve the crisis and to minimize the damage. For lighter and equally absorbing fare, see Morris (2008). The above-mentioned findings strengthen the argument for better regulation prior to liberation, except that regulation is always playing catch-up; regulators seem chronically unable to cope with the challenges posed by openness and innovation; and financial entities, because of herding behavior and moral hazard, seem not disposed to learn from past mistakes.

28. A robust relationship running from trade to growth has eluded economists; nonetheless, tireless econometric effort has yielded enough consoling evidence of gains in productivity and growth deriving from trade. See the surveys by Kneller, Morgan, and Kanchanahatakij (2008); López (2005); and Winters (2004). As Winters (2004: F18) observes, after putting all the evidence to date through the wringer, one emerges with a "strong presumption that trade liberalization contributes positively to economic performance." López comes to broadly the same conclusion after taking into account evidence that the more productive firms become exporters—and it is not exporting that makes them more productive.

2007 allow us to look back at the policy recipes retailed by the WDRs of the 1980s and the first half of the 1990s in a more positive light. Some useful lessons were learned, and the WDRs certainly helped stir debate by spelling out the mainstream thinking and the policies. From this debate has come a more nuanced reading of the Washington Consensus policies, their adaptation and calibration for a variety of situations, and the desirability of prior or parallel institutional developments to maximize the net gains from liberalizing the economy and downsizing the public sector (Williamson 2003). The financial crisis that began in 2007 and 2008 will inform us whether progress of a sort was achieved.[29]

Serious adjustment problems with global implications directly confront one or two of the advanced countries, but a significant slowing of the world economy and high energy and food prices could give rise to or worsen adjustment problems in a number of African, Latin American, and Asian economies. The messages of the WDRs (from the 1980s and 1999/2000) on adjustment, finance, public finance, and trade defined good practice that has largely stood the test of time. The broad principles remain unchanged. Research following the East Asian crisis of 1997 and 1998 added to the literature on shocks and quizzed the role of contractionary monetary policies, but its contribution to policy making is less obvious because, as we are discovering in the case of the United States, public agencies are too often ill equipped to monitor and regulate complex markets where innovation is proceeding apace, to forecast problems, and to make timely interventions. In most developing countries, only very straightforward innovations in the financial sphere and the sphere of public finance can be productively implemented and regulated.

---

29. The crisis, triggered by the collapse of the subprime mortgage sector in the United States, has revealed the continuing inability to anticipate financial and banking shocks (Schroeder 2008) and to identify bubbles at an early enough stage—Robert Shiller is among the few who pointed to the growing housing bubble in the United States (Shiller 2005)—and the reluctance of monetary authorities to nip a boom by means of precautionary credit, interest rate, and regulatory policies that could contain innovations and slow growth and would be politically unpopular. The response to the crisis also shows that the instruments available are few, are slow acting, and when used indiscriminately can store problems for the future. Whether fiscal policy can do better is also questionable: most countries have limited budgetary flexibility; however, western countries have demonstrated considerable aggressiveness in deploying budgetary resources to combat the financial crisis in 2008. What will remain of the Washington Consensus, and what kind of new pragmatic consensus emerges, only time will tell.

The Role of the State

The 1980s saw the beginning of a long, slow retreat from highly interventionist state, a large public sector, and a relatively closed economy. The WDRs in the 1990s (for example, 1991, 1996, and 1997) drove home the message that market institutions and the forces of competition would be far more effective in allocating resources. Building on the WDRs of the 1980s, they argued that a market-guided economy that was more open to trade and to international capital flows would have superior growth prospects.

Following the start of denationalization in Europe in 1985, a shrinkage of the public sector became an integral part of the message on the state, because state-owned or state-controlled assets were viewed as performing less efficiently and less profitably than privately controlled assets, whether in industry, in banking, or in public utilities. The issue of privatization took on much greater urgency after the dismantling of the Berlin Wall confronted the Bank with a major challenge: what position to adopt on the speed and extent of denationalization now that the forces of the market system had apparently carried the day? The Bank embraced privatization as a necessary step for countries seeking the advantages of a market-based system but hedged its bets on the scope and speed of privatization and with respect to the necessary conditions for it to be a success. Instead of a Big Bang, the Bank favored a phased process, starting with smaller manufacturing enterprises that could be easily privatized and following with the larger ones as and when capacity emerged. However, the Bank did urge against long delay that could undermine support for denationalization and dilute the benefits. Advantages also existed in privatizing the banking system (and introducing foreign investment into the sector), the utilities, and some of the natural monopolies. In those cases, however, positive longer-term outcomes in terms of investment, efficiency, and quality of services were linked to creating an effective regulatory infrastructure; receiving an infusion of capital, technologies, and management from foreign strategic investors; and building up local experience with managing these complex entities.[30]

---

30. As the experience with privatized entities has lengthened, the difficulties of effectively regulating prices and quality of services have become more apparent, and the enthusiasm for privatization has been tempered even in the pioneering industrial economies such as the United Kingdom (Kay 2002; Köthenbürger, Sinn, and Whalley 2006; "Special Report: Privatisation in Europe" 2002).

Few had anticipated how messy privatization in the transition economies would be and how uneven the outcomes. Sales to insiders at low prices, asset stripping, and "tunneling" diverted many of the state assets into well-connected hands with long-term consequences for income and asset distributions. Weak managerial capabilities, limited competition, and ineffectual regulation all conspired to limit the anticipated improvements. And inevitably, resistance from vested interests and the absence of credible private buyers meant that many assets remained in the public sector, as for instance, in China, Russia, and other Commonwealth of Independent States countries. On balance—and especially with respect to manufacturing enterprises—privatization was and is a sound idea. Its scope, pacing, and regulation were not well understood in the 1990s. The risks were underestimated, and the challenges of creating a workable regulatory infrastructure confounded newly formed governments and their foreign advisers. The obstacles to creating autonomous and effective regulation have proven to be highly recalcitrant in both developing and developed countries, and the experience with privatized utilities is definitely mixed. No one maintains, however, that the counterfactual—that is, a continuation of the old nationalized system—would have been superior to the partial privatization that ensued.

In reaction to the experience with stalled or misdirected industrialization in the 1960s and 1970s, the *WDRs* on adjustment in the 1980s and on the role of the state in the 1990s stoutly cautioned against industrial policies, at times airbrushing the actions of East Asia's fast developers. The state, argued the Bank, needed to manage the development effort and create a "conducive" macroeconomic and institutional environment, but policy needed to be pursued with the help of market-friendly or market-conforming policies (or, more recently, as a process of discovery). Picking industrial winners and assisting them with targeted incentives was strongly opposed because of the risk that the chosen industries could turn out to be losers and resist closure (then and more recently in the 2005 *WDR*).

In taking a stand against industrial policies, the Bank chose to interpret the "East Asian miracle" as a triumph of market-conforming industrial policies that were continually tested by exposure to international competition through liberalizing trade policies, allowing weak performers to fail.[31] Korea, Singapore, and Taiwan, China, were all depicted as pursuing market-friendly approaches consistent with the lowering of the state's policy-making profile.[32] Through such interpretation, the Bank enlisted the success of East Asian economies to the cause of market-led development, and the WDRs attempted to forge a coexistence between a strong development state and a vigorous market economy. The later emphasis on transactional costs and on institutions was part and parcel of the effort to establish the case for few and streamlined regulations, effective market institutions, and accountable administrative infrastructures as the foundations of a fast-growing economy. The role of the state was to create these, to ensure their smooth functioning through timely interventions and enforcement mechanisms, and to supply those services that the market was unable to provide. The state so depicted was there to serve and complement the market; it was not a powerful entity that managed and directed markets. Instead of defining the role of the state, the WDRs sought to expand the role and significance of markets and to firmly tether this role to institutions. To have assisted in bringing institutions to the center of the discourse on development policy is no mean achievement. We need to be clear, however, that what we now know about the making, the working, and the effectiveness of institutions in promoting growth, reducing poverty, and distributing the benefits relatively evenly is difficult to translate into effective policy instruments that can be put to good use in a variety of developing countries.

---

31. Such a willingness to withdraw support from industries that proved to be unprofitable is not borne out from a review of the experience of the East Asian tiger economies. Korea, for example, did not abandon a single major industry, with the possible exceptions of copper smelting and fertilizer, despite losses incurred over a decade and more. Other East Asian economies have also not shown a readiness to cease supporting their ailing industries. The desirability of the state taking a proactive role in promoting industrialization using directed credit and protection is the theme of books by Chang (2007) and Kozul-Wright and Rayment (2008), who draw attention to the reliance on such policies by western countries at earlier stages of their own development.

32. Hsiao and Hsiao (2003) and Kohli (2004) remind us that both Korea and Taiwan, China, had achieved rates of per capita GDP second only to those of Japan in the late 1930s. Hence, the recovery and resumption of growth in the 1950s and 1960s was foreshadowed by institutional and human capital potential already partly in place, as in pre–World War II Japan and Germany. As Kohli (2004: 5) describes it, "during the 1930s and well into the Second World War, Korea underwent very rapid industrialization." This largely state-sponsored effort, which focused on engineering and chemical industries, extended a base of light industries that had begun to gel in the 1920s. Although the Japanese colonial authorities and firms supplied much of the impetus, Korean business groups emerged and participated in this process. Some of these groups, again under government tutelage, later morphed into the chaebol of the 1960s, including leading firms such as Samsung and Hyundai.

Reducing Poverty

As long as the magnitude of poverty was uncertain and the trickling down of growth was conveniently assumed to be enough to enable the poor to rise out of poverty, the focus was on maximizing growth—a demanding task in itself. Once the Bank undertook the task of measuring poverty and made the elimination of absolute poverty its primary mission and ethical responsibility, almost every *WDR* since 1990 has attempted to identify avenues for reducing poverty and to multiply the number of dedicated policy instruments in the policy toolkit. Poverty reduction should not depend only on whether a country was growing fast or not. Meanwhile, counting the poor and measuring the depth and dynamics of poverty has grown into an ambitious multicountry activity pursued through detailed surveys. The Human Development Index constructed by the United Nations Development Programme for its *Human Development Report* has provided another yardstick for assessing the human condition, and many specialized papers have refined the measures of poverty yet further. Adding the reduction of inequality to the poverty agenda has enlarged the scope of what needs to be accomplished but unfortunately does not augment the policy toolkit.

A related reason for looking more closely at the microlevel is that the data-collecting efforts that gathered momentum in the 1980s and 1990s produced household panel data that made possible analysis of the plight of individual units and assessment of the dynamics of poverty. These data suggest that households affected by shocks have difficulty growing out of poverty, that unequal distribution of income and assets weakened the effects of GDP growth on the poor, and that inequality would, in turn, begin to hold back growth (Kanbur and Vines 2000). The possibility that inequality could exert a negative feedback effect on growth apart from interfering with the distribution of the benefits, if it has validity, strengthens the case for remedial policies. Although the 2006 *WDR* maintains that higher inequality can constrain future prosperity, the matter is by no means settled. Theoretical arguments aside, the practicalities of testing lead, as always, to some findings that support and others that contradict this view (Banerjee and Duflo 2003; Easterly 2007b; Kanbur 2000). Meanwhile, as Kanbur (2000) observes, the objectives of growth and equity are not being jointly realized as was hoped; instead, many countries show signs of greater divergence.

Ad hoc efforts to meet the basic needs of the poor, which were popular in the late 1970s and early 1980s and noted in the 1980 WDR, soon fell from favor. Since then, WDRs have attacked poverty from different directions, trying to construct an effective but pro-poor development strategy.

Today it is a truism that faster growth derived from trade policies, financial deepening, better infrastructure, and industrial or agricultural development will most likely benefit the poor. This was conventional wisdom already in the 1970s. What the WDRs did was add detail and emphasize the gains to be derived from reinforcing the effects of growth with social policies (see Ravallion 2001 and 2002). They made clear that rural roads could improve the lot of poor farmers and that rural poverty could be reduced by adjusting prices of agricultural products and inputs, by introducing new technologies, by improving water management, and by enhancing access of small farmers to credit. These instruments are reliable and have been in use for decades, but they have not eradicated poverty. Even the thinning of the rural population as millions have migrated to cities has left large pockets of poverty in many countries. Furthermore, some poverty is migrating to cities, most notably in Latin America (Ravallion and Chen 2007). Moreover, a deteriorating distribution of income in many developing countries has partially negated the gains from GDP growth for the poor.

The pro-poor policy innovations proposed in the WDRs can be grouped under four categories: services, safety nets, distributive measures, and participatory schemes that are inclusive and give the poor voice. Policies to control population growth, which were actively pursued in the 1960s and 1970s, faded from the WDRs after the 1984 report.

Poverty would fall faster and the distribution of income would become less skewed if the volume and quality of human capital could be raised. In the parlance of the 2004 and 2007 WDRs, this desideratum translates into giving the poor better access to education and health services, in particular, along with other services that make younger people more mobile and employable. How it can be done through public or private providers—especially the latter, in light of government failures—is explored at great length with copious examples. The WDRs have emphasized how to deliver services, how to finance them, and how to make service providers accountable through monitoring and competition. These process issues occupy acres of space in the recent WDRs. Instances of success exist, as well as a number of proposals for improving incentives for providers and for strengthening accountability, but there are no dependable and widely applicable solutions. The rules governing center and local financing of services through user fees and assignment of fiscal responsibilities between different levels are well known (and widely neglected). Community participation and monitoring of providers, which became popular starting about a decade and a half ago, seemed to be a solution, but it works very fitfully. Moreover, most developing countries are far from perfecting the techniques for achieving high-quality services by introducing competition between public and private providers and by providing regulatory oversight. From the limited evidence on the effect of safety nets such as conditional cash transfer programs (in the 2006 WDR), these programs have generally performed well, both in terms of targeting and reducing poverty, in Bangladesh, Chile, Honduras, Nicaragua, and Mexico. On average, the share of program benefits going to the bottom 40 percent of the population was 81 percent (World Bank 2005: 153). As for poverty, communities covered by Mexico's PROGRESA (Programa de Educación, Salud y Alimentación) experienced declines of 17.4 percent in the incidence of poverty compared with the control group. However, in Brazil only a small reduction in the poverty index (1 percentage point) is expected from the federal Bolsa Escola program because of the simulated loss in labor income of children.[33]

The WDRs have added to our knowledge of what has worked where and have enriched our understanding of why so many countries continue to flounder and to waste resources. Countries have not been standing still. In fact, ceaseless experimentation takes place, but progress (aided by impact evaluation studies) in speeding up the process of poverty reduction through better services to build human capital has been slow. The research

---

33. Depending on the overall cost of the program, this reduction in the poverty index need not be seen as insignificant (that is, the benefit-cost ratio might prove to be attractive). See Ferreira, Leite, and Ravallion (2007) on the relative contributions of growth, lower inflation, and social programs to poverty reduction in Brazil. Needs-based cash transfers discussed in the 2006 WDR have been shown to be fairly accurate in Latin America, where countries used a proxy means test (easily observable indicators of income). In other low-income regions, community-based systems have worked well in fairly homogeneous rural communities of Albania, Bangladesh, Ethiopia, Indonesia, Uganda, and Uzbekistan (World Bank 2005: 151). Chile's Puente program and Bangladesh's Income Generation for Vulnerable Group Development Program (run by the Bangladesh Rural Advancement Committee) have been effective in terms of targeting and removing disincentives to "graduate." Most other programs, such as public works, contributory pension, and social pension schemes, run into the problems of forgone earnings, low coverage, and cost-effectiveness. For example, evidence from various countries implementing large social pension schemes indicated that the costs were 1 to 2 percent of GDP (World Bank 2005: 154).

on improving education quality has revealed how weak the effects of class-room size, facilities, and textbooks are and how hard it is to incentivize teachers. Public health services work best when there are "silver bullets," such as clean water, sanitation, a new vaccine or medical prophylactic, or bed nets, but delivering good medical services—especially for increasingly prevalent chronic diseases—is an immense headache. These problems were described by the 1993 WDR.[34] If people are living longer and healthier lives, that is mainly because of better nutrition, cleaner water, a better urban environment, and rising education.

Safety nets—whether these are crop insurance schemes, pensions, food subsidies, or income supports for the poor—have been examined in the WDRs, and again, the added value comes from many examples and a steady accretion of research findings that inform the student and the specialist. They do not necessarily ease the policy maker's life. Designing and implementing cost-effective and fiscally supportable safety nets have proven to be a big test for governments. Given the scale of poverty in many low-income countries, only relatively frugal safety nets can be put in place, which are invariably insufficient. The simple arithmetic of fiscal cost is often at the root of partial failure, not sloppy design or crass inability to implement, although leakages and slippages in intervention are not trivial concerns.

Reading the WDRs encourages one to believe that much can be done to whittle down poverty and to improve distribution. The abundance of examples is certainly informative and encouraging. But poverty is most likely to retreat and to stay down when economies grow fast.[35] If growth

---

34. For example, the 1993 WDR pointed out that the Expanded Program on Immunization, which at that time protected about 80 percent of the children in the developing world against six major diseases (including tuberculosis, measles, and diphtheria), should ideally cover 95 percent of all children. Including micronutrient supplementation such as vitamin A and iodine would enhance the effectiveness of the vaccination programs. School-based health services designed to treat children affected with intestinal worm infections and micronutrient deficiencies through distribution of medications and supplements and that provide health education at the same time were estimated to cost US$1 to US$2 per child per year (World Bank 1993).

35. Son and Kakwani's (2008) efforts to determine whether "growth spells" from 1984 to 2001 were pro-poor (that is, poverty reducing) come to disappointing conclusions. They find that per capita income growth was positive in only 131 (55 percent) of the 237 growth spells they studied, and growth was pro-poor in 55 of these, or in 23 percent of the cases overall. It was anti-poor in 32 percent of the cases overall. Moreover, they find that only the variations in inflation affected whether growth was pro-poor or anti-poor. The share of agriculture in GDP, the extent of openness to trade, and the rule of law did not seem to influence pro-poor growth. In their schema, *growth spells* refers to the periods of time spanning two successive household surveys for a given country. However, see Ravallion (2004) on Kakwani's definition of pro-poor growth.

is slow, services and safety nets are not a substitute and become difficult to finance. In theory, human capital building, tax and transfer schemes, the changing sectoral composition of the economy, and greater productivity should all lead to a more even income distribution. In fact, income distributions are responding slowly, if at all, to policies and structural changes, and in some countries, they are becoming more skewed.

In his 1988 State of the Union address, President Ronald Reagan declared to his audience, "Some years ago the federal government declared war on poverty, and poverty won. Today the federal government has 59 major welfare programs and spends more than a $100 billion a year on them. What has all this money done?"[36] This is the kind of question aid-giving agencies are having to field. Poverty is not winning, but it is far from being eradicated. Moreover, official development assistance (ODA) and the advice on development policy that has come with it appear not to have measurably affected the overall performance of economies. Between 1981 and 2004, the number of people living on less than US$1 per day declined annually by 17 million. A drop of close to 200 million in the early 1980s was largely because agricultural reforms in China substantially raised household incomes (Chen and Ravallion 2007). By 2005, an estimated 1.4 billion people were subsisting on less than US$1.25, with 162 million ultrapoor living on less than 50 cents per day, mainly in Sub-Saharan Africa (A. Ahmed and others 2008; Chen and Ravallion 2008). At the current rate of change, projecting into the future indicates that 800 million people will be living on less than US$1 per day in 2015—the target date for achieving the Millennium Development Goals—and 2.8 billion living on under US$2 per day (Chen and Ravallion 2007).[37]

---

36. In defense of President Lyndon B. Johnson, who initiated the "War on Poverty" and the Great Society programs, Joseph Califano (2008) notes that when Johnson came to office, 22.2 percent of Americans lived in poverty. By the time he left, this percentage had fallen to 13 percent. The 1960s were a period of rapid growth, and poverty was declining sharply from 22.4 percent in 1959 to about 20 percent in 1963. This decline continued until 1973, when a low point of 11.1 percent was reached. Poverty rebounded in the latter part of the 1970s and reached 15.1 percent in 1983. It fell thereafter but was still 12.8 percent when President Reagan made his speech (Hoynes, Page, and Stevens 2005; Mangum, Mangum, and Sum 2003).

37. New purchasing power parity data for China and a revision of the US$1 a day poverty line finds an additional 133 million people living in poverty in 2005 when consumption per person is used and an additional 64 million if income is used (Chen and Ravallion 2008).

Aid and Growth

If the principal mission of the World Bank is to try to rid the world of poverty, then the principal instrument it has is resource transfers. Advice on good policies through the WDRs or other channels is the icing on the cake. Development assistance can make a difference to the lives of people in low-income countries in many ways, and the WDRs are replete with examples of successful projects and myriad beneficial interventions financed by aid programs. However, one inconvenient fact cannot be wished away. Unless development assistance from the World Bank and other donors stimulates growth, its effects on poverty and standards of living will be meager. From early in the history of the WDRs, this issue was noted and discussed, but not much evidence was presented. Resource transfers were assumed to be growth enhancing. Unfortunately, this assumption does not appear to be true. The findings from several score papers overwhelmingly point to a nonexistent, weak, or negative relationship between ODA and growth in recipient countries. Even the finding that aid to countries pursuing good policies raised growth has proven to be very precariously pegged to a specific time period and a specific sample of countries. Change these factors, and the relationship disappears or becomes insignificant.

One measure of the utility of the knowledge encompassed by the shelf of WDRs is how it affects the quality of the Bank's lending and the assistance provided by other donors. If this knowledge leads to better policies, better institutions, and valuable cross-fertilization of development practices among countries, then official development assistance should result in improved performance of borrowers. Moreover, and in parallel, it should be reflected in the allocation of ODA among countries and projects. When the Bank has evaluated its lending operations, on average 50 to 60 percent of projects receive a passing grade or better. Clearly, many Bank-financed projects have yielded good returns and contributed to development.

The picture tends to blur somewhat when we ask whether the Bank and other agencies have become more selective in their lending policies as their knowledge of what works and what is inimical to development has increased. Easterly (2007a: 27) finds no evidence of greater selectivity by the World Bank and other donor agencies and countries with respect to need, policies, and institutions.[38] Forbearing donors have not attempted to penalize policy incompetence or corruption even after the end of the Cold War diminished the contingent necessities of supporting kleptocracies. Easterly (2007a) claims the Bank and other aid agencies have been persistently slow learners. All large public bureaucracies are reluctant to recognize and acknowledge failure; the Bank is no exception, according to Easterly, despite the much greater effort it has put into scrutinizing and diagnosing the twists and turns of development within and among countries. The Bank has been equally slow to spot failures and to adjust its operational practices (see Birdsall 2008 on the seven deadly sins of donors and how to remedy them). Moreover, as pointed out by Celasun and Walliser (2008), the persistent unpredictability of aid flows has been damaging for borrowers by curtailing longer-term investment spending.

A less gloomy picture of how bilateral donors are learning from experience is conveyed by Claessens, Cassimon, and Van Campenhout (2007). They find that assistance is becoming more closely tied to the needs of recipients and the quality of their policies and institutions. However, even these authors still observe considerable variability among donors in degrees of selectivity, suggesting either gaps in perception regarding policies and situations or the continuing force of other imperatives.

Perhaps the thorniest question is about the overall consequences of the assistance provided by the Bank and others. Did it raise growth sufficiently? Did aid and debt relief make the sought-after dent in poverty? Was aid more effective when it flowed to countries that by the standards of highly experienced donor agencies were implementing sound policies on a broad front? Inevitably, such issues are contested terrain, and the guns continue to blaze. A book by Easterly (2006b); a paper by Prasad, Rajan, and Subramanian (2007); a meta-study of 97 papers on aid effectiveness by Doucouliagos and Paldam (2006); a careful survey of the literature by Roodman (2007), which weighs the econometrics of the contending parties; and a study of debt relief by Chauvin and Kraay (2007) provide a reading of the results to date. In capsule, the findings

---

38. From 1979 to 1997, while regularly decrying the increasing indebtedness of borrowing countries, the Bank increased its own financing to highly indebted poor countries even as commercial borrowers pulled out (Easterly 2002).

are discouraging to say the least. Aid and debt relief[39] appear to have had virtually no effect on investment or growth[40] or poverty reduction. Whether they have directly influenced policies and institutions is also open to question, and some research shows that they have not. Prasad, Rajan, and Subramanian (2007: 5) raise additional questions regarding the benefits of external financing to developing countries. According to their estimates, "countries that had high investment rates and lower reliance on foreign capital grew faster—on average by about one percent a year—than countries that had higher investment but also relied more on foreign capital." It would appear that "poor countries have little ability to absorb [foreign capital], especially when provided at arm's length, and ... when it does flow in, it would lead to overvaluation which hurts competitiveness" (Prasad, Rajan, and Subramanian 2007: 6).

These disappointing results suggest, in Roodman's (2007: 275) words, that "aid is probably not a fundamentally decisive factor for development, not as important say as domestic savings, inequality or governance."[41] The heterogeneity of the findings, the continuing controversy over aid effectiveness, and the calls for vastly larger injections of aid raise two deeper issues. First, as observed earlier, despite great advances in methodological sophistication, in techniques of estimation, and in computing software, no econometric finding is ever remotely conclusive. All are at best tentative and provisional because of model uncertainty, inadequate data, endogeneity of variables, omitted variable bias, and aggregation issues, to name just the main culprits. Estimation is complicated by the deep geopolitical roots of ODA (see, for example, Kuziemko and Werker

---

39. Debt servicing problems became noticeable in the late 1970s, and starting with the meeting initiated by the United Nations Conference on Trade and Development in 1977–79, donor countries commenced a steady dribble of debt rescheduling and forgiveness under a variety of terms. In 1996, the Bank announced the heavily indebted poor countries debt initiative and expanded its scope in 1999 for a large number of countries that remained heavily indebted despite two decades of debt relief.

40. Burke and Ahmadi-Esfahani (2006) cannot find a significant effect of aid on growth in even the relatively buoyant Southeast Asian economies—Indonesia, the Philippines, and Thailand. However, Dovern and Nunnenkamp (2007), using a different methodology, show that aid can lead to short-term growth accelerations. How countries would have fared in the absence of any aid is impossible to divine.

41. The mixed outcomes of the Bank's public sector reform lending were recently examined in an Independent Evaluation Group report (World Bank 2008a). Countries receiving International Bank for Reconstruction and Development loans generally did better than countries receiving International Development Association loans; the biggest reform mileage was in public financial management, and the least was in civil service reform and anticorruption.

2006).[42] These roots were revealed by the decline in ODA as a percentage of donor GDPs following the ending of the Cold War. ODA fell from 0.35 percent of GDP in 1986 to 0.25 percent in 1996. This drop partly accounts for the weak or nonexistent relationship between aid and growth. Expensive and unproductive technical assistance and substantial costs of administering aid programs, all of which are lumped into ODA, are also to blame. Hence, important debates smolder indefinitely, leaving policy in limbo. Whether aid giving as it has been practiced to date should continue or be augmented is a vital question. The weight of evidence, however, seems not to convince, or possibly the economic case does not count for much in the scales of decision making. This brings me to the second issue.

Starting with the very first *WDR*, the Bank has argued for more assistance to poor countries through capital and knowledge transfers, and it continues to do so today. It strains credulity to even imagine that low-income countries might derive little benefit from more capital and additional insight on development, but 30 *WDR*s and the immense library of research fail to credibly establish that the gains achieved since the mid-1970s are the outcome of a conceptually and empirically deeper understanding of development and not a function of luck or happenstance or geography or leadership (Sachs 2003).

The debate goes on with voices raised on both sides. Some, such as Jeffrey Sachs (2005), are calling for a Big Push of aid to bring about a surge in growth, terms reminiscent of the 1960s and earlier.[43] Their hopes are buoyed by the technological opportunities that lie within reach if only the resources are forthcoming (Sachs 2008). No doubt a case can be made for larger infusions of ODA by looking into the future, a point I will take up in the final chapter. The inconvenient findings are troubling

---

42. Geopolitics and herding behavior also affect the almost US$15 billion in aid extended by nongovernmental organizations from the Organisation for Economic Co-operation and Development countries, which tend to replicate the allocations of their home governments and their peers. Moreover, nongovernmental organizations favor former colonies and countries with familiar and shared religions, cultural traits, and beliefs (Dreher and others 2008).

43. The revival of terminology popular in the 1960s—*Big Push, poverty traps, takeoff,* and *sustained growth*—has also attracted sharp-eyed empirical scrutiny. Using data for the period 1950 to 2001, Easterly (2006a) cannot find low-income countries that become mired in poverty traps. Economies that can plausibly be described as having experienced a takeoff-like event, such as China; Hong Kong, China; Singapore; Taiwan, China; and Thailand, are exceedingly few, and none were recipients of a large aid injections.

for the World Bank, although they do not nullify the messages conveyed by the WDR. What they do make one wonder is why the advice given through policy dialogues, technical assistance, and lending operations to the developing countries that accepted assistance from the Bank did so little good for growth. Such policy advice—duly rendered operational and embedded in a scholarly apparatus—was clearly seen as adding value and contributing to the performance of the borrowing nations at least as much as the loans and credits. Could it be, for instance, that reforms that were introduced starting in the 1980s—reforms that initiated the building of market-friendly institutions, introduced macrostability, began improving the business climate, and paved the way to greater economic openness—are only now starting to bite after a lag of a decade and more? This is an attractive proposition, but could it be true? Do we just have to be patient? The recent accelerations in the growth of many countries in Sub-Saharan Africa and the higher average rates of growth in Latin America are a positive sign. However, it is hard to disentangle the effects of freer trade and large injections of resources into these regions following the rise in prices of energy and primary commodities since 2005. Also notable is that China and India—two of the most dynamic economies, which have accounted for most of the drop in poverty since the early 1990s—have followed a slow and cautious path to reform. They still sustain a large state sector, as well as a major state role in guiding the market, and they rank fairly low with respect to the "Doing Business" indicators. Moreover, other East Asian economies that went further with denationalization, openness, and building market institutions are now confronting a slowing of economic growth and an upward creep in economic inequality.

A WDR Policy Scorecard

In sum, the Bank through its WDRs has been powerfully instrumental in raising awareness on the extent of poverty and in exhaustively cataloguing the many ways of erasing it. Whether the policy medicines are potent enough is less than obvious, but certainly the challenges and policy options have been widely disseminated. Very likely, much of the poverty reduction stems directly—and indirectly—from GDP growth. In this regard, the Bank has begun pinning more hope on growth derived through gains in TFP than from substantial increases in capital spending, which was the message of the early Big Push literature. The WDRs have progressively leaned toward human and knowledge capital to secure the sought-after traversal to higher and sustained rates of growth that can also bring significant gains to the poor. Provision of services to augment human capital and raise its quality is also central to the strategy for gaining the upper hand on poverty and containing income inequality. The approach has its attractions, and the knowledge economy is in the policy foreground; nevertheless, the past experience of the high-achieving economies is not reassuring on this score. Fast growth has a large price tag: knowledge matters, but in the earlier stages, capital matters more. The WDRs are silent on what it takes to reach 35 percent rates of capital investment. For 7 and 8 percent rates of growth, nothing less is sufficient, and at this point, the slower-growing low-income countries of South Asia and Sub-Saharan Africa are falling far short of this level (see table 3.2). Most worrying is that the lower-middle-income countries that have far to climb up the greasy pole are also experiencing a decline in investment.

Consonant with the market-based philosophy espoused by the Bank, starting in the mid 1980s, the WDRs have called for a smaller state, a shrunken public sector, and the growing of a forest of market institutions. A scaling back of the state was in the cards. How far it should go,

Table 3.2: Average Investment of Slow-Growing South Asian and Sub-Saharan Africa Countries and India, 1990–2006

Indicator	1990–99	2000–06
South Asia		
Investment rate	20.2	21.7
GDP growth	4.6	4.9
GDP per capita growth	2.1	2.7
Sub-Saharan Africa		
Investment rate	16.4	18.4
GDP growth	2.4	4.1
GDP per capita growth	–0.3	1.3
India		
Investment rate	23.6	28.6
GDP growth	5.6	6.9
GDP per capita growth	3.7	5.3

Source: World Development Indicators database.

which services and utilities should be privatized, and how actively the state needs to engage in erecting regulatory institutions is contested terrain.[44] The financial debacles and concern regarding the quality of services in high-income countries are warning signals whose import has yet to be sufficiently internalized.

In conformity with current academic thinking, the WDRs have gone looking for illustrative stories and policy gold in the burgeoning empirical literature on microeconomic issues. This practice is sensible, but perhaps we need to be more keenly aware of the limitations of the research being conducted in coming to grips with empirical realities, teasing out causal relationships, and identifying policies that can produce results under varying conditions. For example, on global inequality—a matter of burning interest—the most painstaking review of the studies to date concludes sadly that

> it is not possible to reach a definitive conclusion regarding the direction of change in global inequality over the last three decades of the twentieth century. The different studies arrive at widely varying estimates [because] of varying data sources and methodologies.... [A]ll studies suffer from a variety of sources of uncertainty that include inter alia: measurement error in national accounts, in household surveys, and in within country price data used for PPP [purchasing power parity] estimation; standard index number and multilateral comparison problem with PPP estimates; and non-comparability of household surveys.... Given these uncertainties and the range of estimates of change in global inequality ... there is insufficient evidence to reject the null hypothesis of no change in global interpersonal inequality over 1970–2000. (Anand and Segal 2008: 90–91)

For more discussion on global inequality, see Ferreira and Ravallion (2008: 10–15).

In some cases, the narrow focus of the research and the desire to minimize econometric bias are "motivating the discipline to study randomized experiments either natural or controlled," modeled on agricultural crop experiments or clinical trials to test the potency of drugs (Mookherjee 2005: 11). The randomized approach avoids the risk of "arbitrariness with respect to theoretical formulation or structural relationships.... The purpose (of the randomized exercises) is not to understand the underlying

---

44. Following the partial government takeover of some banks in Europe and the United States in response to the banking crisis of 2007–08, the terms of the debate on the role of the state have clearly changed.

structure of the system of relationships generating the outcomes, only the statistical outcome impact of certain policy treatments" (Mookherjee 2005: 11).[45] As a consequence, the work at the frontiers of development economics may be adding relatively little to the fund of fresh and insightful theories. Without new and well-articulated theories to thread together empirical findings into a compelling story, the progress toward better policy has been slow (Kanbur 2005).

Thirty volumes of the WDR encapsulate a vast body of knowledge on development, track the changes in circumstances and in (Western) mainstream thinking, and bring the reader face to face with thousands of interesting experiments and stories. They constitute an imposing array of books offering a panoramic view of development. Two questions are uppermost as I come to the final chapter of this book. First, what are the frontiers toward which the WDR should be steering? Should the Bank take more of a lead, as it once did, given its proximity to the activity of development and its awareness of which way the winds are beginning to blow? Should the WDR continue to offer an increasingly compendious review of the literature? Or should it retrieve the ambition, the spirit, and the heft of the original WDR and issue a report, not necessarily every year, that directs the attention of policy and opinion makers to key emerging development issues and proposes a strategy for achieving results?

---

45. Ravallion (2008) observes that the policies and settings that can serve as the grist for randomized experiments are themselves nonrandom. From these, only a subset of the relatively simple programs can be selected that permit a clear separation of participants and nonparticipants. And the experiments illuminate only a tiny number of parameters in specific settings, which is of limited assistance to policy makers.

4

WHERE TO NOW?

There can be no doubt that the global economy accumulated more economic wealth between 1975 and 2006 than during any period in the past. It is always hazardous to measure the economic attributes of earlier periods; however, the guesstimates for the eight centuries extending from AD 1000 to the eve of the Industrial Revolution show that global gross domestic product (GDP) grew from US$121 million to US$371 million, and living standards of the average English or Chinese citizen changed little. Populations crept upward ever so slowly at 0.2 percent per year, kept in check by horrendously high mortalities and by agricultural and energy resource constraints. For the vast majority, even under the umbrella of a social compact, existence (in the language of Hobbes) could be nasty and brutish and was almost always short. Better data from about 1800 show that parts of the global economy were beginning to cast off the tethers that had been responsible for maintaining a low-level equilibrium across the world for several millennia. Between 1870 and 1950, despite the cruel wars and depressions that periodically caused immense economic damage, the size of the global economy rose from US$1,111 billion to US$5,337 billion, implying a growth rate of 2 percent per year. Between 1950 and

1975, the pace picks up to an average of 4.7 percent per year. And in the most recent stretch, from the mid 1990s up to 2006, growth was at its highest ever—5.2 percent per year—compared with that of earlier times (Maddison 2007).[1]

When the "technology of development" is so widely shared—not the least through the WDRs—why are there so many laggards? Why is there a great and widening divergence? Why aren't the ranks of "tiger economies" growing by the year? This topic is so fascinating that it attracts a steady trickle of imaginative and illuminating books.[2] Each book has contributed to our knowledge of the circuitous pathways to development and has sensitized us to the obstacles along the way. Every year, along comes a WDR—plus other reports—that adds more details on development, more analysis, more layers of complexity, more anecdotes, more factual information. If only this knowledge could render policy making less of an art and less subject to slippages and uncertainties, the whole world would be developed and growing by 7 percent per year, much like the more fortunate East Asian economies, several of which were forging ahead before the first WDR was written and which have occasionally flouted some of the messages in the WDRs while sustaining their remarkable and largely unwavering performance.

Perhaps the biggest lacuna in the corpus of knowledge contained in the WDRs is a lucid and detailed diagnostic explaining why even with good policies, the growth of the typical developing country rarely climbs much above 3 to 5 percent per year, which is impressive by historical standards, but countries in a hurry to catch up aspire to faster rates of growth. Figures 4.1 and 4.2 show the steady 1.8 percent per year growth of per capita GDP in the United States over a 140-year span and the faster 5.8 percent per year increase in the per capita GDP of the Republic of Korea over a 23-year period. The stability of this growth over extended periods, during which policies and circumstances varied, is quite remarkable and again raises questions regarding what economic policies are able to accomplish.

---

1. Lucas (2003) estimates that world output grew fourfold between 1960 and 2000, which translates into a per capita increase of 2.3 percent per annum.

2. Among them are G. Clark (2007), Collier (2007), Diamond (1999), Goldstone (2008), C. Jones (2008), Landes (1999), North and Thomas (1976), Rosenberg and Birdzell (1986), Sachs (2008).

Figure 4.1: Per capita GDP Growth of the United States, 1870–2003

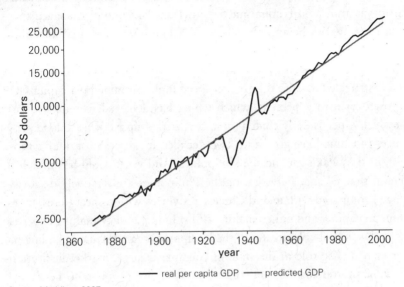

year

Source: Maddison 2007.

Figure 4.2: Per capita GDP Growth of Korea, 1960–2003

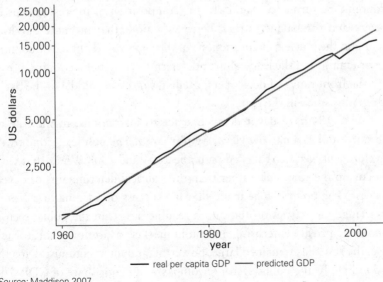

year

Source: Maddison 2007.

Since 1978, policy makers in the developing economies have benefited from vast transfers of capital and of knowledge on economic management—with the WDRs being only one among hundreds of formal and informal conduits for the transfer of policy-making expertise. However, the Ghanas, the Mexicos, the Pakistans, and the Philippines of the world have struggled to raise the growth speed limit. Sustained per capita GDP growth of 6 to 7 percent, which China has achieved seemingly effortlessly, has persistently eluded these countries. Impoverished inland provinces in China have grown for two decades at rates almost double those attained by Pakistan and the Philippines. And yet it could be difficult to claim that Ghana, Pakistan, or the Philippines are relatively disadvantaged compared with inland Chinese provinces with respect to resources, human capital, and policy-making skills. In fact, policy-making expertise is and was probably greater in the Philippines than in Guangxi, Ningxia, or Gansu. The role of the state in Guangxi is large, market institutions have a shorter history, and the business environment is no better and might be a good deal less welcoming for private business.

Possibly the answer does not lie mainly in the characteristics of the business environment, the readiness of market institutions, or the supply of human capital—the ground plowed over by the WDRs. Policies and the quality and determination of the leadership leave a deep imprint on economic performance. Similarly, the composition of interest groups in society and the balance struck between actions that promote development and the rent-extracting actions of the elites can reinforce or counter the orientation of the leadership and determine whether a country moves into the front ranks of developers, oscillates near the middle of the pack, or remains stuck in the rear.

The WDRs have devoted much space to institutions, to the role of the state, and to a narrow view of governance. The political economy of development has been touched on in the 2004 and 2008 WDRs, but with a focus on the economic rather than the political determinants of development. The point can be made that the success of a China or a Korea or a Singapore rested on the state's readiness to trim the public sector, encourage private enterprise, and build market institutions, but in each case, the state has remained large, powerful, and interventionist. Directly and indirectly, the public sector encompasses a major share of GDP. The small, fast-growing Nordic countries are not too dissimilar. The public sector is large, the state is active in promoting new industries through the national innovation system, and its not-so-hidden hand is everywhere, as it is in Singapore. The state in Brazil and Mexico has a lesser role, and market institutions have had a longer time to take root. The volume of human capital is surely adequate to support rapid growth, the domestic market is large, the geographic neighborhood is dynamic enough, but the achievements pale before those of China and now even India.

The interest of policy makers lies not in whether the state should be large or small or more or less interventionist; the interest is in what specific forms of intervention over a period of time yield the best results under similar external circumstances. The same is true regarding institutions. Everyone can see that market institutions in successful East Asian industrializing countries are at best functional and at worst weak and minimally supportive. The interesting issue is how an assortment of institutions of varying capabilities and degrees of maturity can, with the help of a strong developmental state, produce good results using the local knowledge that policy makers surely have (Rodrik 2007). In a world where conditions in any country are always less than ideal, we need to be able to explain how countries can transform a fishing vessel into a serviceable cruise liner while on the high seas and in the absence of a detailed blueprint.

Undoubtedly, the WDRs are doing a creditable job of deepening knowledge and collecting an immensity of experience, but in doing so there is a risk that they might be rendering policy making more complex. So many more necessary conditions are being identified while the sufficient conditions seem ever more elusive. In successful economies, policy makers worked with simple decision rules and with reference to a few—or just one—practical model. By keeping things straightforward and above all practical, they made and implemented decisions quickly. That mistakes were also made is certainly true—they are still being made, although thanks to the WDRs, we cannot cite ignorance—but in a simpler decision environment, it was and is easier to rectify them without lengthy research.

In short, by striving to convey the full richness of research and practical experience on a topic, the WDRs might be catering more to the student of development than to their primary audience of policy makers looking for practical guidance and rules of thumb. This closing section briefly alludes to few of the topic areas where there is an urgent need for raising awareness and mobilizing effort across countries, for identifying key issues, and for providing policy makers with a framework for organizing information and formulating policies.

Putting Knowledge to Work

Few could deny the salience of technological progress in explaining growth most emphatically after the mid 18th century. The earlier references to the growth "residual" and to total factor productivity underscore the contribution of science. In our times, making science flourish and making the scientific endeavor productive are easily among the leading objectives of countries strongly committed to promoting industrial competitiveness and growth and to improving the quality of life. Technology policies and national innovation systems are becoming a preoccupation of policy makers even in the low-income countries, and by styling itself as a knowledge bank, the World Bank has evinced an awareness of this trend.[3]

Increasingly the questions policy makers are asking revolve around identifying technologies with the greatest longer-run potential in terms of growth and employment.[4] These questions lead to further questions about, for example, the volume and allocation of public funds to catalyze and build capacity in the selected areas, the ways to share the burdens of investment and risk with the private sector, the scale and range of incentives to be offered to firms and researchers, the rules governing intellectual property, and the means for expeditiously commercializing research findings. Smart policies are inseparable from targeting areas for technology development and steering public and private resources into these areas generally for long periods of time. They entail investment in specialized skills with support from public funding of scholarships, and they call for public spending on universities, research institutes, incubators, intermediaries, and science

---

3. The 1998/99 WDR addressed technology development and the pursuit of innovation. Others, such as the 2008 WDR, have devoted a chapter (or a box) to this topic.

4. Phillips (2008) lists some of the challenges as well as the mechanisms for ferreting out technologies and forecasting change.

parks (Howells 2006; Romer 2000; Yusuf 2008). The public sector generally must foot part of the bill for venture capital, and in many instances, whether it is pharmaceuticals, armaments, electronics, or software, the public sector is a major purchaser. There is no dearth of material on the knowledge economy (see, for example, Foray 2004) and on innovation systems, but middle- and low-income countries are looking for strategies and ways of implementing such systems, which the Bank could highlight. Doing so might require a reappraisal of the Bank's belief in minimizing the involvement of the state in open-ended infant-industry activities with no definite payoff and its strong views on anything that smacks of industrial targeting.

Warming Climate, Scarce Water

The climate change that lies in our future will bit by bit transform the physical world and demands adjustments and adaptations on many fronts. Low-income countries lying in the tropical belt will be affected the worst by climate extremes, higher temperatures,[5] desertification, water scarcity, coastal flooding, and far more hazardous epidemiological circumstances.[6] Among these changes, the long-run effects of seasonal water shortages and exceedingly variable rainfall arguably could impose the heaviest burdens on rural and urban inhabitants alike. A succinct summary of the economic issues being debated with respect to climate change can be found in Heal (2008).[7] The seriousness of global warming is unfolding daily in scientific and popular publications. The Intergovernmental Panel on Climate Change report (IPCC 2007), the *Stern Review* (Stern 2007), and detailed exegeses on these reports provide the closest reading

---

5. One of the deadliest and thus far relatively neglected weather-related catastrophes is the heatwave, which has wreaked havoc even in developed countries. The examples of Chicago in 1995, France in 2003, and Hungary in 2007 come to mind. See Klinenberg (2003) for a detailed account of how heat and humidity resulted in 700 excess deaths in Chicago during the week of July 12, 1995.

6. Dell, Jones, and Olken (2008), drawing on data from the past 50 years, emphasize the negative effects of higher temperatures for the poorer countries.

7. A similarly compact account of the ethical issues associated with discounting future costs is provided by Broome (2008). On the issue of discounting and providing for future generations, see Summers and Zeckhauser (2008). Dyson (2008) also offers a typically lucid review of two major publications, one by William Nordhaus exploring the implications of different rates of discounting and the other by Ernesto Zedillo.

of where matters rest, and some plausible and alarming scenarios are spelled out in Campbell (2008). Additional information is flowing in thick and fast, very little of it reassuring. As fresh water becomes increasingly precious, markets alone might not be able to handle rising and competing demands.[8] It has frequently been noted that the sharpest conflicts in the future could erupt over water resources. These conflicts might arise between users located at different points along a major waterway, between rural and urban consumers of surface or underground water, and among countries that share water resources. A number of populous countries face the predicament of having to divide among themselves the bounties of a shared river or a subterranean aquifer. The populations and needs of these countries are rising even as the future supplies of water are set to dwindle with the retreat of mountain glaciers, deforestation, and sparser rainfall in upstream catchment areas (Orlove, Wiegandt, and Luckman 2008).[9] Under such circumstances, food security will surely reemerge as a paramount concern imperiling the stability of several low-income countries with large rural populations and perhaps also jeopardizing crucial elements of partial and hard-won trade liberalization—one of the key benefits of globalization.

Securing, conserving, fairly allocating, and efficiently using water resources will be at the very heart of development as these issues were some decades ago (Pearce 2006; Rogers 2008; UNDP 2007). These issues could once again challenge the broad skills of the Bank: operational, analytic, technological, and diplomatic. The Bank's role in crafting the Indus Basin treaty (a slow process that commenced in 1951 and came to a close in 1960) and in helping to finance the network of dams and canals in the Punjab ranks as one of its finest achievements, and efforts on a similar scale but in many regions might be required in the future. A *WDR* could chalk out a framework for tackling the problems associated with dwindling supplies of

---

8. Water stress is mounting in parts of Asia, which has 60 percent of the world's population but only 27 percent of the world's fresh water. In Africa, the situation is even more serious, with close to two-thirds of the population relying on limited and highly uncertain sources of supply and with some estimates suggesting that 40 percent of the existing supplies of irrigation water will not be sustained. (Smil 2008b: 198). See also Smil (2008c) on the advances in the capacity and efficiency of facilities desalinating water through reverse osmosis, which offers hope for parched coastal communities with access to affordable energy supplies.

9. Ten major watersheds lie in Tibet, and the rivers flowing from them provide water to almost one-half of the world's population.

fresh water and advance the dialogue on desirable actions among affected countries. Among the actions to be explored are building a storage and distribution infrastructure, developing sharing arrangements and institutions to strengthen water markets, and investing in sewage facilities to reduce the contamination of available fresh water. We can also include new technologies to purify or desalinate water; investment in the infrastructure that cities would need to use water of different grades for different purposes; investment in urban distribution systems to cut the 20 to 25 percent losses from leakages; technologies for minimizing the losses from evaporation and increasing the efficiency with which farmers use water ("Running Dry" 2008); new cropping patterns using genetically engineered crops that are tolerant of water stress and salty or brackish water (Hindo 2008; "Next Green Revolution" 2008); exploitation of the potential of urban agriculture through "sky farming," which minimizes water loss and pollution and also lessens the energy costs of shipping fresh food from distant places for urban consumption; planting of vegetation that provides cover but minimizes the loss of moisture through evapotranspiration; and, last but not least, resettlement of people currently living in areas that will be receiving a declining amount of fresh water (or will be endangered by rising sea levels).[10] This is not the only niche for the Bank that could be an

---

10. The wide-ranging increase in commodity prices since 2000 and the steep rise in the prices of foodstuffs that started in 2007 could have significant positive implications for the low-income economies with large rural populations. Higher agricultural prices, on balance, benefit the poor, and as they are likely to persist, offer a golden opportunity to do away with agricultural price supports and trade barriers in developed countries. The gains, mainly accruing to a number of lower- and middle-income countries that export foodstuffs, range from US$460 billion to US$2.5 trillion (Anderson and Winters 2008). However, importers of foodstuffs will need to take account of the changing circumstances, and water-stressed regions will have to reconsider the benefits of exporting "virtual water" (Allan 2003). At least three kinds of strategic opportunities have arisen that could be grist for a *WDR*. First is the opportunity to begin building research, innovation, and extension systems that will enhance urgently needed agricultural technology capability in low-income countries. Such capability has lagged, especially in Africa, affecting the availability of crop varieties that are more productive (and less dependent on natural gas–based nitrogen fertilizer for their yields), richer in nutrients, more resistant to disease, and better able to survive water stress (Paarlberg 2008). The future of agriculture depends on the infusion of technology. Second, the future of smallholder-based agriculture needs to be reconsidered in the light of ongoing climatic changes and estimates of the population that viable rural systems could support over the longer term. Rather than entrenching populations in rural areas with the help of institutions and infrastructure, sketching scenarios of urban development for a faster rural exodus would be more helpful. Third, stimulating agricultural economies could set the stage for the kind of growth spurt and the associated declines in poverty that occurred in China and Vietnam (Lin 1992; Rozelle and Swinnen 2007; World Bank 2008b) in the 1980s and 1990s. The chances of this rejuvenation happening can be increased if, down the road, the Doha Round is revived by highlighting the scale of the benefits for all participants.

outgrowth of climate change; however, it is one that could harness the existing or latent strengths of the Bank—possibly more so than carbon trading, for example. And to reiterate the earlier point, this problem is a topic for a *WDR*, possibly cast in the mold of the earliest reports, that succinctly maps out issues and strategy. The details and an exhaustive review of the literature can be left to specialized reports.

The Geography of Human Habitation

Climate change coupled with resource and energy scarcities will call for a very different kind of urban environment. The cities we now live in arose with minimum planning in a world where energy was cheap and water plentiful. The advent of the automobile and, more recently, of advanced telecommunications and the Internet[11] has encouraged horizontal expansion and the increasing consumption of housing space. More space, as incomes rise, is associated with higher costs for space heating and cooling. Urban sprawl eats up prime agricultural land in the vicinity of cities and necessitates expensive supporting networks of infrastructure to provide transport, energy, water, and sanitation services.[12]

Initial construction costs aside, there are additional recurring costs of maintenance and replacement, plus the losses from transferring electricity and water over vast networks of wires and pipes. Many of today's megacities were built up piecemeal without an eye to the efficiency of land use—from a long-term standpoint—or to cost containment in terms of energy, congestion, and time devoted to intraurban travel. In a crowded, largely urban world constrained by increasing scarcities of water and energy, urban planners will need to partially reconstruct many of the existing megacities in the developing world and to carefully plan the expansion of existing

Defining the benefits and elucidating the political economy of sharing and of the ways of surmounting likely hurdles could, together with the above, mean that a decisive victory might be won in the long struggle against poverty.

11. Computerization and the increasing reliance on information technologies have added to the energy intensity of urban living. Running and cooling faster microprocessors and vast server farms consume 10 percent of all the electricity generated in the United States. Creating, packaging, storing, and moving 10 megabytes of data consume 900 grams of coal (Hamm 2008; Mckenna 2006).

12. Among the worst instances is the "decentralized dense sprawl" of the Los Angeles area, with its high population density, congestion, air pollution, and lack of both public transportation and recreational amenities (Eidlin 2005). Sprawl, which is in part the outcome of land-use restrictions in the central city, pushes urban development outward and contributes to greater greenhouse gas emissions (Glaeser and Kahn 2008).

urban centers with an eye not only to resource conservation, but also to convenience, livability, and the health of urban inhabitants. For example, monocentric cities with a radial pattern of roads that give rise to congestion during peak hours will need to morph into polycentric cities with ring roads, public transport services, and other changes in travel and commuting patterns and residential development. Floor area ratios will have to be raised so as to encourage densification, especially around nodes. Mixed use of land will be needed to minimize the proliferation of office canyons that are only used for part of the day. Ribbon development along the main transport arteries will have to be actively discouraged. Technological advances in transport, in road-user charges differentiated by time of day, in waste disposal, and in recycling will need to be incorporated in existing cities and become an essential feature of new urban areas.

There is scope for significant technological gains in the design and construction of buildings, which collectively account for 45 percent of gross energy consumption and greenhouse gas emissions ("Science/Technology: Construction" 2008). What are now viewed as somewhat exotic "eco-friendly" and "green" technologies will need to become the norm. All this improvement will entail huge new expenditures, but more than that, it calls for fundamental shifts in urban living conditions in arguably more compact cities, in the direction of technological advances,[13] in the rapid incorporation of the technologies, and in urban planning for the longer term that anticipates massive systemic reform.

Some of the spatial issues are tackled by the 2009 WDR; however, there remains an awareness-raising and strategy-defining role for the Bank to play in helping urbanization come to terms with the looming scarcities of energy and water and with the need to both manage and safeguard ecosystems.[14] The future of urbanization is intertwined with climate change[15] because there are cities whose prospects are uncertain because they are located in

---

13. Downsizing, material conservation, and heightened advantages of further miniaturization (which Japanese firms have raised to a fine art) could spur a new round of innovation (Phillips 2008).

14. The energy needs of modern living are examined in detail by Smil (2008a), and the links between energy use on the one hand and urbanization, transport, health, and climate change on the other are explored by Haines and others (2007); Wilkinson, Smith, Beevers, and others (2007); Wilkinson, Smith, Joffe, and Haines (2007); and Woodcock and others (2007). Humanity's transformation of ecosystems and the effect of cities is the topic of a valuable paper by Kareiva and others (2007).

15. Urbanization appears to be on an inexorable upward trend, especially in Asia and Africa, and it has major implications for climate change, both local and global (Grimm and others 2008; Montgomery 2008).

low-lying coastal areas or in areas where warming, water scarcity, and the costs of supplying water from elsewhere will seriously affect habitation.[16] Some cities, therefore, might not be worth expanding or rebuilding, and the time is now to start thinking about the geography of human settlement.

This situation leads to the whole question of future regional development and poverty alleviation in the more inhospitable corners of our planet and migration. Migration will be the only cure for poverty in these parts of countries where the potential for agricultural or urban development is minimal and becoming less promising day by day as global warming tightens its grip. Migration out of these areas will need to be channeled to cities with longer-term growth possibilities. Bringing infrastructure and services to areas that are certain to become depopulated would be a waste of resources. Thus, regional development has to be redirected and intermeshed with urban strategies. Moreover, in many instances, migration out of parts of the tropics will be unavoidable, and multilateral arrangements will be required to absorb people in places where the climate and water resources are conducive to habitation and economic activity. The sociopolitical upheavals that this migration will involve are immense. A *WDR* could launch and help focus the debate. It could also initiate a parallel debate on the future role of the state and of global governance arrangements in a world where inframarginal discussions will be made—by the state—on where and how people can live in order to fit into the global budget of resources and global public goods. Markets will certainly help, but the enormity of the tasks ahead will be far beyond the capacities of the market, given how little time is left before irrevocable and painful changes in the environment are upon us.

Resilient Complex Societies

As societies develop, the degree of complexity of numerous interlocking systems has increased—infrastructure, industry, finance, energy, health, and transport to name a few. This complexity mirrors technological sophistication

---

16. Gulledge (2008) notes that the United States has the largest number of coastal cities that would be vulnerable to rising sea levels. Delta areas are also highly susceptible. A one meter rise in the sea level would inundate the entire Mekong Delta, which is home to 20 million people and is a major producer of rice.

and underpins prosperity. However, complexity and its associated interdependencies are also a source of vulnerability: they can rapidly magnify a problem by diffusing a shock widely throughout a regional or a national economy (MacKenzie 2008a, 2008b). We are all aware of how urban life can be brought to a halt by a major electricity outage. Shocks administered by a lethal outbreak of disease,[17] an earthquake, a weather-related event, a terrorist strike on a key urban or energy node, or a climatic event that dramatically affected the water supply and sewage systems of a region that was densely populated, water stressed, or both could trigger sudden and disastrous outcomes for urban societies in particular.[18] Such events could result in very large migrations in a short period of time, and these migrations could quickly overwhelm organizations and services in affected areas. We have had a foretaste with recent earthquakes, droughts, tsunamis, and hurricanes ("East Africa: Disasters" 2008). Avian flu and bovine spongiform encephalopathy (BSE, or "mad cow disease") have caused immense damage and disrupted production of beef and poultry as well as trading patterns. So far, a disease outbreak affecting humans on a large scale has been mercifully avoided, but specialists warn us that it is in the cards. Any outbreak of sufficient lethality would be exceedingly difficult to contain given how integrated the world has become ("Infectious Disease" 2006; Smil 2005).[19] The contagiousness of the financial crisis linked to subprime mortgages that started in 2007 and the resulting squeeze on interbank lending in many of the leading industrial countries is another example of this phenomenon.

Climatic, economic, demographic,[20] and political trends strongly argue for building resilience into the complex, globally integrated urban

---

17. For example, the outbreaks of avian flu in Southeast Asia have radically changed the structure and composition of the trade in poultry products (Nicita 2008).

18. Posner (2007) notes that scientific advance can increase the probability of catastrophic risks. He goes on to observe that low-probability risks are inherently harder to deal with.

19. The limited capacity to cope with a surge in health care requirements and some of the reasons for this decreased capacity are delineated in a study of the state of Indiana in the United States (Avery and others 2008). One major problem is the depleted shelf of potent antibiotics (especially those effective against gram-negative bacteria); the thin pipeline of new antibiotic drugs; limited funding available for research on such drugs; and the time it takes to develop, test, and win approval for new vaccines (Groopman 2008; and Baker 2007 for a more positive reading on the future course of antibiotic development).

20. The youthfulness of populations in many developing countries, the high ratio of males to females, insufficient stable job opportunities, and limited scope for emigration could become a source of social turbulence (Hudson and den Boer 2004; World Bank 2006).

societies that are mushrooming all around.[21] Such resilience is a function of the quality, design, and robustness of the infrastructure (soft and hard);[22] organization; good contingency planning; fail-safe information technology (IT) systems; plenty of built-in redundancies; social capital;[23] well-financed institutions for absorbing shocks; and institutions and instruments for insuring against risks and pooling those risks internationally.[24] In a crowded, warming world with lopsided demographic structures and substantial income disparities, shocks are likely to be more frequent and deadlier. How to partially shockproof societies that are likely to be at the epicenter of such events is a major challenge. And how to prepare their neighbors and the rest of the world is a major secondary concern. There is a dearth of thinking on this problem and a lack of preparedness, which is apparent from the disorganized and clumsy responses to recent crises and the absence of long-run efforts to strengthen global capabilities for worsening crises. The WDR can become a vehicle for ideas for factoring such longer-term capabilities into the normal activity of development.

An Equal Marriage of Politics and Economics

It was Gunnar Myrdal (1968) who, by drawing attention to the frequently ineffectual nature of the soft state, imported politics into the analysis of development. Few would doubt that the distribution of political and economic power determines the direction and dynamics of development

21. Sheffi (2005) discusses resilience in organizations.

22. A recent study by the U.S. Department of Transportation indicates just how vulnerable the infrastructure is to adverse weather extremes and how much needs to be done to change standards of design and construction (Kintisch 2008). Other research shows how the design of infrastructure impinges on and threatens vital ecosystems (Doyle and others 2008).

23. The work of Diego Gambetta and Robert Putnam on trust and social capital is relevant in this regard. See, for example, Bacharach and Gambetta (2001); Gambetta (1988, 2006); and Putnam (2000, 2007).

24. The importance of the Internet and the extent to which it is worming its way into every corner of our lives has given rise to worries about the consequences of a collapse of this complex system. These worries have been fanned by accidents affecting undersea cables, attacks on major hubs, and denial of service attacks. Again the answer is built-in resilience through greater cooperation among operators, greater bandwidth, redundancy, and more effective management ("Science/Technology: How Likely Is Internet Collapse?" 2008). Catastrophe bonds, weather derivatives, and insurance pools are among the instruments now available, although the market's appetite for derivatives is modest, as it is for disaster insurance.

(Bardhan 2006; Feng 2003). But the Bank's charter forbids commentary on the politics of a country. "The Bank is not to be influenced by the political character of the country requesting credits" (Shihata, Tschofen, and Parra 1991: 72). The WDRs talk of the role of the state in largely apolitical terms and "have suffered from an enforced reticence on political matters. Generally anything that might offend politicians of particular countries has been avoided so there is a pervasive weakness in the reports on matters of political economy" (Stern and Ferreira 1997: 571). The discussion of political economy in the 2004 WDR is on mechanisms for making service providers more accountable by giving people more voice and access to better information; the 2008 WDR calls for building coalitions of stakeholders that will give agricultural producers, small and large, a greater voice and the ability to advance the cause of agricultural development. These suggestions are constructive; however, the inability to explain fluctuations in growth rates, the weaknesses of policies and the failure of implementation, the factors that make democracy more or less effective and contribute to "democratic capital,"[25] the disappointing consequences of official development assistance at the macrolevel, the factors contributing to the failure of states and the measures needed to retrieve failed states from political paralysis and cycles of violence,[26] the extreme seriousness of future challenges, and the changing constellation of what Fareed Zakaria (2008) calls "the rise of the rest"[27] all suggest that economics needs to forge much closer ties with the social disciplines, with the engineering sciences, and with the branches of technology that have a large hand in defining the physical environments we live in. Other disciplines such as engineering are seeing the value of multidisciplinary training. Economists remain highly specialized, and most

25. See the succinct review of the political economy literature by Alesina (2007). See also S. Ahmed and Varshney (2008) and "India: Democracy Is Embedded" (2008) on the political economy of India's development.

26. Failed states lead to great hardship for their citizens and can have spillover effects on countries near and far. Containing violence and constructing the social fabric for recovery is a difficult process that is attracting increasing attention. See Ghani and Lockhart (2008); Haims and others (2008).

27. A new and more diffuse power structure is emerging, and among the leading powers, new and old, there is an upsurge of competition and of rivalries that threatens to unravel trade agreements (Mahbubani 2008). Robert Kagan (2008: 4) believes that after a short spell of integration the world is entering an age of divergence: "Struggles for status and influence in the world have returned as central features of the scene. The old competition between liberalism and autocracy has also reemerged, with the world's great powers increasingly lining up according to the nature of their regimes."

view development from extremely narrow perspectives. This narrow outlook is leading to the accumulation of the increasingly specific findings I referred to above. However, given the diversity of talent in the Bank and its capacity to tap resources externally, the institution is well placed to explore fresh analytic and interdisciplinary angles,[28] strike out in new directions, and experiment with new policy recipes. This is a worthy ambition for the next 30 years.

The unfinished development agenda is large, and there is much for the Bank to do. The *WDR* can again become a vehicle for mobilizing global opinion and for guiding strategy. Something comparable to the vision that gave birth to the first *WDR* could be recovered or rediscovered. Exhaustive *WDR*s packed with myriad microempirical findings may be running into diminishing returns outside and inside the Bank. So many other similar reports are on the market that the voice of the *WDR* and its uniqueness are in danger of being lost. At a time when the Bank—along with other international financial institutions—is attempting to reinvent itself and define its longer-term role, reinventing the *WDR*, differentiating it from the herd, and using it to deliver messages on crucial elements of development strategy would signal that the Bank is ready once again to pick up the mantle of leadership on development.

---

28. The Independent Evaluation Group report (World Bank 2008a: 41) observes that "the Bank's understanding of political economy is improving, but much of it is still at a general level without connection to details of the [public sector reform] agenda.... The Bank has done some work and could do more to understand the political foundations of governance."

THE WORLD DEVELOPMENT REPORT AT THIRTY: A BIRTHDAY TRIBUTE OR A FUNERAL ELEGY?

ANGUS DEATON

Shahid Yusuf's review of the *World Development Reports* (*WDRs*) is elegant and insightful, but also wistful and nostalgic. He clearly believes that the *WDRs* have known better days, and I agree with him. He is positive about the future, but I am not sure I agree; I think the problems that afflict the *WDRs* have deep causes that will not soon go away.

In my comments, I shall follow the same general outline as does Yusuf. I will begin with my understanding of the function of the reports, and I will review some of the most influential reports—and their possible influence on development thinking—as well as the general tone and content of recent reports. Like Yusuf, I shall not be afraid to use the exercise as an excuse to think about economic development more generally and about the role of the World Bank in particular.

In what follows, I shall draw freely on the review of Bank research—including the *WDRs*—that was carried out by an outside panel consisting of Abhijit Banerjee, Nora Lustig, and Ken Rogoff, with myself as chair. Our report, *An Evaluation of World Bank Research, 1998–2005*, has been available on the Bank's Web site since September 2006 (Banerjee and others 2006). I note, however, that although the report is a joint document, the review panel is in no way responsible for the views expressed here, which are entirely my own.

The (Multiple) Roles of the *World Development Report*

The *World Development Report* is the flagship publication not of the World Bank as a whole, but of its Research Department, headed by the Bank's chief economist. The chief economist always has overall responsibility for the report and on occasion uses it as a vehicle for publicizing his or her own views about development policy or the importance of particular topics. Joe Stiglitz on information, Nick Stern on the investment climate, and François Bourguignon on equity are recent examples. In all cases, the *WDR* provides a summary of Bank thinking and research on a particular topic—or on an interrelated set of topics—and tries to position its own views in the forefront of current development thinking and debate. Yusuf writes that "The *WDR* can again become a vehicle for mobilizing global opinion and for guiding strategy," summarizing both its aim and the view that it is currently failing, although it has succeeded in the past. *World Development Reports* summarize not only the Bank's own research, but also outside academic research, not only from economics, but increasingly from other subjects, including political science, sociology, psychology, and epidemiology. These summaries reputedly put the *WDRs* on many college reading lists, though I am unaware of any evidence. Because the *WDR* is perceived as very important within the Bank, intense internal competition surrounds the choice of topic, with different groups jockeying for prominence for their own pet issue or research topic. This role does much to ensure the continuation of the reports and may be as important in doing so as any success in mobilizing global opinion and guiding strategy.

The evidence that the *WDRs* have—or ever had—such an influence is notably thin. Citation counts are presented, which are unimpressive to my eyes, but are scarcely relevant. The reaction of the intended audience—policy makers and their advisers around the world, newspaper editorialists, or even teachers of economic development—is not well measured by citations in the ISI Web of Knowledge database or on Google Scholar.

But even in a time when economic development and foreign aid are very much in the public and academic minds, and when the *New York Times* has a world poverty correspondent, neither the *Times* nor the *Journal of Economic Literature* anxiously awaits the appearance of a new *WDR*. (Compare this situation, for example, with the extensive reaction to the new poverty counts in late August 2008.) Newspapers in Delhi, Kampala, or Cape Town may evince more excitement, and reactions there could usefully have been documented. Other commentators in this volume are better placed to assess this international reaction and to comment on whether the policy makers and advisers routinely use the *WDRs*. On the publicity side, my impression is that the most heavily publicized of the recent *WDRs* was *World Development Report 2000/2001: Attacking Poverty*, which became a news item, not for its content, but for the internal disarray that it revealed within the Bank, particularly on the role of growth in poverty reduction.

The production of the *WDRs* is expensive, something that is not discussed in Yusuf's essay. At any given time, approximately eight full-time researchers are at work on the current, previous, or next report. Measured in numbers of people, this team constitutes about 10 percent of the Bank's research effort, which takes no account of the fact that the *WDR* team is typically drawn from among the Bank's best and most senior researchers. Nor does it count the financial costs of the world tour that follows the publication of each report. If the reports have not been successful, it is not for want of commitment by the Bank. Yet research in the Bank, like the Bank as a whole, is under increasing budgetary pressure. Now is surely a good time to think about whether the value of this one item is worth what it costs, for which we would need a much fuller accounting of costs and benefits than is currently provided.

The Quality and Intellectual Legacy of the *World Development Reports*

The research review panel summarized its views of the *WDRs* as follows:

> The *World Development Reports* have sometimes been instrumental in changing the way that the world thinks about some aspect of development, such as poverty, health, or population. In recent years, they have, to an extent, become the victims of their own success. Because they are seen as so important, they must incorporate the views of large numbers of people, inside and outside the Bank. In consequence, they often seek to minimize conflict and to emphasize "win-win" situations instead of trade-offs. They often lack sharpness and focus, and are sometimes incoherent, especially when it proves impossible to reconcile the views of the various commentators and authors.... [T]heir regular appearance contributes to the Bank's standing in the development community even if, to some extent, they are trading on their past reputation (Banerjee and others 2006: 8).

If this view differs from Yusuf's, it is only in emphasis.

The three best remembered *WDRs* are those on fertility, on poverty, and on health. The 1984 fertility report took the previously standard, though even then rapidly fading, view that population growth was indeed a problem for economic development, that more mouths meant less for each (the lump fallacy), and that the "tragedy of the commons" meant that the individual decisions of parents about their fertility were unlikely to lead to good outcomes. Perhaps the most important intellectual legacy of this report was the establishment of a National Academy of Sciences panel under the chairmanship of Sam Preston, which produced an authoritative modern account of the issue and which takes a very different view from the *WDR* (Preston, Lee, and Greene 1986).[1] Yusuf comments that the Bank dropped the issue after the report, and indeed the tide was turning against the international population control movement from the mid-1980s on. Yet much harm had already been done, as documented in Matthew Connelly's (2008) *Fatal Misconceptions*, which while not painting the World Bank as the principal villain in this shameful history, does not absolve it either. In any case, the population report was clearly an example not of Bank intellectual leadership, but of the Bank being well behind then-current best thinking.

The 1990 poverty report is famous for introducing the international dollar-a-day poverty standard and the associated counts. These counts have continued to date, regularly updated by Martin Ravallion and his team, who were also the original authors. They have had an immense effect on development practice and on development debate, not least through the use of the dollar-a-day standard to define the first of the Millennium Development Goals (MDGs) and the appointment of the Bank as the subsequent scorekeeper. It is worth noting that this intellectual contribution, one of the Bank's most prominent, was not in the area of policy making or of theory, but in the area of measurement. The dollar-a-day standard illustrates how important measurement and scorekeeping have been in development and in the assessment of the Bank itself. Yet measurement plays little role in Yusuf's paper, an issue to which I will return.

---

1. Yet the idea of a population threat is a hydra that will never die, and it is showing signs of life again in the wake of the current boom in world food and commodity prices, as well as in Jeffrey Sachs's most recent book *Common Wealth* (Sachs 2008).

The dollar-a-day standard is not without its problems and detractors. It provides the measurement underpinnings not only for the first MDG, but also for at least part of the Bank's current, almost exclusive focus on poverty reduction. One of the problems comes from the fact that the measures are tied to the purchasing power parities from the International Comparison Program (ICP), so that the global poverty line and the associated counts change with every revision of the ICP, whose own measurements are sometimes on shaky ground. The latest (2005) version of the ICP, which had greater cooperation from China and India than ever before, brings hundreds of millions of Chinese and tens of millions of Indians into the international poverty counts who were previously thought to have escaped (see Chen and Ravallion 2007, 2008). Although Chen and Ravallion take the view that the 2005 ICP is simply better—because it is more comprehensive and because it better controls for the quality of goods and services across countries—this argument is by no means obviously or unqualifiedly correct, and a real risk exists that the constantly shifting standard will eventually bring the counts into disrepute. That previous estimates are discarded with every new round of the ICP certainly undermines public understanding of what is happening to global poverty and causes a great deal of confusion—as demonstrated, for example, by the immediate reaction in the Indian press to the latest counts. For example, Surjit Bhalla, a longtime critic of the Bank's poverty work, noted that if the latest ICP estimates are correct, and if India's growth rates are correct, Indian living standards in 1950 could not easily have supported life.

More fundamentally, the success of the dollar-a-day measure carries with it the risk that the objective of the Bank becomes not just the elimination of poverty, but the elimination of dollar-a-day poverty. Given the uncertainties of just who is poor by this criterion—with hundreds of millions of people being reclassified with each new set of measures—directing all attention to people below the line and ignoring those just above it makes no sense. Of course, the problem is more general than the international lines. Many local domestic lines that are used by the Bank for country policy advice have a substantial arbitrary component, and many have little local political legitimacy. Governments are—or at least should be—responsible to all of their citizens, not just to those below an arbitrary and uncertain poverty line.

The 1993 *WDR* on health is also famous, mostly for its introduction of the disability-adjusted life year (DALY), although this concept and its subsequent sweeping of the world is attributable less to Bank researchers than to Chris Murray, who was a consultant to the *WDR*. The DALY, like the dollar-a-day standard, has become a central tool of health measurement around the world for computing the burden of disease associated with different conditions, for permitting a combination of mortality and morbidity, and for assigning priorities. Again, many may criticize the DALY measures, particularly the arbitrariness of the weights that they attribute to different diseases—adding together migraines, quadriplegia, or schizophrenia—as well as of the dangers of using DALYs as a guide to policy and taking seriously the discounting of the lives of people with disabilities and diseases. The success of the concept may owe as much or more to the vacuum that it filled than to its own conceptual soundness. But the 1993 *WDR*, more than any other Bank report, put the Bank on the map as a major player in global health. It is also famous for reputedly persuading Bill Gates that international health was important, certainly an excellent example of the *WDR* mobilizing global opinion and shaping strategy.

It is noteworthy that both the 1990 poverty report and the 1993 health report are best known for their introductions of new tools for *measurement*. Although it is too early to know which recent *WDRs* will be as influential, my guess would be the report on service delivery, which also introduced new measurements, from the Bank's important surveys on absenteeism among health and education workers around the world. New measures changed and shaped the debate more than new analysis. This fact is perhaps not surprising. More than other international agencies, the Bank is well equipped with data and with high-quality researchers and consultants who are able to present these data in new ways that have long-lasting influence on the way that people think about development successes and failures.

The *World Development Indicators*

In the early days of the *World Development Reports*, many of us would wait anxiously for a new one, and when it arrived, we would ignore the words up front and turn quickly to the tables at the back. These tables became the *World Development Indicators* (*WDI*), later spun off into an immensely successful stand-alone product. In the early days, the production of the *WDI* was essentially a retail operation, with the Bank assembling information that others had collected. Over time, the Bank has become a major data provider in its own right—for example, collecting household surveys, conducting the Doing Business and Investment Climate surveys, and—most recently—managing the latest round of the International Comparison Program. In consequence, an increasing fraction of the data in the *WDI* is generated in-house. The WDI database is accessed by tens of millions of subscribers around the world and is used not only by academic researchers, but also by economic commentators, policy makers, and policy advisers around the world. Of the 18.8 million registered online users, 10 million are in low- and middle-income countries. The provision of these data is exhibit A in the Bank's case to be a knowledge bank, and their development is an achievement for which the *WDRs* should take much of the credit.

Declining Fortunes: From a Star Is Born to a Red Dwarf or Even a Black Hole?

Yusuf's paper leaves the strong impression that the *World Development Reports* are not what they once were, and some of these concerns are also reflected in the summary statement from the panel review quoted previously. The *WDRs* certainly suffer from being the consensus reports of a large bureaucracy among whose members serious differences of opinion exist that cannot be resolved without confusion, banality, and contradiction. Despite the Bank's increasing importance in measurement and data provision, the *WDRs* have not had a distinguished history of handling empirical evidence; too often bad—or simply incredible—evidence is presented along with useful and interesting new findings. Some of this history reflects unresolved differences being papered over by any evidence that can be brought to hand. Some of it is the enthusiasm of young researchers, whose fascination with new techniques has not always been tempered or restrained by the more seasoned judgment of their managers, among whom statistical and econometric expertise has not always been a priority. In fairness, economics as a whole has moved from a subject dominated by prior theorizing to one dominated by empirical evidence, and the transition from one to the other has been far from smooth. As a result, there has been little help from the outside.

More fundamentally, we also need to ask whether the decline in the *WDRs* reflects a decline in the quality of thinking in the Bank, or at least in its Research Department. I do not think that a decline is the major source of difficulty, but there are causes for concern. In the earliest days of the *WDRs*, the Bank's Research Department could and did attract leading scholars in international development. Very high salaries and generous pension arrangements were certainly part of the attraction, but so was the sense of moral purpose—that working for the World Bank, thinking about economic development and the alleviation of poverty, and passing on expertise were a good way to spend a working life. Not only did the Bank attract good new PhDs, but it also attracted a substantial number of assistant professors who decided that policy advice plus research was more fulfilling than teaching and research. A good deal of this thinking still goes on, and some of the young researchers in the Bank are clearly very good indeed. But the salaries (and pension benefits) are now much less, and very much so relative to academic salaries, which have risen rapidly in the meantime. The original pension arrangements have also made it possible for some of the Bank's best thinkers to quit the Bank for academia and think-tanks—Harvard, Princeton, and particularly the Center for Global Development—while they still have many years of useful contributions ahead of them. I suspect that more than any of these factors, however, the decline in the attractiveness of being a Bank researcher results from a growing skepticism that the Bank is doing much for international development and about whether aid, particularly as dispensed by the Bank, does much for economic growth and the reduction of poverty.

One version of the history of development economics within the Bank runs in terms of a steady broadening of focus, with each step a response to failure at a previous narrower focus. In the earliest days of the institution, much of its expertise was in engineering, with specialists who could help countries construct roads, dams, ports, or even whole industries. Economic policies were a matter of planning, of coordinating the engineers and their projects. By the 1950s and 1960s, it became clear that many of these projects were not contributing to the social good. One distinguished set of intellectual responses explored the idea that projects that were profitable at distorted market prices might not do much to help development—or might even hurt it—because the prices were so misleading. In response, and within the general framework of optimal growth theory, researchers, including Bank researchers, developed systems of cost-benefit analysis based on shadow prices that were supposed to be used by the Bank and client countries to evaluate projects. When, in turn, these procedures foundered on their simplistic treatment of policy making—few governments of developing countries could accurately be described as social planners optimizing an infinite stream of consumption—the Bank moved toward more systematic and comprehensive policy reform, in which market prices—and macroeconomic policy—were to be "got right" first.

In the ruins of the structural adjustment programs, the Bank moved out into an even broader agenda of political and institutional reform, which brings us more or less up-to-date. One notable feature of the broadening is the diminution of expertise. The engineers knew what they were doing, even if their expertise did not extend to ensuring that their dams or steelworks were socially beneficial. The growth and welfare economists of the 1950s and 1960s had a sophisticated understanding of their models, though not of the motives of policy makers. A broader spectrum of economists understands the consequences of price distortions or of unsustainable macroeconomic policies. And although we are not entirely without expertise, reforming governance and institutions is a much taller order than building a water delivery system or even a petrochemical plant.

One interpretation of this much simplified narrative is that the problem was not well conceived from the start, that the very idea of outside expertise helping countries to develop is misconceived—and possibly even harmful. As we move from posing questions to engineers to posing questions to political scientists, the answers may move from telling us "how to" to telling us "not to." In their recent summary of thinking in political science, Moss, Pettersson, and van de Walle (2008, p. 269) note that large aid flows "may undercut the very principles the aid industry intends to promote: ownership, accountability, and participation," essentially because the presence of the large donors inhibits the development of the democratic contract that would allow development to proceed. If this argument is correct—and I think it plausible, but I do not know for sure, or what kinds of aid (international public goods, some health interventions?) are exempt—then the development expertise that is the center of the World Bank's mission may not exist in useful form or, at the least, needs to be fundamentally rethought and restricted. And if the *World Development Reports* are the handbooks of development expertise as contained by the Bank, they too may have a limited future.

In the end, I suspect that the nostalgia in Yusuf's history is not for a *World Development Report* but for the World Bank itself.

THE WORLD BANK AND THE EVOLVING POLITICAL ECONOMY OF DEVELOPMENT

KEMAL DERVIŞ

Shahid Yusuf's essay on 30 years of *World Development Reports* (*WDRs*) is a masterful overview of what has at the same time been 30 years of development economics at the World Bank. I will first focus on one key aspect of the overview: the evolution of the political economy of development economics at the World Bank, influenced, of course, by my own perceptions of the 1980s and 1990s, two decades I spent at the World Bank. I will then turn to the future and to one key dimension that I think has been missing in the *WDRs*.

There is no doubt that development economics at the World Bank, and with it the *WDRs*, have been and will continue to be influenced by the political and intellectual environment of the times. The Executive Board does influence the management and the staff, not only because it has some "decision powers" over policies and strategies but also, and perhaps even more, because positive recognition by the board is a sought-after prize, and criticism is perceived as a big setback. Positive recognition by the president of the institution and by the chief economist is also something very valuable, influencing careers and promotions. The ideological and intellectual orientations of the president and of the chief economist clearly influence the work of economists at the World Bank.

Shahid Yusuf stresses these influences in his overview, showing how development economics at the World Bank and the content of the *WDRs* moved from strong faith in planning and in the role of the state, along with the quantitative models championed by Hollis Chenery and his colleagues in the late 1970s, to the structural adjustment approach of the 1980s and early 1990s. This period coincides broadly with what are often called the Reagan-Thatcher years, marked by much greater emphasis on the market, on "getting prices right," and on both liberalization (particularly trade liberalization) and privatization. The second half of the 1990s saw renewed emphasis on poverty reduction and on the need for proactive poverty-reducing social policies, particularly after James Wolfensohn took over as president in 1996, with Bill Clinton in the White House and Tony Blair soon after at 10 Downing Street. I agree with much of Yusuf's analysis, but I do believe it somewhat exaggerates the influence politics and ideology have had in the two-plus decades reviewed.

Several factors make it difficult for any particular political ideology to "take over" the World Bank—and I believe that is a very fortunate state of affairs. Moreover, although the influence of the U.S. and U.K. treasuries is, of course, very important, particularly on big programs, it is less so regarding the economic work done and the many and very decentralized interactions that take place with member countries. Although its headquarters are in Washington, D.C., and English is clearly the language in which World Bankers work, the World Bank is, both by the composition of its staff and by the very nature of the business it conducts, a truly international institution. In decades past, no small group of governments has easily been able to direct the work of the thousands of economists and other professionals who make up the staff. Over many decades, the institution has—as have many other institutions—developed its own "DNA," which is deeply rooted in the experience staff members gain around the world and the interactions staff members have with professionals and citizens in places as diverse as Brazil, China, the Arab Republic of Egypt, India, Malawi, Nigeria, and Vietnam, to name just a few.

The Executive Board also is—and has been—a very diverse body. Much of the world is represented and expresses itself. It is true that the voting weights are outdated and do not today reflect the realities of the 21st century. A significant change in the "weights" countries have at the Bank is overdue and is essential for the overall legitimacy of the institution. Nonetheless, diversity of voice exists, and different coalitions form and then dissolve over time, depending on the topic at hand or the particular period concerned. A good and articulate executive director from a smaller country can have substantial intellectual influence. Finally, presidents and senior managers have visions and have shown leadership, but to be successful, they must also convince the staff, listen to the accumulated experience, and be open to feedback.

In my experience, the driving force of the changes in emphasis so well described by Shahid Yusuf in the 30 *WDRs* reviewed, as well as in the content of development economics at the World Bank, has been more the evolution of academic thinking than of politics as such. That aspect, too, is emphasized in the essay, but I would stress it even more. Since Robert McNamara and Hollis Chenery, the institution's strongest links have always been to the academic work on development, and the *WDRs* themselves are expressions of that link. For example, the work done at Princeton introducing relative prices and price-sensitive demand and supply functions into the older, rigid Leontief input-output models was adopted by the Development Research Center of the World Bank and facilitated a more market-oriented approach to development policy. That academic work imported into and championed by the World Bank in the late 1970s turned planning models into policy and market simulation models, which were later widely used to analyze the structural adjustment policies of the 1980s. Both continuity and strong interaction with academia existed throughout that process, with political ideology playing a lesser role. As another example, one can mention the very wide use of domestic resource cost estimates and effective protection rates to measure the social costs of price distortions and trade policies, which owed more to the academic work ongoing at the time than to ideology. Two Bank chief economists were, with Béla Balassa (also a senior presence at the World Bank throughout the late 1970s and 1980s), intellectual originators of these concepts; however, Anne Krueger was politically right of center, whereas the late Michael Bruno was close to the Israeli Labor Party.

More recently, the academic work on the role of institutions in development and labor markets, as well as on the microeconomics of information and market structure, has strongly affected the economic work at the World Bank after the mid-1980s and the *WDRs* in the 1990s. Chief economists such as Stanley Fischer, Larry Summers, Joseph Stiglitz, Nicholas Stern, and François Bourguignon have clearly been impressive academics, and their academic and policy analysis achievements brought them to their positions more than any political or ideological bent they may have had. This is not to say that all economic work at the Bank has been of the highest quality. Too much of it has allowed simplistic and, yes, sometimes "politically correct" cookie-cutter prescriptions to pass as analysis. But it has been the creative and academically grounded work that in the end earned recognition and respect.

I am not sure how strong a difference exists between Shahid Yusuf and myself in assessing the weight of the different influences on the *WDRs*. But I do want to stress the power of the link between academia and economics at the World Bank, the strong institutional DNA built over decades with a value system emphasizing analytical skills and academic recognition, and the difficulty of linking the choice and role of chief economists in a simple way to primarily political or ideological factors.

It is interesting to note that the United Nations Development Programme's *Human Development Reports* (*HDRs*) provide another example of how an institution's DNA and intellectual tradition cut across the tenures of chief executives with very different political homes. The *HDRs*, which have succeeded in providing tough competition to the *WDRs* in terms of influence and attention, have from the start emphasized poverty reduction, income distribution, and the role of public policy. And yet the *HDRs* were launched under William H. Draper, appointed with the then determining influence of the U.S. Republican administration of the late 1980s.

The second point I would like to make, looking at 30 years of *WDRs*, relates to the almost exclusive focus on the "country" or "nation-state" as the unit of analysis. It is true that the first *WDRs* contained global projections that later were spun off and became the *Global Economic Prospects* series, but only a very weak link exists between the projections and the development policy analysis contained in the *WDRs*. The latter is country focused, and the international economy, as such, is not in the forefront of analysis. This country focus does, in fact, faithfully reflect what is practiced by most academic economists when they run growth regressions or when they do case study work trying to distill the lessons of development policy experience. The unit of observation is almost always the country, without much attention to the international system within which country policies have to operate.

The importance of export orientation, openness to trade, human capital policies, investment rates, or financial sector policies is most often analyzed giving individual countries equal weights as units of observation. China and Lesotho each constitute one observation point per year of available data when regressions are run. This equal-weight and nation-state-focused nature of much of comparative development economics has at least two weaknesses. The first weakness relates to the relevance of the findings. Suppose, for example, that one finds that total factor productivity growth is more important than capital accumulation in explaining differences in growth performance—except for India and China, which are, in Yusuf's words, "accumulating physical capital and pouring it into industry at a feverish pace." Should one then turn the statement around and say that capital accumulation is the dominant factor for half of the developing world because these two giants account for about half of the population of developing countries? To what extent should size matter when drawing conclusions? This question has no easy answer; it presents theoretical and empirical challenges. Nevertheless, I do think that the fact that much data come by country units should not make us forget the extreme size differences involved.

Another dimension of this problem relates to policy space. The degree of freedom of the policy maker and the effects policies can have are clearly affected by the world economic environment, but more so for smaller countries and very open economies. Take an example that is currently particularly relevant. It is well known in theory that international capital mobility constrains monetary policy. The nature and effects of policy responses by the Brazilian, South African, or Turkish central banks to the crisis level challenges that emerged in 2008 greatly depend on the interest rate policies of the Federal Reserve and of the European Central Bank. Analyzing macroeconomic or structural policies of particular countries without putting them explicitly in a global context is increasingly difficult. Systemic international developments affect most elements of development policy, including labor market, agricultural, tax, energy, trade, and financial sector policies. Given the degree of interdependence that characterizes the 21st-century world, country-focused analysis increasingly must be complemented by analysis of the world economy as a system. What may be needed is a kind of hierarchical analysis, where local development; national development; regional development (Africa, Latin America, the Middle East, and so on); and global development are parts of a systemic approach that tries to capture what matters at what level and what freedom of action policy makers have at these various levels.

Some *WDRs* have gone beyond the country as the basic unit of analysis, including the 2009 *WDR* on spatial issues. An explicitly multilevel approach could mark a new start for the *WDRs* and respond to the realities of the new global world of the 21st century. The *WDR* planned for 2010 on the topic of development and climate change, chosen by Bob Zoellick, could become a path-breaker in that respect. Clearly, climate is a global issue and a global public good. The importance of climate-related policies for development can be analyzed only in an explicitly multilevel framework, where global, regional, and country-level policies interact to determine outcomes that cut across national boundaries.

THE INDOMITABLE IN PURSUIT OF THE INEXPLICABLE: THE WORLD DEVELOPMENT REPORTS' FAILURE TO COMPREHEND ECONOMIC GROWTH DESPITE DETERMINED ATTEMPTS, 1978–2008

WILLIAM EASTERLY

The intellectual tragedy of 30 years of *World Development Reports* (*WDRs*) is that they never accepted the reality of the great unpredictability and uncertainty of economic growth in the short to medium run. The *WDRs* keep trying to find ways to raise growth in the short to medium run when the economics profession does not have this knowledge. They seek to explain short-term fluctuations in growth when there is no evidence base for such explanations. As a result, they fall prey to many of the classic heuristic biases about randomness (à la Kahneman and Tversky), including frequent use of circular reasoning, and they lose the opportunity to carry on a fruitful debate about the best way to handle this uncertainty and to make development more likely in the long run (Gilovich, Griffin, and Kahneman 2002; Kahneman, Slovic, and Tversky 1982).

What is the state of our knowledge about growth? First of all, country growth rates are not persistent over time, which was documented as long ago as Easterly, Kremer, Pritchett, and Summers (1993). High growth is mostly transitory, reverting to the global mean in the following period. This finding was bad news when most of the candidate explanations of growth were very persistent country characteristics. Of course, there could have been time-varying variables that explained the time-varying element of growth. Unfortunately, the second characteristic of our growth knowledge is that we have failed to identify any such robust time-varying variables (or for that matter any robust persistent variables). Levine and Renelt (1992) established this failure convincingly early in the growth literature. It further showed itself in the 145 different variables found to be "significant" in growth regressions with fewer than 100 observations (Durlauf, Johnson, and Temple 2005). The last hope was Bayesian model averaging to identify the small number of variables that were robust in most regressions (Doppelhofer, Miller, and Sala-i-Martin 2004). Even this hope vanished recently when Ciccone and Jarociński (2008) showed that Bayesian model averaging gave completely different "robust" variables for different equally plausible samples (World Bank versus Penn World Tables or successive revisions of the Penn World Tables).

In defense of the WDRs, the economics profession was also slow to admit the inexplicability of growth fluctuations. However, a wide spectrum of economists has by now conceded we don't know how to raise growth in the short to medium run (Easterly 2001; Lindauer and Pritchett 2002; Harberger 2003; "Barcelona Development Agenda" 2004;[1] Rodrik 2006; Solow 2007; Spence Commission 2008).

A random effects regression on the panel of per capita growth rates from 1960 to 2005 reveals that only 8 percent of the cross-time, cross-country variation in growth is due to permanent country effects; the other 92 percent is transitory (which is equivalent to stating the lack of persistence of growth rates identified in Easterly, Kremer, Pritchett, and Summers 1993). The transitory does not have to be mechanically "random" in the sense of coin-flipping; it could well be one-off movements caused by human action. It could be an entrepreneur finding a "big hit" in exports, like cut flowers in Kenya or garments in Bangladesh; it could be a smart policy move that

---

1. The "Barcelona Development Agenda" is a consensus document resulting from a meeting of economists in Barcelona, Spain, in 2004. Signatories of the document include Olivier Blanchard, Guillermo Calvo, Stanley Fischer, Jeffrey Frankel, Paul Krugman, Dani Rodrik, Jeffrey Sachs, and Joseph Stiglitz.

was in the right place at the right time; or it could be a bubble caused by an information cascade or other kinds of herding. On the negative side, it could be a dramatic mistake by a policy maker or a private entrepreneur. Still the transitory might as well be random in the sense that we cannot usually explain or replicate what just happened.

Hence, many of the classic Kahneman-Tversky heuristic biases about randomness have played themselves out in *WDRs*.[2] Take, for example, the fallacy of the "hot hand," when a basketball player makes a string of baskets in a row. The hot hand bias is to falsely conclude that the player's skill has temporarily moved to a higher level, whereas actual calculation shows that a player is no more likely to make the next basket after a hot streak than at any other time. The problem is that we expect randomness to show up as alternating hits and misses when in fact it often displays streaks of hits. Another way of stating this fallacy is Kahneman and Tversky's sarcastically named "law of small numbers" (Kahneman, Slovic, and Tversky 1982). In the case of the *WDRs*, we falsely draw conclusions about how to achieve superior long-run performance from too small a number of observations, without allowing for the large role of transitory factors in a small sample. The small numbers refer both to a small number of "successes" and a small number of annual observations (even 25 years may not be long enough, as will be discussed).

WDRs abound with statements reflecting this fallacious viewpoint, as summarized by Yusuf:

> If [China and India] can rack up rates of investment and growth that are the envy of the world under the most makeshift of institutional conditions, need other countries more attuned to the market strive after greater perfection? China was growing when it had few if any market institutions; as its institutional structure has strengthened, it has continued growing with investment serving as the principal driver without a clear relationship running from the specifics of institution building to growth.

China and India definitely reflect some genuine success, but their sudden shift upward in growth is also bound to reflect some inexplicable, transitory factors that do not help us understand success (and it is even worse to break up their performance into subperiods, as with China in the last sentence).

---

2. A wonderfully entertaining summary of this and other related research is a recent book for nontechnical audiences by Mlodinow (2008).

One systematic way of showing the hot hand fallacy at work is by simulating a mechanical procedure to identify "success." The example I use is not from WDRs but from the Spence Commission (2008); however, the WDRs (as shown by the quotes above) definitely do informally what the Spence Commission did more formally, so this example is just a way to formalize a comment on the WDRs' worldview.

The Spence Commission identified "success" as (essentially) any 25-year period of gross domestic product (GDP) per capita growth above 5 percent.[3] This procedure sounds like a pretty good bet, but in fact it was very likely to pick up a large element of transitory performance for two reasons:

1. Selecting on high values of the growth outcome will very likely include large positive realizations of the transitory component. This problem is all the more likely because the permanent component of growth outcomes exceeds 5 percent in only 1.8 percent of realizations (whereas the temporary component will exceed 5 percent by itself in 26 percent of realizations).

2. Selecting on the time period (*any* 25-year period out of a 45-year sample from 1960 to 2005) further biases the episodes toward those that had large positive transitory outcomes. The time period is selectively biased to be one that started and ended so as to include a large number of large positive transitory outcomes.

A Monte Carlo simulation based on the parameters from the random effects regression shows that the Spence Commission's definition of "success" will occur in about 9 percent of countries, which is far more than the 1.8 percent of countries that have a genuine permanent country growth above 5 percent (granted the assumptions about the permanent and transitory components being normally distributed). In the event, the Spence Commission found 13 "success stories."[4] Interestingly, India did not make

---

3. I say "essentially" because the commission inexplicably used total GDP growth rather than per capita growth. Its criterion was GDP growth above 7 percent, so with population growth usually about 2 percent, I convert this criterion to a per capita growth criterion of above 5 percent.

4. I did 25,000 runs of per capita growth in countries for 45 years, in which growth is the sum of two orthogonal components: a normally distributed permanent component $N(0.0176438, 0.0155495)$ and a normally distributed transitory component $N(0, 0.0506495)$. The means and standard deviations are taken from the random effects regression over 1960 to 2005 of all countries

it on the Spence exercise, suggesting that informal discussions of success stories are even looser than the excessively loose Spence criterion.

The Spence Commission spent a lot of time analyzing these high-growth countries as if they completely reflected fundamentals. However, the other bad news about the bias toward including a large transitory element is that this procedure will likely not even pick the right countries. The same Monte Carlo simulation reveals that about 37 percent of the countries that are in the top 9 percent according to the Spence criteria are *not* in the top 9 percent of permanent country growth rates. The Spence Commission successes (just like the *WDR* success story analyses)—even as they are carefully being picked apart to discern their innermost secrets—are bound to include some ringers that just got lucky.

Why is such flawed analysis pursued by such talented and well-trained economists? Yusuf notes with frustration that "even with good policies, the growth of the typical developing country rarely climbs much above 3 to 5 percent per year [1 to 3 percent per capita]." Yusuf notes that this figure "is impressive by historical standards, but countries in a hurry to catch up aspire to faster rates of growth." The Spence Commission and the *WDRs* just cannot accept that 5 percent per capita growth is rare (expected to occur in 1.8 percent of the sample). It is easy to see the appeal of a definition that makes this yearned-for outcome 4.8 times more likely, and so economists are often willing to overlook that this increased likelihood is likely spurious.

So we see "growth booms" as attainable because we think they reflect an intentional shift in the country's fundamentals upward, which could be replicated elsewhere. Again, this assumption could possibly be right, and we could have confirmed it if we had achieved any success in explaining cross-time variations with some variables capturing fundamentals—but we have not done so. Or the *WDRs* could successfully be doing qualitative analysis that would help identify ways to trigger a growth boom. However,

with complete data so as to have a balanced panel (95 countries). The Spence Commission found 13 "success stories," but the commission does not say how large its sample of countries with the necessary data was. Thirteen would be 9 percent if the sample was 144 countries, which sounds a little too high for countries having complete data. Of course, one run of 100 or so countries is not large enough to give a precise estimate of the percent likelihood of "success"; such a small sample estimate could vary considerably around the expected value computed from a large value of Monte Carlo simulations.

Yusuf's review shows instead the frequent changes in messages, the sloppy vagueness of explanatory factors, and a complete lack of success stories in replicating growth booms through expert advice in the *WDRs*. It seems like the hot hand fallacy may instead explain our unproductive fascination with growth booms.

This heuristic bias is so hardwired into us as humans that we actually do worse than rats on the hot hand fallacy. In a classic laboratory experiment, subjects were shown a light that flashed either red or green. They were allowed to watch for a while and then were asked in successive rounds to predict the next flash. The experiment was rigged so that red was randomly flashed twice as often as green, although the subjects were not told so. The rats pursued the optimal strategy of always guessing red. The humans did not. The humans thought they perceived occasional "hot streaks" of green and would then guess green. As Mlodinow (2008) says "humans usually try to guess the pattern, and in the process we allow ourselves to be outperformed by a rat."

Another heuristic bias is called the "halo effect." This effect is the well-documented tendency (verified in many psychology experiments in the laboratory) to assume that an individual who excels on one dimension will also have superior talents on other dimensions (as subjectively evaluated by the observers in the experiments, for which there is no factual basis whatsoever by the design of the experiment).[5] So, for example, we expect our successful male politicians to also be good husbands (despite abundant evidence to the contrary). And *Fortune* magazine's annual ranking of the World's Most Admired Companies ranks companies on eight very different dimensions, which are all suspiciously correlated with the company's latest financial performance and with each other. So Cisco Systems was highly rated on quality of management, quality of people, innovativeness, and so forth in 2000, when its stock value was high. When the stock collapsed after 2001, observers suddenly detected that every dimension got worse at the same time: the same management and people had overnight become low quality and not innovative (Rosenzweig 2007: 61–62).

One particularly remarkable laboratory finding came from an experiment in which subjects observed two people executing a task. The

---

5. This effect is also the subject of an excellent book for nontechnical audiences (Rosenzweig 2007).

experiment had been carefully rigged so that the two people's performance was equal. The subjects were told that one of the two people would receive a large payment and that this assignment would be *random*. The subjects were then asked to describe the performance of the two agents. Despite the subjects' knowledge that the payment was random, they gave superior marks on multiple performance attributes to the agent who received the payment.

In the *WDRs*, a country that excels in achieving high growth is assumed to also excel in having wise leaders, good institutions, entrepreneurial citizens, and so on. The latter characteristics are hard to measure objectively, so these subjective assumptions are hard to prove or disprove. Then, to go from the halo effect to pure circular reasoning, we conclude that these wise leaders, good institutions, and entrepreneurial citizens explain the high growth.

Perhaps the worst single offender with respect to the halo effect and circular reasoning in the *WDRs* was the introduction of the concept of the "investment climate." This concept absorbed one entire *WDR* and yet lacked any theoretical definition or any agreed-upon measurement. Something so vague is bound to be seen wherever good outcomes are happening and then flexibly deployed to "explain" success. Yusuf diplomatically acknowledges these problems: "Nick Stern, the Bank's chief economist from 2000 to 2003, was instrumental in making the assessment of the investment climate in member countries an integral part of the Bank's economic analysis of countries. His conception of the determinants of this climate was sweeping …." It was so sweeping as to use what Yusuf politely calls an "eclectic selection of evidentiary material." Yet the appeal of circular reasoning through the halo effect still holds: "Did Botswana, Chile, China, India, and Mauritius as well as the East Asian economies achieve growth mainly by mending the investment climate …?"

The halo effect contaminates the endless and increasingly useless analysis of the East Asian success stories. Hong Kong, China; Taiwan, China; the Republic of Korea; and Singapore are very unlikely to be ringers; they almost certainly represent genuine long-run success on growth rates. Yet the halo effect falsely anoints every single aspect of these countries as also being ultra-exceptional and then jumps to the unwarranted conclusion that every such factor contributed to the remarkable success. The successful

East Asian characteristics are subjectively chosen, and it is even worse that they seem to keep changing with whatever is the latest fad in development thinking. Yusuf states:

> East Asian economies, by virtue of their successful growth performance, became the ones to emulate. The message distilled from their experience was that market-guided industrialization within the milieu of a relatively open economy could result in rapid growth if industries were able to compete in export markets.
>
> . . .
>
> [T]he success of a China or a Korea or a Singapore rested on the state's readiness to trim the public sector, encourage private enterprise, and build market institutions, but in each case, the state has remained large, powerful, and interventionist. Directly and indirectly, the public sector encompasses a major share of GDP.
>
> . . .
>
> Everyone can see that market institutions in successful East Asian industrializing countries are at best functional and at worst weak and minimally supportive. The interesting issue is how an assortment of institutions of varying capabilities and degrees of maturity can, with the help of a strong developmental state, produce good results using the local knowledge that policy makers surely have.

Then, to make things yet worse, we jump to conclusions from an even smaller number of recent observations in which the Gang of Four slowed down:

> Other high-performing countries in East Asia have seen their growth performance flag while their institutions have matured, albeit slowly. However, all these economies have also witnessed a decline in investment and a partial withdrawal of the state from the forefront of economic decision making.

As if this were *still* not bad enough, the analysis of the few top performers is contaminated even further by yet another selection bias: the survivor bias. Suppose that a set of drivers was going from New York to Washington, D.C., driving Lamborghinis at 150 miles per hour down I-95. We are in Washington and interview the Lamborghini drivers who arrive. We wax ecstatic at the drivers' trip to Washington in under two hours (compared with the usual minimum of four hours), their willingness to take bold risks, and the overall superiority of the speeding Lamborghini drivers to the other plodding drivers on I-95. Because we observe only the ones who arrive in Washington, we are unaware that many (plausibly a large majority) of the Lamborghini speedsters were pulled over and arrested for reckless driving and never made it to Washington, not to mention a few who were killed or maimed in traffic accidents because of their insanely risky driving. So on average, the hockey moms driving minivans, who arrive in Washington in five hours or so, outperformed the Lamborghini drivers. Our conclusion that going 150 miles per hour in a Lamborghini is a formula for success in getting to Washington is false; we were led astray by survivor bias.

We induce a survivor bias when we analyze only the top "success stories." I doubt very much that the success of the Gang of Four is entirely explained by survivor bias. But this example does show the risks of praising every aspect of the experience of the Gang of Four. Some strategies may have been very risky, and by concentrating only on the success stories, we miss the experience of other countries that may have followed the same strategy and crashed and burned. Survivor bias makes the whole methodology of obsessively dissecting every aspect of the success stories very suspect. The remedy is simple: to assess the growth payoff from factor X, we should study *all* countries—both those that had factor X and those that did not—and ask, "What was the average payoff?" So take, for example, the conclusion sometimes reached that the Gang of Four's success is due to authoritarian leaders pursuing industrial policies. But the track record worldwide of dictators picking winners is very poor, so why are we so sure that this factor contributed to the success of the Gang of Four? And even if it did, which is basically nonfalsifiable, why do we think it is replicable elsewhere—that finding which is most relevant and *is* falsifiable?

Of course, the general enterprise of assessing all possible factor Xs to find the secrets to growth success has not been helpful either (see the previous discussion of growth literature), but at least this exercise was not contaminated by survivor bias. We have still learned something from the failure of growth regressions: that there is no universal factor X that works everywhere to reliably raise growth—because if there had been, it surely would have shown up as a robust determinant of growth in our extensive effort at cross-country regressions.

On a more positive note, how *should* we deal with a world where there is so much uncertainty about growth determinants? Despite this uncertainty, a substantial number of countries (Australia, Japan, the Gang of Four, and countries in Europe and North America) have already achieved a high level of per capita income, which must reflect good average growth

performance over some suitably long period. The problems with randomness get progressively alleviated the longer we make the period of analysis.
Studying the *level* of per capita income rather than growth rates as a measure of success or failure is one way to focus on the long run. The *WDRs*
have been forced by the peculiar conventions of development economics to exclude most of the countries that actually succeeded the most at
development, and so they rarely invoke any lessons from the long histories
of countries that are now rich (except for the Gang of Four), as compared
with those that are still poor. In contrast, a slew of papers that were published in top journals in economics studied levels for the whole sample and
attributed development success to long-run factors such as property rights,
democracy, trade openness, and technological creativity. These papers have
their own problems resolving correlation and causation, but they are still
clearly superior to the methodology of the *WDRs*; the latter have been led
fatally astray by glaring biases in the treatment of transitory components
of volatile short- to medium-run growth rates.

Perhaps one way to unify the findings of the levels regressions—a
theoretically appealing way to understand how systems can handle vast
short-run uncertainty—is to hypothesize that systems that respect individual rights do the best in the long run on economic development. Such
individual rights include property rights, rights to dissent from prevailing
conventional wisdom, rights to trade whatever with whomever you want,
rights to enter new industries and start up new firms, rights to advocate
new political directions, and so on. The theoretical appeal of this hypothesis is that individual rights can handle systemic uncertainty by exploiting
individuals' superior localized knowledge and powerful incentives to solve
their own local problems, which will lead to superior performance even if
no policy maker at the top knows how to raise growth rates.

This possibility is obviously just the beginning of such a discussion,
and this brief discussion is a long way from confirming this or any other
hypothesis. The sad thing about the *WDRs* is that they missed out on such
fruitful and deeper long-run discussions about the best systems for achieving development under uncertainty by diverting all their energies to a futile
attempt to find patterns in this uncertainty. Are our heuristic biases, like
those described here, so strong that future *WDRs* will continue this tragic
intellectual failure? As usual, it is hard to predict.

THE EVOLUTION OF DEVELOPMENT ECONOMICS AND EAST ASIA'S CONTRIBUTION

TAKATOSHI ITO

Shahid Yusuf has summarized the 30-year history of the *World Development Report* (*WDR*) in light of the intellectual evolution of economic development philosophy. The review is quite extensive, and it goes beyond a summary of the history of the *WDR*. The reader benefits from Yusuf's insights about how development economics has changed and how political priorities in development have changed over more than the 30 years (the history starts well before the *WDR* was born). Yusuf's writing is filled with the pride that the *WDR* was the first major publication of this kind by an international financial organization.

In the essay, chapter 2 reviews the historical development of the *WDR* from volume 1 to volume 30. Chapter 3 covers crucial issues that have been debated, and chapter 4 explores the direction for the future.

Comments on the Essay

In explaining the history of the *WDRs*, Shahid Yusuf has successfully identified three different threads: changes in the president and chief economist of the World Bank, changes in *WDR* emphasis, and changes in development economics literature. Those who were remote from politics in Washington, D.C., and the World Bank would learn with interest how changes in the presidency have altered both the Bank's and the *WDRs'* emphasis.

In 1978, President Robert McNamara and Chief Economist Hollis Chenery created the first *WDR*. According to Yusuf, Chenery "encouraged McNamara to pursue the idea of an annual publication," and "McNamara entrusted Chenery with the task of preparing a flagship report." The first report was only 68 pages long. Increasing length has both benefits and costs. Yusuf admits that the report has become so large that few now read beyond the executive summary.

Transition from McNamara and Chenery to President A. W. Clausen and Chief Economist Anne Krueger shifted the Bank's emphasis from a dual objective of growth and poverty alleviation with macroeconomic emphasis on the availability of external finance, to microeconomic advice on getting the prices right. Krueger, "a staunch advocate of market solutions, ... hitched the Bank's approach to development firmly to market forces." In the 1980s, the political environment of Ronald Reagan and Margaret Thatcher also influenced thinking in development economics. Yusuf notes that the pendulum swung from state help to the market because of the failure of the state in many regions, but the pendulum swung too far because of ideology.

A big change occurred when James Wolfensohn became president in 1995. It is interesting to know that Wolfensohn "desire[d] to contain the influence of economists in the Bank." Was this economics in the narrow sense? I ask this question because both Amartya K. Sen and Douglass North, who were supporters of Wolfensohn, are economists—Nobel laureates—after all. Joseph Stiglitz, chief economist from 1997 to 2000, is also a Nobel laureate. It must have been a shift of emphasis within economics broadly defined.

In the 2000/2001 *WDR*, Yusuf describes the following new consensus. "Growth was necessary but not sufficient," which he observes completes "almost [a] full circle ... to the views expressed in the earliest *WDRs*.... It had to be supported by infrastructure and other services so as to build human capital, especially among the poor, and to lessen the inequity of assets and incomes." Is this observation encouraging or discouraging? The Bank's views shift as Bank executives—president and chief economist—change, as explained well in the earlier pages. The new consensus is more a matter of course than a big surprise or new insight for Asians and continental Europeans. In those economies, the government has played an important role in education, from primary to advanced, as well as in social and economic infrastructures. Deregulation and liberalization were conducted in a gradual manner. Is going full circle over some 20 years a reflection of the changing ideology and political environment of American economics and politics? Maybe the history suggests that the World Bank should be modifying its tradition so that presidents, vice presidents, and high-ranking economists from France, Germany, Japan, and other non-Anglo-Saxon economies are represented in addition to mainstream fashion in American economics. Appointing a chief economist from China may be a good start.

Yusuf concludes the summary of his 30-year history by noting three shifts over the years:

1. From state directed to market guided
2. From structural issues to sectoral issues
3. From macroeconomic concerns to microeconomic concerns

This summary succinctly captures the changes of emphasis over three decades quite well. They all seem reasonable, but again the balance is important. In this connection, it is commonly believed that a division of labor exists between the International Monetary Fund (IMF) and the World Bank. The IMF is in charge of macroeconomics and sectoral issues rather than microeconomics and structural issues. From this point of view, the shift in emphasis from macro to micro in the World Bank makes sense. This shift may be viewed as a welcome retreat from "mission creep." But in terms of the second shift, shouldn't the World Bank continue to address structural issues as well as sectoral issues?

In chapter 3, Yusuf takes up important topics where debates continue. In the section on "Growth through Perspiration," the debate over the source of growth, whether capital accumulation or total factor productivity (TFP), is reviewed. Certainly, increasing investment is important, but it is difficult for some countries to achieve. TFP is also difficult to promote by policy, although education and knowledge would possibly increase TFP. In the section "From Machines to Institutions," Yusuf reviews the debate over whether growth comes first and institutions follow or whether good institutions are a prerequisite for growth. The idea of "Inspired Growth" became popular in the literature of new growth theory, but in reality the bulk of growth comes from capital accumulation. In the section "Resource Balances and Capital Flows," various issues on use of foreign capital are reviewed. The so-called Washington Consensus is discussed. Then the discussion on the "Role of the State" is a recap of the changes in thinking over time. As Europe has implemented denationalization since the mid-1980s, the role of the state has been reconsidered downward. The WDR, however, took a position that privatization and denationalization should be done in a gradual manner. That idea seems to be a departure from the more radical thinking of Big Bang. However, Yusuf seems to disagree with the WDR interpretation of the East Asian miracle as an unqualified endorsement of market economy; the government did not withdraw from failing industries. East Asia remains a paradox in the mainstream view of the role of state. The section "Reducing Poverty" describes changing thinking about poverty reduction, from meeting the basic needs in the late 1970s and early 1980s to promoting "pro-poor" development strategy. The pro-poor policy is to promote human capital development that would contribute to decreasing poverty and encourage less unequal distribution of income. The section on "Aid and Growth" gives an important recap on the use and effectiveness of aid—a first step to rid the world of poverty. A consensus hardly exists in the academic literature about how big aid should be.

In a section called "A WDR Policy Scorecard," Yusuf gives a high mark to the WDR for having been "powerfully instrumental in raising awareness on the extent of poverty and in exhaustively cataloguing the many ways of erasing it." It identified the importance of capital investment and, later, human and knowledge capital for growth. But Yusuf admits that the "WDRs are silent on what it takes to reach 35 percent rates of capital investment."

Chapter 4 is about the future of the WDR, "Where To Now?" Yusuf lists the future challenges. First, he shows the long-term data of per capita GDP growth of the Republic of Korea and the United States. Both show the steady growth of income with some fluctuations around the trend, with the U.S. growth rate lower than Korea's (figures 4.1 and 4.2). The point of the figures is whether economic policy made any change over the long-term natural force (autonomous growth). It seems a bit unfair to show the two more or less successful cases and a good period for Korea. In addition, the long-term data mask the occasional deceleration and acceleration.

Yusuf then explains the importance of institutions. His understanding seems to be much more reasonable than what is commonly seen as the Washington Consensus, however. The following sentences struck me most as a promising starting point for future direction:

> The interest of policy makers lies not in whether the state should be large or small or more or less interventionist; the interest is in what specific forms of intervention over a period of time yield the best results under similar external circumstances. The same is true regarding institutions. Everyone can see that market institutions in successful East Asian industrializing countries are at best functional and at worst weak and minimally supportive.

Yusuf raises five specific topics that he considers key for the future of the *WDRs*: "Putting Knowledge to Work," "Warming Climate, Scarce Water," "The Geography of Human Habitation," "Resilient Complex Societies," and "An Equal Marriage of Politics and Economics." Each of these topics has a large literature behind it and controversial, ongoing debate in front. This comment is not the place for lengthy arguments; however, let me point out some important missing pieces. As mentioned in the beginning of this section, a puzzle remains: When the "technology of development" is so widely shared—not the least through the *WDRs*— why are there so many laggards? Why is there a great and widening divergence? Why aren't the ranks of "tiger economies" growing by the year? These questions should be highlighted. The World Bank may put more focus on the least developed countries, defying the logic of development and growth that predicts a takeoff. *WDRs* may have been putting too much emphasis on analyzing successful middle-income developing countries, and the World Bank has been busy lending to those good-credit borrowers. Memory of poor performance of the "laggards" may have been erased with debt reduction. The World Bank may be well advised to shift its resources from China and India—where the private sector as well as the World Bank can do a lot—to Africa and to the poorer countries of Latin America and Central Asia. The future research plan should include a serious analysis of the laggards, however painful and politically difficult it may be.

Big Push, Development, and Growth: A Synthesis

In the past, economic development and economic growth were two different subjects. On the one hand, development deals with long history, institution building, big government policy, structural changes, and transition of industrial structures, for example, from an agrarian economy to a manufacturing economy, and to a service-oriented, advanced economy. Quantifying development success or failure is often very difficult, but case studies are needed. On the other hand, (old) growth economics stresses the commonalities across countries. When a country is equipped with capital, labor, and technology, then growth occurs. With the initial state of income level, the production function, and the saving rate being given, the rest is automatic. No policy is needed. No institution is needed. Convergence to the steady state is autonomous and guaranteed.

With the emergence of new growth theory, the line between development and growth theories has been blurred. Emphasis on institutions—repeatedly mentioned by Yusuf—is a hallmark of new growth theory. Factors that influence growth (convergence) are now on the right-hand side of growth regressions. However, new growth theory emphasizes standardization and quantification so that cross-country regressions can be implemented. Also, regressions need a long enough data series with a fixed starting year, often taken as 1960. Policy change and reforms and structural breaks cannot be treated at the same level of detail as in standard development economics.

The most difficult part of development and growth is the miracle of lifting a low-income country from a low-growth trap to a reasonably high-growth path. The four tigers—Hong Kong, China; Taiwan, China; Korea; and Singapore—made that transition in the 1970s. East Asian economies made the transition in the 1980s, and China and India accomplished it in the early 1990s. Once the country moves from a low-income, low-growth state to low-income, high-growth state, then the "convergence" of growth theory works, unless political meddling hinders the process. The initial miracle—Big Push or takeoff in the old development theory—is the key and not known even in the series of WDRs. The takeoff part desperately needs a building up of institutions, reforms, policy interventions, and so on. Once a country is on the

Figure C.1: The Transition to a High-Growth Path

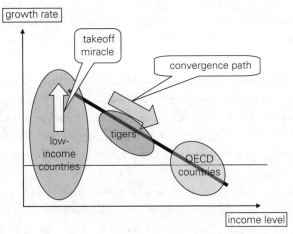

Source: Author.

convergence path, a gradual withdrawal of policy interventions may be desirable, and old and new growth theories apply. This view is shown in figure C.1 (see also Ito 1995, 1998). A similar pattern is empirically established in Ito (2000).

It is obvious from figure 1 that linear growth regressions that mix pre-takeoff countries and tiger-OECD countries would not yield clear-cut results. The importance of institutions matters most for the takeoff.

Underappreciation of East Asian Experiences

A delicate relationship has existed between East Asia and the World Bank over what is the right development strategy. Policy makers in East Asian economies felt that government interventions in identifying sunrise industries and allocating scarce resources, including foreign exchanges, were helpful in industrialization. However, these government interventions were regarded as a source of distortion and corruption in the rest of the world and in mainstream World Bank thinking. Yusuf mentions the East Asian tigers as a case for openness:

> These economies were portrayed as single-mindedly pursuing growth through the export of manufactures, relying mainly on market forces to guide the allocation of resources and exploiting the advantages of greater openness to gain access to

overseas markets and to ensure the competitiveness of their industries. Although the degree to which market forces were responsible for directing resource flows to areas of comparative advantage was far less than was assumed, and although most tiger economies nurtured industries behind trade barriers, the East Asian economies, by virtue of their successful growth performance, became the ones to emulate.

This quotation is a very diplomatic description of the political-economy controversy that took place between East Asia and Washington, D.C., in the 1980s. In this respect, it was not the *WDR*; rather, a special World Bank study that resulted in *The East Asian Miracle* (World Bank 1993) was comprehensive in taking up both views and striking a good intellectual balance.

The high economic growth of the four tigers was followed by the growth of several southeast Asian countries, including Indonesia, Malaysia, and Thailand. As a region, Asia seemed to be a successful case. The Asian crisis of 1997 and 1998 dented Asian confidence. However, since 2001, the Asian region, with China and India, has become the center of world growth again. Asia presents a difficult case for both those who advocate market solutions and those who are more sympathetic to government interventions. The *WDR* could have taken East Asian experiences more carefully with respect to the true reasons for success and transferability of the lessons to other regions. The crucial differences between the Asian developing countries and developing countries in other regions, especially the laggard countries, should be identified and analyzed.

In summary, the East Asian miracle seems to be a miracle still—a miracle of takeoff, a transition from a low-income, low-growth state to low-income, high-growth state. That magic should be the focus of the *WDR* in the future, and the experiences of East Asia, including China and India, will be worth taking seriously.

THE WORLD DEVELOPMENT REPORT: DEVELOPMENT THEORY AND POLICY

JOSEPH E. STIGLITZ

I had responsibility, to varying degrees, for five different *World Development Reports* (*WDRs*). The first, on the role of the state, was begun by my predecessor; the next two, *Knowledge for Development* and *Entering the 21st Century*, I saw through from beginning to end; and the final two, *Attacking Poverty* and *Building Institutions for Markets*, were initiated while I was chief economist but completed after I left.

Many of the *WDRs* that had gone before focused on a particular aspect of development, a particular sector—education, health, agriculture. I saw the *WDR* as an opportunity to redefine broader views about development.

One of the hardest struggles—and I was only partially successful— was to change the concept of the *WDR*. Traditionally, it has summarized "received wisdom." The goal was to summarize the received wisdom in a few, easily understood "messages." The messages, in turn, were intended to set the policy agenda: they were messages that World Bank staff could bring to developing countries around the world. I was worried about this approach for several reasons. It smacked too much of a "one-size-fits-all" cookie-cutter approach—unless the messages were so anodyne as to be almost meaningless. And I was very much of the view that the role of outside advisers was to share experiences and general principles. Democratic development required that each country make its own decisions—in the simple way we put it, "the country was in the driver's seat." Our role was to help the country think through these decisions.

In this perspective, the objective of the *WDR* was to begin a global dialogue, a democratic conversation about some of the most contentious issues in development. It did not bother me that we might not know the right answer. Indeed, it bothered me more that we sometimes pretended to know more than we did. To me, the role of an outside adviser was more to ask the right questions—or to help those in the developing countries ask those questions—than to give the right answer.

The Role of the *WDR* in Thinking about Development More Broadly

To me, then, the *WDR* was an instrument to begin the change in thinking about development. Even before I came to the Bank, I was convinced that the Washington Consensus doctrines represented the wrong approach, at least for many countries. The economic theories on which the Washington Consensus rested had long been discredited. My own work on imperfect and asymmetric information and incomplete markets had contributed to undermining the theoretical foundations. And the World Bank's own report on the East Asian Miracle—on which I had worked—had shown that the most successful countries had not followed these recipes (World Bank 1993). But a gap remained between these insights from modern economic research and the perspectives of many policy makers.[1] I knew that many people in the Bank still believed in those ideas, and I saw the *WDR* as a way of beginning a global conversation—inside and outside the Bank. Not surprisingly, as each *WDR* went through the process of development within the Bank, difficulties were encountered. Many were uncomfortable with the ideas; many with the underlying economic analysis, which often exposed the limitations of models that had traditionally been relied on by those within the Bank; and many more were uncomfortable with the policy conclusions that emanated from the analyses.

---

1. I used the keynote addresses to the Annual Bank Conference on Development Economics in the first two years that I served as chief economist to focus attention on that gap—and to work to reduce it (see Stiglitz 1998a, 1999).

But the controversies were, perhaps, even more tense at the level of the Board. We touched on raw nerves. For the first time, we began to question the positions taken by the United States or other Group-of-Seven countries. To me, it was clear: we were international civil servants representing the interests of the developing countries. Inevitably, sometimes that would go against the position of the United States, whose policies were often driven by special interests. I was perhaps more aware of this than previous chief economists, who had come from academia. I had come directly from serving as chairman of the Council of Economic Advisers under President Bill Clinton. I had seen these special interests at work. The council had argued, on a number of occasions, against the positions taken by the U.S. Treasury and the U.S. trade representative. At the time, I was lucky, because the U.S. executive director, Jan Percy, was also focused on the concerns of the developing countries, and she was sufficiently influential within the administration that she could push back against Treasury, when necessary.

Knowledge for Development

Some examples illustrate. In the 1998 *WDR* on knowledge, we had to discuss, if ever so briefly, the role of intellectual property. I had opposed Trade-Related Aspects of Intellectual Property Rights (TRIPS), the intellectual property provision of the Uruguay Round, when I was on the Council of Economic Advisers.[2] So, too, had the U.S. Office of Science and Technology Policy. We thought it was bad for U.S. science, for global science, and for developing countries. I had seen firsthand how TRIPS was shaped, not by the concerns of U.S. science, but by our pharmaceutical and entertainment industries. I had no illusions: it was special-interest legislation. But my concerns about the adverse effects on developing countries were strengthened after I came to the World Bank. It was increasingly clear that what separated developing countries from developed countries was not just a gap in resources but a gap in knowledge, and it was imperative that this gap be closed. I had come to that view when I participated some years earlier in the World Bank's study on East Asia.[3] The unprecedented success of these

---

2. Part of my opposition was in fact based on my own research on the determinants of technological progress. It was simply not true (as the advocates of stronger intellectual property rights seem to claim) that stronger intellectual property rights lead to faster innovation and growth.

3. A version of our report was published as *The East Asian Miracle* (World Bank 1993).

countries was based on their closing the knowledge gap through heavy investments in education and technology. I reformulated that idea in my Prebisch lecture (Stiglitz 1998b) on development as transformation, and it is a view I have continued to develop with my colleague Bruce Greenwald.[4] It was a view that was strongly shared by the president, Jim Wolfensohn, who saw the Bank as a knowledge bank. But TRIPS made access to knowledge more difficult, adding new impediments in the struggle to close the knowledge gap.

In the *WDR*, we called for a more balanced view of intellectual property rights, recognizing that the "optimal" system for developing countries would be different from that for more developed countries. That call has now been taken up in the World Intellectual Property Organization, where the developing countries have called for a development-oriented intellectual property regime. In the decade since the *WDR* on knowledge, the limitations of America's intellectual property regime have come to be recognized even in the United States, and there are increasing calls for reform (see, for instance, Stiglitz 2006: chapter 4; see also Stiglitz 2004b, 2007).

I anticipated, though, that we would encounter trouble from the United States even with our carefully phrased call for a balanced intellectual property regime. But I also knew that we should be criticized by developing countries for not being more critical of TRIPS. We did our homework, consulting extensively with various executive directors. So when the United States launched its expected attack, saying that the *WDR* should take a stronger stance in favor of "stronger" intellectual property rights, several developing countries were prepared to launch a counterattack, urging us to take a more critical stance. So effective was their attack that the United States staged a hasty retreat.

Corruption

My first *WDR* also engendered a political controversy, because it raised, for the first time, the issue of corruption. This *WDR*, like most of the other *WDRs*, reflected both my interests and concerns and those of the Bank president. The year before coming to the Bank, I had given a keynote

---

4. In particular, we have asked, how can one design an economy (society) to best enhance its learning capacities? See Greenwald and Stiglitz (2006).

address (Stiglitz 1997a) at the Annual Bank Conference on Development Economics on the issue of the balance between market and government (see also Stiglitz 1997b).

In my work on the economics of the public sector, I had helped develop the market failures approach to the role of government (see Atkinson and Stiglitz 1980; Stiglitz 1986): markets often failed to yield efficient (let alone socially just) outcomes; well-structured government interventions could make everyone better off. I had attempted to identify what the government should do and how it should do it. While I was at the Council of Economic Advisers, I became involved in another project: Vice President Al Gore's initiative on "Reinventing Government," which tried to make government more efficient, more effective, and more responsive to citizens' wants and needs. If one believed (as I did) that the government had an important role, it was important for the government to perform its role well.

My own research (and that of others) had ended the theoretical debate about Adam Smith's invisible hand: markets were not, in general, efficient (see Greenwald and Stiglitz 1986; for a more general interpretation, see Stiglitz 1991). But many conservatives responded that, while government *might* effect a Pareto improvement, in practice, governments typically made things worse. Clearly, *sometimes* they did so, but also, in the most successful countries, the government had played an important role. However, if the government was to play the role it should in helping to create a fair and efficient society, one had to do what one could to improve the efficiency and effectiveness of the public sector.

In developing countries, one of the factors impeding the effectiveness of the public sector was corruption. The Bank's charter precluded the Bank from getting engaged in *political* matters, and some on the Board viewed corruption as a matter of politics—not economics. I had thought that the boundary was less clear than it seemed. To me, the issue of privatization of social security was an intensely political matter; so too was the issue of whether central banks should focus exclusively on inflation. There had been intense political fights on these issues in the United States—in which the Clinton administration seemed to take the opposite view from that taken by the World Bank and the International Monetary Fund (IMF). The administration's research on corruption showed that corruption affected economic growth, and economic policies (such as wages paid to civil servants) affected the level of corruption. This research demonstrated that corruption was well within the remit of the Bank. The *WDR*, and the research that went into it, thus had a profound effect on the direction of Bank and IMF policy: after Paul Wolfowitz became president, the Bank seemed to behave as if corruption was *the* most important development issue. Although the Bank clearly went overboard, and although there was undoubtedly some corruption in the corruption agenda, that *WDR*'s effects on the Bank and on the broader developmental dialogue were deep and long lasting.

Poverty

Every 10 years, the Bank has been doing a *WDR* on poverty. The Bank had helped focus attention on the large number of people in poverty—a focus that increased with the Millennium Development Goals enunciated just as I was leaving the Bank. The *WDR* was a natural follow-up to work we had been doing, called *Voices of the Poor* (Narayan and others 1999, 2000; Narayan and Petesch 2002). We had asked, "What aspects of their lives contributed most to the suffering of the poor?" We discovered—not surprisingly—that the poor were concerned not only about their lack of income but also about their lack of security and lack of voice. We had concluded that the exclusive focus on income (as in the 1990 *WDR*) was wrong, and under the direction of Ravi Kanbur, we decided to take a broader perspective. Not surprisingly, again, the approach drew political criticism—including from the U.S. secretary of treasury (and former World Bank chief economist), Lawrence Summers.

The debate was part of a broader development controversy. Some argued for trickle-down economics: countries should maximize growth, and that would be the most effective way of reducing poverty. Most of those within the Bank had moved away from that view. The evidence was overwhelming that growth did not *necessarily* reduce poverty. Trickle-down economics did not *necessarily* work. If growth was accompanied by increasing inequality, poverty could actually increase. The problem was that many of the Washington Consensus policies that the Bank and the IMF had argued for in the past had contributed to—or had at least been associated with—increasing inequality. And that was especially true of policies like capital market liberalization, which the U.S. Treasury had advocated. Such policies had not led to any or much increased growth[5] but had led to more instability, and the greater instability had led to more inequality—which was particularly pronounced in the context of the East Asian crisis.

To be sure, one could not have sustained poverty reduction without growth, which was why we had begun to focus on poverty-reducing growth strategies. The Comprehensive Development Strategies on which the Bank was then focusing[6] called attention to important complementarities that had often been missed in the past: trade liberalization might, for instance, by itself lead to more poverty, because jobs were destroyed faster than they were created. Only if accompanied by policies to enhance access to credit and technology might trade liberalization lead to reduced poverty.

Thus, the 2000/2001 *WDR* suggested not only that the policies being pushed by the U.S. Treasury might be bad for poverty in the narrow income sense, but also that they were even worse if poverty was more broadly conceived. For if capital market liberalization or trade liberalization was associated with greater economic instability, then the insecurity to which it gave rise might contribute even more to the worsening plight of those at the bottom.

Other policy controversies were also directly implicated. The Washington Consensus policies had argued for privatization of social security, but private social security accounts left individuals exposed to the vagaries of the market (all too evident in the 2008 market crash) and did not even insulate against the risks of inflation. Unionization and collective bargaining, part of the core labor standards around which broad global consensus existed, had attempted to increase worker security. Yet Washington Consensus policies had often argued for greater labor market flexibility, code words for eliminating or reducing hard-fought-for social protections. Although the evidence and the theory of the effects of such policies on growth or stability were ambiguous (Stiglitz, Easterly, and Islam 2001; see also Stiglitz and

---

5. This view has now become accepted even by the IMF (see Prasad and others 2003; Stiglitz and Ocampo 2008; Stiglitz and others 2006). My theoretical work had explained why that might be so (see, for example, Stiglitz 2004a).

6. The intellectual foundations of these strategies were, in part at least, provided by my Prebisch lecture (Stiglitz 1998b).

Rey 1993), such policies clearly may contribute to greater poverty in the broader sense.

Similarly, one of the criticisms of IMF (and, to a lesser extent, World Bank) loans, with their extensive conditionalities, is that they undermined democratic processes—reducing the scope for the voice of those affected. But such policies could be criticized as contributing to "poverty" in the broader sense, which recognizes the role of voice.

Our commitment to giving more voice to those in the developing countries—and making the WDR a vehicle through which democratic dialogue on development issues would be engendered—was reflected in the process of writing the WDR. We had organized extensive consultations throughout the world, posting each draft of the WDR on the Internet. This approach served us well in the ensuing controversy.

The U.S. Treasury demanded that the income aspect of poverty be given primacy. This demand went against the global consensus that had been generated in the process of our global discussions. Ravi Kanbur's resignation created a global furor. The Bank had to give weight to the process by which the WDR had been written, including the large number of consultations with scholars, government officials, and nongovernmental organizations in developing countries and in the development community. In the end, the Bank was forced to accept as the final draft a version that was close to that *before* the U.S. Treasury had unilaterally demanded its invasive changes.

Institutions

The 2000/2001 report was undoubtedly the most controversial WDR. But almost every WDR involved internal debate and discussion—precisely because the WDRs involved issues of importance where important differences of opinion existed.

Under Wolfensohn, the Bank had moved beyond projects to policies—and beyond policies to institutions. As the 1997 WDR emphasized, the public sector made a difference. But some governments—and some governmental institutions—were more successful than others. Some were less corrupt or corruptible than others. Within economics, the awarding of the Nobel prize to Doug North highlighted the importance of institutions.

But what makes for good institutions? And how can we create them? During the East Asian crisis, there was much discussion of the weaknesses of the East Asian institutions—financial institutions, financial regulatory bodies, corporate governance. Many were told to imitate U.S. institutions. Since then, confidence in what makes for good institutions has weakened. The Enron and WorldCom scandals highlighted weaknesses in accounting, financial institutions, and corporate governance in the United States. But the subsequent passage of the Sarbanes-Oxley Act gave renewed confidence in the institutions of the United States: its public institutions had faced up to the underlying weaknesses in corporate governance and had taken action. I was more skeptical. I had argued that perhaps the most fundamental flaw had to do with stock options, which provided incentives for bad accounting and short-sighted behavior (Stiglitz 2003b). But nothing was done. I and others had worried too about the bonus system that had encouraged excessive risk taking and the lack of regulation. I had worried that securitization was increasing problems of information asymmetries and decreasing the quality of lending (Stiglitz 2003a). Few would say today that the institutions of the U.S. financial sector—its rating agencies, its regulatory authorities, or its commercial or investment banks—are exemplary.

Although these ambiguities formed a backdrop to the heated debates in the formulation of the *WDR*, the real controversy concerned the role of institutions: did they "fill in" for market failures, or did they often help to preserve existing inequalities, frequently giving rise to inefficiencies in the attempt to do so? My own research had shown that the naive view that nonmarket institutions helped to remedy market failures (for example, by providing insurance when markets failed to do so) was wrong or at least needed to be more nuanced. Nonmarket institutions could actually be dysfunctional, enlarging market inefficiencies (Arnott and Stiglitz 1991).

But the distributional critique of institutions was, in a sense, even more fundamental.

Urbanization

Not all the *WDRs*—even those that raised big issues—were controversial. As we ended the 20th century and looked toward the next, we decided to use the 1999/2000 *WDR* to focus on some of the big megatrends and, in particular, on urbanization. Historically, most people living in developing countries have lived in the rural sector. And even today, the vast majority of those in poverty live there. Yet there have been large migrations from the rural to the urban sector, and in some places (such as China), such rapid development of some parts of the rural sector has occurred that it has become urbanized.

Urbanization—and development urbanization—bring their own advantages (ideas can spread more rapidly) and problems (especially with respect to housing, the environment, and transportation). This *WDR* helped push forward the thinking that will be needed if these problems are to be addressed.

The *WDR* and Specific Policy Issues

Although to me the most exciting aspect of the *WDR* has been the role it has played in rethinking basic issues of development, in doing so, it has helped the rethinking of numerous specific issues. I mention four that were highlighted in the *WDRs* with which I was involved. Sometimes a case for a particular policy was built up over several years—and over several *WDRs*.

Primary versus Secondary Education

The Bank had long emphasized the role that education (including female education) played in development. It had—rightly, I think—emphasized primary education. It had done so because many developing countries spent large fractions of their education budgets on tertiary education, of benefit only to the elites. But the Bank had, we concluded, gone too far. The countries that succeeded best in development (those in East Asia) had also invested heavily in higher education. They had realized that one had to close the knowledge gap, which required individuals with high levels of education.

Health

The 1993 *WDR* focused on health. Health is an important determinant of productivity. Access to health care is an important determinant of health, but knowledge about health is as, or even more, important, one of the points emphasized in the 1998/99 *WDR*. For instance, many people in developing countries suffer from inadequate nutrition, but even within their existing budgets, such countries could do better. Knowledge about how to avoid dehydration was critical in preventing a large fraction of children's deaths from diarrhea. Knowledge about where to place latrines in relation to sources of drinking water could prevent many gastrointestinal diseases.

Social Insurance

The 1997 *WDR* argued that developing countries suffered as often from too little government action, from a failed state, as they did from too much government. The 1998/99 *WDR* helped to explain one pervasive source of market failure of particular importance in developing countries: imperfect information. This is of especial importance in helping to explain the absence of insurance markets. Finally, the 2000/2001 *WDR* emphasized the importance of security—including health and economic security—as an aspect of poverty.

Together, these three *WDRs* provided a compelling case for government action in the area of social insurance—an area to which the Bank was paying increasing attention, especially in the context of the problems arising from the East Asian crisis and the transition from communism to a market economy.

The debate on this issue within the Bank has not been easy, with some arguing for a more limited role than others do.[7] Although the Bank had pushed many countries to privatize their social security systems, the outcomes of some of the privatizations were less than fully satisfactory. The problems in transition were not trivial. Because the government was deprived of essential cash flows, severe fiscal problems were artificially created, in some cases contributing to severe economic crises. Argentina is an admittedly controversial case in point. Many blamed its crisis on its fiscal problems, but had it not privatized its social insurance system, its budget would have been nearly in balance. Transaction costs turned out to be large. And the imposition of burdens of risk on individuals was far from trivial. When the United States had a national debate on privatization of its social security system, support was overwhelming for keeping it public; in

---

7. A sense of the debate is given by *New Ideas About Old Age Security* (Holzmann and Stiglitz 2001), and especially chapter 1 (Orszag and Stiglitz 2001).

the 2008 crash, there was a national sigh of relief that social security had not been privatized.

Access to Finance

The standard economic model that ignores information imperfections may work well in some countries in some sectors; it does not work well in most sectors in most developing countries. That was one of the important messages of the 1998/99 WDR.[8]

The 2000/2001 WDR emphasized that growth might be necessary to reduce poverty, but it was not sufficient. One had to look for growth policies that alleviated poverty and enhanced equality. In the case of some policies, a trade-off between growth and equality may not even exist. One example is providing universal education. Making sure that every child can live up to his or her potential reduces poverty, enhances equality, and promotes growth.

So, too, does access to finance. Standard economic models denied the possibility of credit rationing. Yet modern economic theories, based on the economics of information, highlighted in the 1998/99 WDR, explain why it is likely to occur and why alternative ways of providing finance, such as the peer-monitoring microcredit schemes pioneered by the 2006 winner of the Nobel prize, Muhammad Yunus and the Grameen Bank and the Bangladesh Rural Advancement Committee, are likely to be far more effective (see also Stiglitz 1990).

The Bank has taken an increasingly active role in promoting microcredit and access to finance, an agenda to which the 1998/99 WDR may have contributed.

Concluding Remarks

Throughout its history, the WDR has played an active role in shaping thought and policy, both within the World Bank and in the wider development community. It was sometimes overly ambitious, hoping to be able to summarize in a few clear messages the received wisdom on a key aspect

---

8. Like most WDRs, this one was built on extensive work done within the World Bank in earlier years (see, for instance, Hoff, Braverman, and Stiglitz 1993).

of development. The world is too often too complicated for that to be done. When the WDR did so, it risked reemphasizing the obvious or what was well accepted, or conducting the discussion at such a high level of abstraction as to be of limited use. Occasionally, it became the publication vehicle for official Bank doctrines—a summary of beliefs of the moment. Even here, it served a helpful role, at least for students of the evolution of economic thought, for they could see how thinking about development evolved over the years.

But to me, at least, its greatest contributions occurred when it helped to frame controversial issues, when it pushed the boundaries of thinking, when it opened up new frontiers—thinking about issues that had previously received too little attention—when it sparked a global debate. In those cases, the WDR's effect was not only immediate, but also likely to be long lasting.

Appendix A

List of
World Development Reports,
1978–2008

#	Year	Staff director	President	Title
1	1978	D. C. Rao	Robert S. McNamara	Prospects for Growth and Alleviation of Poverty
2	1979	Shankar Acharya	Robert S. McNamara	Structural Change and Development Policy
3	1980	Paul Isenman	Robert S. McNamara	Poverty and Human Development
4	1981	Robert Cassen	Robert S. McNamara	National and International Adjustment
5	1982	David Turnham	Alden W. Clausen	Agriculture and Economic Development
6	1983	Pierre Landell-Mills	Alden W. Clausen	Management in Development
7	1984	Nancy Birdsall	Alden W. Clausen	Population Change and Development
8	1985	Francis X. Colaço	Alden W. Clausen	International Capital and Economic Development
9	1986	Anandarup Ray	Alden W. Clausen	Trade and Pricing Policies in World Agriculture
10	1987	Sarath Rajapatirana	Barber B. Conable	Industrialization and Foreign Trade
11	1988	Johannes F. Linn	Barber B. Conable	Public Finance in Development
12	1989	Millard F. Long	Barber B. Conable	Financial Systems and Development
13	1990	Lyn Squire	Barber B. Conable	Poverty
14	1991	Vinod Thomas	Barber B. Conable	The Challenge of Development

15	1992	Andrew Steer	Lewis Preston	*Development and the Environment*
16	1993	Dean T. Jamison	Lewis Preston	*Investing in Health*
17	1994	Gregory Ingram	Lewis Preston	*Infrastructure for Development*
18	1995	Michael Walton	James D. Wolfensohn	*Workers in an Integrating World*
19	1996	Alan H. Gelb	James D. Wolfensohn	*From Plan to Market*
20	1997	Ajay Chhibber	James D. Wolfensohn	*The State in a Changing World*
21	1998/99	Carl Dahlman	James D. Wolfensohn	*Knowledge for Development*
22	1999/2000	Shahid Yusuf	James D. Wolfensohn	*Entering the 21st Century: The Changing Development Landscape*
23	2000/01	Ravi Kanbur and Nora Lustig	James D. Wolfensohn	*Attacking Poverty*
24	2002	Roumeen Islam	James D. Wolfensohn	*Building Institutions for Markets*
25	2003	Zmarak Shalizi	James D. Wolfensohn	*Sustainable Development in a Dynamic World: Transforming Institutions, Growth, and Quality of Life*
26	2004	Shantayanan Devarajan and Ritva Reinikka	James D. Wolfensohn	*Making Services Work for Poor People*
27	2005	Warrick Smith	James D. Wolfensohn	*A Better Investment Climate for Everyone*
28	2006	Francisco Ferreira and Michael Walton	Paul Wolfowitz	*Equity and Development*
29	2007	Emmanuel Y. Jimenez	Paul Wolfowitz	*Development and the Next Generation*
30	2008	Derek Byerlee and Alain de Janvry	Robert B. Zoellick	*Agriculture for Development*

Appendix B

Citations of World Development Reports in Peer-Reviewed Articles, 1990–2005

Year	Title	Cited year 1990	1991	1992	1993	1994	1995	1996	1997	1998	1999	2000	2001	2002	2003	2004	2005	2006	Total cites	Cites/ year
1990	Poverty	1	31	45	31	23	30	33	50	41	27	28	17	20	18	15	10	6	426	25.1
1991	The Challenge of Development		2	30	62	38	30	27	37	35	26	17	27	13	7	11	9	0	371	23.2
1992	Development and the Environment			2	36	55	49	53	59	71	52	52	55	41	37	25	24	12	623	41.5
1993	Investing in Health				6	63	89	149	219	235	229	189	171	152	134	127	95	34	1,892	135.1
1994	Infrastructure for Development					2	16	51	62	57	52	32	29	25	24	30	21	5	406	31.2
1995	Workers in an Integrating World							33	67	51	48	38	15	24	15	16	11	7	325	27.1
1996	From Plan to Market							2	39	70	73	74	36	23	23	15	9	4	368	33.5
1997	The State in a Changing World								4	74	113	115	84	67	60	43	35	15	610	61.0
1998/99	Knowledge for Development									2	26	34	42	25	22	17	11	3	182	20.2
1999/2000	Entering the 21st Century										11	54	61	48	53	15	21	7	270	33.8
2000/01	Attacking Poverty											4	74	152	205	147	140	50	772	110.3
2002	Building Institutions for Markets												0	8	23	41	55	21	148	24.7
2003	Sustainable Development in a Dynamic World													0	8	32	59	21	120	24.0
2004	Making Services Work for Poor People														0	7	27	16	50	12.5
2005	A Better Investment Climate for Everyone															0	4	1	5	1.7
	Total citations per year	1	33	77	135	181	214	348	537	636	657	637	611	598	629	541	531	202	6,568	

References

Acemoglu, Daron, Simon Johnson, and James A. Robinson. 2001. "The Colonial Origins of Comparative Development: An Empirical Investigation." *American Economic Review* 91 (5): 1369–401.

Acemoglu, Daron, and Fabrizio Zilibotti. 2001. "Productivity Differences." *Quarterly Journal of Economics* 116 (2): 563–606.

Aghion, Philippe, Diego Comin, and Peter Howitt. 2006. "When Does Domestic Saving Matter for Economic Growth?" NBER Working Paper 12275, National Bureau of Economic Research, Cambridge, MA.

Ahmed, Akhter U., Ruth Vargas Hill, Lisa C. Smith, Doris M. Wiesmann, and Tim Frankenberger. 2008. *The World's Most Deprived: Characteristics and Causes of Extreme Poverty and Hunger.* Washington, DC: International Food Policy Research Institute.

Ahmed, Sadiq, and Ashutosh Varshney. 2008. "Battles Half Won: The Political Economy of India's Growth and Economic Policy since Independence." Commission on Growth and Development Working Paper 15, World Bank, Washington, DC.

Albouy, David Y. 2008. "The Colonial Origins of Comparative Development: An Investigation of the Settler Mortality Data." NBER Working Paper 14130, National Bureau of Economic Research, Cambridge, MA.

Alesina, Alberto F. 2007. "Political Economy." *NBER Reporter* 3: 1–5.

Alesina, Alberto F., William Easterly, and Janina Matuszeski. 2006. "Artificial States." NBER Working Paper 12328, National Bureau of Economic Research, Cambridge, MA.

Alesina, Alberto F., and Eliana La Ferrara. 2004. "Ethnic Diversity and Economic Performance." NBER Working Paper 10313, National Bureau of Economic Research, Cambridge, MA.

Alexandratos, Nikos. 2005. "Countries with Rapid Population Growth and Resource Constraints: Issues of Food, Agriculture, and Development." *Population and Development Review* 31 (2): 237–58.

Allan, J. A. "Tony." 2003. "Virtual Water: The Water, Food, and Trade Nexus—Useful Concept or Misleading Metaphor?" *Water International* 28 (1): 4–11.

Allen, Robert C. 2001. "The Rise and Decline of the Soviet Economy." *Canadian Journal of Economics* 34 (4): 859–81.

Altonji, Joseph G., Prashant Bharadwaj, and Fabian Lange. 2008. "Changes in Characteristics of American Youth: Implications for Adult Outcomes." NBER Working Paper 13883, National Bureau of Economic Research, Cambridge, MA.

Álvarez, Roberto, and J. Rodrigo Fuentes. 2005. "Paths of Development, Specialization, and Natural Resources Abundance." Inter-American Development Bank, Washington, DC.

Amsden, Alice H. 1989. *Asia's Next Giant: South Korea and Late Industrialization*. New York and Oxford, U.K.: Oxford University Press.

———. 2007. *Escape from Empire: The Developing World's Journey through Heaven and Hell*. Cambridge, MA: MIT Press.

Anand, Sudhir, and Paul Segal. 2008. "What Do We Know about Global Income Inequality?" *Journal of Economic Literature* 46 (1): 57–94.

Anderson, Kym, and L. Alan Winters. 2008. "Now Is the Time to Reduce International Trade and Migration Barriers." VoxEU.org, Centre for Economic Policy Research, London.

Ang, James B. 2008. "A Survey of Recent Developments in the Literature of Finance and Growth." *Journal of Economic Surveys* 22 (3): 536–76.

Armstrong, Mark, and David E. M. Sappington. 2006. "Regulation, Competition, and Liberalization." *Journal of Economic Literature* 44 (2): 325–66.

Arnott, Richard, and Joseph E. Stiglitz. 1991. "Moral Hazard and Non-market Institutions: Dysfunctional Crowding Out or Peer Monitoring." *American Economic Review* 81 (1): 179–90.

Arrunada, Benito. 2007. "Pitfalls to Avoid When Measuring Institutions: Is *Doing Business* Damaging Business?" *Journal of Comparative Economics* 35 (4): 729–47.

Asian Development Bank. 2005. *Connecting East Asia*. Manila: ADB Press.

Atkinson, Anthony, and Joseph E. Stiglitz. 1980. *Lectures in Public Economics*. New York: McGraw-Hill.

Avery, George H., Mark Lawley, Sandra Garrett, Barrett Caldwell, Marshall P. Durr, Dulcy Abraham, Feng Lin, Po-Ching C. DeLaurentis, Maria L. Peralta, Alice Russell, Renata A. Kopach-Conrad, Lalaine M. Ignacio, Rebeca Sandino, and Deanna J. Staples. 2008. "Planning for Pandemic Influenza: Lessons from the Experiences of Thirteen Indiana Counties." *Journal of Homeland Security and Emergency Management* 5(1): article 29.

Ayres, Robert U. 1999. "What Have We Learned?" *Technological Forecasting and Social Change* 62 (1): 9–12.

Bacharach, Michael, and Diego Gambetta. 2001. "Trust in Signs." In *Trust in Society*, ed. Karen S. Cook, 148–84, New York: Russell Sage Foundation.

Baker, Robert 2007. *Quiet Killers*. Phoenix Mill, UK: Sutton Publishing.

Balassa, Béla. 1971. *The Structure of Protection in Developing Countries*. Baltimore, MD: John Hopkins University Press.

Banerjee, Abhijit, Rukmini Banerji, Esther Duflo, Rachel Glennerster, and Stuti Khemani. 2008. "Pitfalls of Participatory Programs: Evidence from a Randomized Evaluation in Education in India." Policy Research Working Paper 4584, World Bank, Washington, DC.

Banerjee, Abhijit, Angus Deaton, Nora Lustig, and Ken Rogoff. 2006. *An Evaluation of World Bank Research, 1998–2005*. Washington, DC: World Bank. http://siteresources.worldbank.org/DEC/Resources/84797-1109362238001/726454-1164121166494/RESEARCH-EVALUATION-2006-Main-Report.pdf.

Banerjee, Abhijit V., and Esther Duflo. 2003. "Inequality and Growth: What Can the Data Say?" *Journal of Economic Growth* 8 (3): 267–99.

———. 2004. "Growth Theory through the Lens of Development Economics." MIT Department of Economics Working Paper 05-01, Massachusetts Institute of Technology, Cambridge, MA.

"Barcelona Development Agenda." 2004. Consensus document resulting from Forum Barcelona 2004, Barcelona, Spain, September 24–25. http://www.barcelona2004.org/esp/banco_del_conocimiento/docs/CO_47_EN.pdf.

Bardhan, Pranab. 1970. *Economic Growth, Development, and Foreign Trade: A Study in Pure Theory*. New York: John Wiley & Sons.

———. 2005. "Theory or Empirics in Development Economics." *Economic and Political Weekly* 40 (40): 4333–35

———. 2006. "Political Economy of India." In *The Oxford Companion to Economics in India*, ed. Kaushik Basu. New Delhi: Oxford University Press.

Bates, Robert H. 2008. *When Things Fell Apart: State Failure in Late-Century Africa*. Cambridge, U.K.: Cambridge University Press.

Baumol, William J., and William G. Bowen. 1966. *Performing Arts: The Economic Dilemma*. New York: Twentieth Century Fund.

Bayly, Christopher A. 2002. "'Archaic' and 'Modern' Globalization in the Eurasian and African Arena, ca. 1750–1850." In *Globalization in World History*, ed. A. G. Hopkins. New York: W. W. Norton.

Ben-David, Dan, and David H. Papell. 1997. "Slowdowns and Meltdowns: Postwar Growth Evidence from 74 Countries." NBER Working Paper 6266, National Bureau of Economic Research, Cambridge, MA.

Benhabib, Jess, and Mark M. Spiegel. 1994. "The Role of Human Capital in Economic Development Evidence from Aggregate Cross-Country Data." *Journal of Monetary Economics* 34 (2): 143–73.

Berg, Elliot. 1981. *Accelerated Development in Sub-Saharan Africa: An Agenda for Action.* Washington, DC: World Bank.

Bernanke, Ben S., and Refet S. Gurkaynak. 2001. "Is Growth Exogenous? Taking Mankiw, Romer, and Weil Seriously." NBER Working Paper 8365, National Bureau of Economic Research, Cambridge, MA.

Bhagwati, Jagdish N., and Anne O. Krueger. 1973. "Exchange Controls, Liberalization, and Economic Development." *American Economic Review* 63 (2): 419–27.

Bideleux, Robert. 1985. *Communism and Development.* New York: Methuen.

Bils, Mark, and Peter Klenow. 2000. "Does Schooling Cause Growth?" *American Economic Review* 90 (5): 1160–83.

Birdsall, Nancy. 2008. "Seven Deadly Sins: Reflections on Donor Failings." In *Reinventing Foreign Aid*, ed. William Easterly, 515–51. Cambridge, MA: MIT Press.

Blanchard, Olivier J. 2008. "The State of Macro." NBER Working Paper 14259, National Bureau of Economic Research, Cambridge, MA.

Bleakley, Hoyt. 2008. Comments on "When Does Improving Health Raise GDP?" by Quamrul H. Ashraf, Ashley Lester, and David N. Weil. In *NBER Macroeconomics Annual 2008*, ed. Daron Acemoglu, Kenneth Rogoff, and Michael Woodford. Chicago: University of Chicago Press. Remarks delivered at the 2008 NBER Macro Annual.

Blonigen, Bruce. 2008. "Doha's Woes and the Long-Gun Structural Issues Facing Trade Negotiations." VoxEU.org, Centre for Economic Policy Research, London.

Boarini, Romina, and Hubert Strauss. 2007. "The Private Internal Rates of Return to Tertiary Education: New Estimates for 21 OECD Countries." OECD Economics Department Working Paper 591, Organisation for Economic Co-operation and Development, Paris.

Bordo, Michael. 2007. "The Crisis of 2007: Some Lessons from History." VoxEU.org, Centre for Economic Policy Research, London.

Bosworth, Barry P., and Susan M. Collins. 2007. "Accounting for Growth: Comparing China and India." Working Paper 12943, National Bureau of Economic Research, Cambridge, MA.

Bourguignon, François, and Christian Morrison. 2002. "Inequality among World Citizens: 1820–1992." *American Economic Review* 92 (4): 727–44.

Broome, John. 2008. "The Ethics of Climate Change: Pay Now or Pay More Later?" *Scientific American* (June): 97–102.

Brunnschweiler, Christa N., and Erwin H. Bulte. 2008. "Linking Natural Resources to Slow Growth and More Conflict." *Science* 320 (5876): 616–17.

Bruno, Michael, and William Easterly. 1998. "Inflation Crises and Long-Run Growth." *Journal of Monetary Economics* 41 (1): 3–26.

Burke, Paul J., and Fredoun Z. Ahmadi-Esfahani. 2006. "Aid and Growth: A Study of South East Asia." *Journal of Asian Economics* 17 (2): 350–62.

Cai, Fang, and Meiyan Wang. 2008. "A Counterfactual Analysis on Unlimited Surplus Labor in Rural China." *China and World Economy* 1 6(1): 51–65.

Califano, Joseph A. Jr. 2008. "The Price of Forgetting a Presidency." *Washington Post*, May 31, A13.

Campbell, Kurt M. 2008. *Climatic Cataclysm: The Foreign Policy and National Security Implications of Climate Change.* Washington, DC: Brookings Institution.

Caselli, Francesco, and Wilbur John Coleman II. 2006. "On the Theory of Ethnic Conflict." NBER Working Paper 12125, National Bureau of Economic Research, Cambridge, MA.

Cass, David. 1965. "Optimum Growth in an Aggregative Model of Capital Accumulation." *Review of Economic Studies* 32 (3): 233–40.

Celasun, Oya, and Jan Walliser. 2008. "Predictability of Aid." *Economic Policy* 23 (55): 545–94.

Chang, Ha-Joon. 2007. *Bad Samaritans: Rich Nations, Poor Policies, and the Threat to the Developing World.* London. Random House.

Chaudhury, Sushil. 1995. *From Prosperity to Decline: Eighteenth Century Bengal.* New Delhi: Manohar.

Chauvin, Nicholas M. Depetris, and Aart Kraay. 2007. "What Has 100 Billion Dollars Worth of Debt Relief Done for Low-Income Countries?" World Bank, Washington, DC.

Chen, Shaohua, and Martin Ravallion. 2007. "Absolute Poverty Measures for the Developing World, 1981–2004." Policy Research Working Paper 4211, World Bank, Washington, DC.

————. 2008. "The Developing World Is Poorer Than We Thought, but No Less Successful in the Fight against Poverty." Policy Research Working Paper 4703, World Bank, Washington, DC.

Chenery, Hollis. 1950. "The Engineering Bases of Economic Analysis." PhD dissertation, Harvard University, Cambridge, MA.

Chenery, Hollis, Montek S. Ahuluwalia, C. L. G. Bell, John H. Duloy, and Richard Jolly. 1974. *Redistribution with Growth: Policies to Improve Income Distribution in Developing Countries in the Context of Economic Growth.* London and New York: Oxford University Press.

Chenery, Hollis and Michael Bruno. 1962. "Development Alternatives in an Open Economy: The Case of Israel." *Economic Journal* 72 (285): 79–103.

"China: Labor Shortages Trump Rural Surplus." 2008. *Oxford Analytica*, January 3.

Chung, Young-lob. 2007. *South Korea in the Fast Lane*. Oxford, U.K.: Oxford University Press.

Ciccone, Antonio, and Marek Jarociński. 2008. "Determinants of Economic Growth: Will Data Tell?" Working Paper 852, European Central Bank, Frankfurt am Main, Germany.

Claessens, Stijn, Danny Cassimon, and Björn Van Campenhout. 2007. "Empirical Evidence on the New International Aid Architecture." IMF Working Paper 277, International Monetary Fund, Washington, DC.

Clark, Andrew E., Paul Frijters, and Michael A. Shields. 2008. "Relative Income, Happiness, and Utility: An Explanation for the Easterlin Paradox and Other Puzzles." *Journal of Economic Literature* 46 (1): 95–144.

Clark, Gregory. 2007. *A Farewell to Alms*. Princeton, NJ: Princeton University Press.

Clarke, Peter. 2008. *The Last Thousand Days of the British Empire*. New York: Bloomsbury Press.

Coakley, Jerry, Farida Kulasi, and Ron Smith. 1988. "The Feldstein-Horioka Puzzle and Capital Mobility: A Review." *International Journal of Finance and Economics* 3 (2): 169–88.

Coatsworth, John H., and Jeffrey G. Williamson. 2002. "The Roots of Latin American Protectionism: Looking before the Great Depression." NBER Working Paper 8999, National Bureau of Economic Research, Cambridge, MA.

Cole, Harold L., Lee E. Ohanian, Alvaro Riascos, and James A. Schmitz Jr. 2004. "Latin America in the Rearview Mirror." NBER Working Paper 11008, National Bureau of Economic Research, Cambridge, MA.

Collier, Paul. 2007. *The Bottom Billion: Why the Poorest Countries Are Failing and What Can Be Done about It*. New York: Oxford University Press.

Commission on Growth and Development. 2008. *The Growth Report: Strategies for Sustained Growth and Inclusive Development*. Washington, DC: World Bank.

Connelly, Matthew. 2008. *Fatal Misconceptions: The Struggle to Control World Population*. Cambridge, MA: Belknap.

Corbo, Vittorio L., and Leonardo T. Hernández. 2006. "Successes and Failures in Real Covergence: The Case of Chile." In *Living Standards and the Wealth of Nations: Successes and Failures in Real Convergence*, ed. Leszek Balcerowicz and Stanley Fischer, 115–45. Cambridge, MA: MIT Press.

Cord, Robert. 2007. *Keynes*. London: Haus Publishing.

Coyle, Diane 1998. *The Weightless World*. Cambridge, MA: MIT Press.

Crafts, Nicholas. 2004a. "Globalization and Economic Growth: A Historical Perspective." *World Economy* 27 (1): 45–58.

———. 2004b. "Productivity Growth in the Industrial Revolution: A New Growth Accounting Perspective." *Journal of Economic History* 64 (2): 521–35.

Crossman, Richard, ed. 1950. *The God That Failed: Six Studies in Communism.* London: Hamish Hamilton.

Dasgupta, Sukti, and Ajit Singh. 2005. "Will Services Be the New Engine of Indian Economic Growth?" *Development and Change* 36 (6): 1035–57.

De Haan, Jakob, Susanna Lundström, and Jan-Egbert Sturm. 2006. "Market-Oriented Institutions and Policies and Economic Growth: a Critical Survey." *Journal of Economic Surveys* 20 (2): 157–91.

Dell, Melissa, Benjamin F. Jones, and Benjamin A. Olken. 2008. "Climate Change and Economic Growth: Evidence from the Last Half Century." NBER Working Paper 14132, National Bureau of Economic Research, Cambridge, MA.

DeLong, J. Bradford. 2000. "Cornucopia: the Pace of Economic Growth in the Twentieth Century." NBER Working Paper 7602, National Bureau of Economic Research, Cambridge, MA.

Deming, David, and Susan Dynarski. 2008. "The Lengthening of Childhood." NBER Working Paper 14124, National Bureau of Economic Research, Cambridge, MA.

Devarajan, Shantayanan, William Easterly, and Howard Pack. 2001. "Is Investment in Africa Too High or Too Low? Macro- and Micro-Evidence." *Journal of African Economies* 10 (Suppl. 1): 81–108.

"Developing Countries Face Power Deficit." 2008. *Oxford Analytica*, March 26.

Diamond, Jared M. 1999. *Guns, Germs, and Steel: The Fates of Human Societies.* New York: W. W. Norton.

Dixit, Avinash. 1996. *The Making of Economic Policy.* Cambridge, MA: MIT Press.

———. 2007. "Evaluating Recipes for Development Success." *World Bank Research Observer* 22 (2): 131–57.

Djankov, Simeon, Ira Lieberman, Joyita Mukherjee, and Tatiana Nenova. 2002. "Going Informal: Benefits and Costs." World Bank, Washington, DC.

Domar, Evsey D. 1946. "Capital Expansion, Rate of Growth, and Employment." *Econometrica* 14 (2): 137–47.

Doppelhofer, Gernot, Ronald Miller, and Xavier Sala-i-Martin. 2004. "Determinants of Long-Term Growth: A Bayesian Averaging of Classical Estimates (BACE) Approach." *American Economic Review* 94 (4): 813–35.

Doucouliagos, Hristos, and Martin Paldam. 2006. "Aid Effectiveness on Accumulation: A Meta Study." *Kyklos* 59 (2): 227–54.

Dovern, Jonas, and Peter Nunnenkamp. 2007. "Aid and Growth Accelerations: An Alternative Approach to Assessing the Effectiveness of Aid." *Kyklos* 60 (3): 359–83.

Doyle, Martin W., Emily H. Stanley, David G. Havlick, Mark J. Kaiser, George Steinbach, William L. Graf, Gerald E. Galloway, and J. Adam Riggsbee. 2008. "Aging Infrastructure and Ecosystem Restoration." *Science* 319 (5861): 286–87.

Dreher, Axel, Dirk-Jan Koch, Peter Nunnenkamp, and Rainer Thiele. 2008. "NGO Aid: Well Targeted to the Needy and Deserving?" VoxEU.org, Centre for Economic Policy Research, London.

Durlauf, Steven N., Paul A. Johnson, and Jonathan R. W. Temple. 2005. "Growth Econometrics." In *Handbook of Economic Growth*, vol. 1A, ed. Philippe Aghion and Steven N. Durlauf, 555–677. Amsterdam: North-Holland.

Durlauf, Steven N., Andros Kourtellos, and Chih Ming Tan. 2008. "Are Any Growth Theories Robust?" *Economic Journal* 118 (527): 329–46.

Dyson, Freeman. 2008. "The Question of Global Warming." *New York Review of Books* 55 (10): 43–45.

"East Africa: Disasters Overwhelm Regional Governments." 2008. *Oxford Analytica*, January 10.

Easterlin, Richard E. 1998. *Growth Triumphant: The Twenty-First Century in Historical Perspective (Economics, Cognition, and Society)*. Ann Arbor, MI: University of Michigan Press.

Easterly, William. 2001. *The Elusive Quest for Growth: Economists' Adventures and Misadventures in the Tropics*. Cambridge, MA: MIT Press.

———. 2002. "The Cartel of Good Intentions: The Problem of Bureaucracy in Foreign Aid." Center for Global Development Working Paper 4, Institute for International Economies, Washington, DC.

———. 2005. "National Policies and Economic Growth: A Reappraisal." In *Handbook of Economic Growth*, ed. Philippe Aghion and Steven N. Durlauf, 1015–59. Amsterdam: Elsevier.

———. 2006a. "Reliving the 1950s: The Big Push, Poverty Traps, and Takeoffs in Economic Development." *Journal of Economic Growth* 11 (4): 289–318.

———. 2006b. *The White Man's Burden: Why the West's Efforts to Aid the Rest Have Done So Much Ill and So Little Good*. New York: Penguin Press.

———. 2007a. "Are Aid Agencies Improving?" *Economic Policy* 22 (52): 633–78.

———. 2007b. "Inequality Does Cause Underdevelopment: Insights from a New Instrument." *Journal of Development Economics* 84 (2): 755–76.

Easterly, William, Michael Kremer, Lant Pritchett, and Lawrence Summers. 1993. "Good Policy or Good Luck? Country Growth Performance and Temporary Shocks." *Journal of Monetary Economics* 32 (3): 459–83.

Eichengreen, Barry. 2007. "The Asian Crisis after Ten Years." University of California, Berkeley, CA.

Eichengreen, Barry, and Richard Baldwin, eds. 2008. *Rescuing Our Jobs and Savings: What G7/8 Leaders Can Do to Solve the Global Credit Crisis*. A VoxEU.org Publication. London: Centre for Economic Policy Research.

Eidlin, Eric. 2005. "The Worst of All Worlds: Los Angeles, California, and the Emerging Reality of Dense Sprawl." *Transportation Research Record* 1902: 1–9.

Eifert, Benn, Alan Gelb, and Vijaya Ramachandran. 2008. "The Cost of Doing Business in Africa: Evidence from Enterprise Survey Data." *World Development* 36 (9): 1531–46.

Ellman, Michael. 1979. *Socialistic Planning*. Cambridge, U.K.: Cambridge University Press.

Etzkowitz, Henry, and Sandra N. Brisolla. 1999. "Failure and Success: The Fate of Industrial Policy in Latin America and South East Asia." *Research Policy* 28 (4): 337–50.

FAO (Food and Agriculture Organization). 2006. "FAOSTAT Statistical Database." FAO, Rome.

Felton, Andrew, and Carmen M. Reinhart. 2008. *The First Global Financial Crisis of the 21st Century*. London: Centre for Economic Policy Research.

Feng, Yi. 2003. *Democracy, Governance, and Economic Performance*. Cambridge, MA: MIT Press.

Ferguson, Niall. 2002. *Empire*. New York: Basic Books.

Ferreira, Francisco H. G., and Louise C. Keely. 2000. "The World Bank and Structural Adjustment: Lessons from the 1980s." In *The World Bank: Structure and Policies*, ed. Christopher L. Gilbert and David Vines, 159–95. Cambridge, U.K.: Cambridge University Press.

Ferreira, Francisco H. G., Phillippe G. Leite, and Martin Ravallion. 2007. "Poverty Reduction without Economic Growth? Explaining Brazil's Poverty Dynamics, 1985–2004." Policy Research Working Paper 4431, World Bank, Washington, DC.

Ferreira, Francisco H. G., and Martin Ravallion. 2008. "Global Poverty and Inequality: A Review of the Evidence." Policy Research Working Paper 4623, World Bank, Washington, DC.

Findlay, Ronald, and Kevin H. O'Rourke. 2008. "Lessons from the History of Trade and War." VoxEU.org, Centre for Economic Policy Research, London.

Fogel, Robert W. 2000. "Simon S. Kuznets: April 30, 1901–July 9, 1985." NBER Working Paper 7787, National Bureau of Economic Research, Cambridge, MA.

———. 2005. "Reconsidering Expectations of Economic Growth after World War II from the Perspective of 2004." NBER Working Paper 11125, National Bureau of Economic Research, Cambridge, MA.

Foray, Dominique. 2004. *The Economics of Knowledge.* Cambridge, MA: MIT Press.

Forrester, Jay W. 1971. *World Dynamics*. Cambridge, MA: MIT Press.

Frankel, Jeffrey A. 2003/04. "Program Report: International Finance and Macroeconomics." *NBER Reporter* (Winter): 1–8.

Frankel, Marvin. 1962. "The Production Function in Allocation and Growth: A Synthesis." *American Economic Review* 52 (5): 996–1022.

Fukuyama, Francis. 1989. "The End of History?" *National Interest* 16 (Summer): 3–18.

Galor, Oded, and Andrew Mountford. 2008. "Trading Population for Productivity: Theory and Evidence." CEPR Discussion Paper 6678, Centre for Economic Policy Research, London.

Gambetta, Diego. 1988. *Trust: Making and Breaking Cooperative Relations*. Oxford, U.K.: Cambridge, MA: Basil Blackwell.

———. 2006. "Trust's Odd Ways." In *Understanding Choice, Explaining Behaviour: Essays in Honour of Ole-Jørgen Skog*, ed. Jon Elster, Olav Gjelsvik, Aanund Hylland, and Karl Moene, 81–100. Oslo: Unipub Forlag/Oslo Academic Press.

Gerschenkron, Alexander. 1962. *Economic Backwardness in Historical Perspective*. Cambridge, MA: Belknap Press.

Ghani, Ashraf, and Clare Lockhart. 2008. *Fixing Failed States: A Framework for Rebuilding a Fractured World*. New York: Oxford University Press.

Gilbert, Christopher L., Andrew Powell, and David Vines. 2000. "Positioning the World Bank." In *The World Bank: Structure and Policies*, ed. Christopher L. Gilbert and David Vines. Cambridge, U.K.: Cambridge University Press, 39–86.

Gilovich, Thomas, Dale Griffin, and Daniel Kahneman. 2002. *Heuristics and Biases: The Psychology of Intuitive Judgment*. New York: Cambridge University Press.

Glaeser, Edward L., and Matthew E. Kahn. 2008. "The Greenness of Cities: Carbon Dioxide Emissions and Urban Development." NBER Working Paper 14238, National Bureau of Economic Research, Cambridge, MA.

Goldstone, Jack A. 2008. *Why Europe? The Rise of the West in World History 1500–1850*. New York: McGraw-Hill.

Gómez-Ibáñez, José A. 2006. *Regulating Infrastructure: Monopoly, Contracts, and Discretion*. Cambridge, MA: Harvard University Press.

Gourinchas, Pierre-Olivier, and Olivier Jeanne. 2003. "The Elusive Gains from International Financial Integration." NBER Working Paper 9684, National Bureau of Economic Research, Cambridge, MA

Greenwald, Bruce C., and Joseph E. Stiglitz. 1986. "Externalities in Economies with Imperfect Information and Incomplete Markets." *Quarterly Journal of Economics* 101 (2): 229–64.

———. 2006. "Helping Infant Economies Grow: Foundations of Trade Policies for Developing Countries." *American Economic Review* 96 (2): 141–46.

Grimm, Nancy B., Stanley H. Faeth, Nancy E. Golubiewski, Charles L. Redman, Jianguo Wu, Xuemei Bai, and John M. Briggs. 2008. "Global Change and the Ecology of Cities." *Science* 319 (5864): 756–60.

Groopman, Jerome. 2008. "Superbugs: The New Generation of Resistant Infections Is Almost Impossible to Treat." *New Yorker*, August 11.

Gulledge, Jay. 2008. "Three Plausible Scenarios of Future Climate Change." In *Climatic Cataclysm: The Foreign Policy and National Security Implications of*

Climate Change, ed. Kurt M. Campbell, 49–96. Washington, DC: Brookings Institution.

Guryan, Jonathan, Erik Hurst, and Melissa Schettini Kearney. 2008. "Parental Education and Parental Time with Children." NBER Working Paper 13993, National Bureau of Economic Research, Cambridge, MA.

Haims, Marla C., David C. Gompert, Gregory F. Treverton, and Brooke K. Stearns. 2008. "Breaking the Failed-State Cycle." Occasional Paper 204, RAND Corporation, Santa Monica, CA.

Haines, Andrew, Kirk R. Smith, Dennis Anderson, Paul R. Epstein, Anthony J. McMichael, Ian Roberts, Paul Wilkinson, James Woodcock, and Jeremy Woods. 2007. "Energy and Health 6: Policies for Accelerating Access to Clean Energy, Improving Health, Advancing Development, and Mitigating Climate Change." *Lancet* 370 (9592): 1264–81.

Hamm, Steve. 2008. "It's Too Darn Hot." *BusinessWeek*, March 20.

Hansen, Alvin H. 1939. "Economic Progress and Declining Population Growth." *American Economic Review* 29 (1): 1–15.

Hanushek, Eric A. 2006. "School Resources." In *Handbook of the Economics of Education*, ed. Eric A. Hanushek and Finis Welch, 865–908. Amsterdam: North-Holland.

Hanushek, Eric A., and Steven G. Rivkin. 2006. "Teacher Quality." In *Handbook of the Economics of Education*, ed. Eric A. Hanushek and Finis Welch, 1051–78. Amsterdam: North-Holland.

Hanushek, Eric A., and Ludger Woessmann. 2007. "The Role of Education Quality in Economic Growth." Policy Research Working Paper 4122. World Bank, Washington, DC.

Harberger, Arnold. 2003. "Sound Policies Can Free Up Natural Forces of Growth." *IMF Survey* 32 (13): 213–16.

Harrod, R. F. 1939. "An Essay in Dynamic Theory." *Economic Journal* 49 (193): 14–33.

Hausmann, Ricardo, Lant Pritchett, and Dani Rodrik. 2004. "Growth Accelerations." NBER Working Paper 10566, National Bureau of Economic Research, Cambridge, MA.

Hayami, Yujiro. 2003. "From the Washington Consensus to the Post-Washington Consensus: Retrospect and Prospect." *Asian Development Review* 20 (2): 40–65.

Heal, Geoffrey. 2008. "Climate Economics: A Meta-Review and Some Suggestions." NBER Working Paper 13927, National Bureau of Economic Research, Cambridge, MA.

Heckman, James J., and Paul A. LaFontaine. 2008. "The Declining American High School Graduation Rate: Evidence, Sources, and Consequences." *NBER Reporter* 1: 3–5.

Helpman, Elhanan. 2004. *The Mystery of Economic Growth.* Cambridge, MA: Harvard University Press.

"High Seas, High Prices." 2008. *Economist* 388 (8592): 64.

Hill, K., W. Selzer, J. Leaning, S. J. Malik, and S. S. Russell. 2008. "The Demographic Impact of Partition in the Punjab in 1947." *Population Studies* 62 (2): 155–70.

Hindo, Brian. 2008. "Monsanto on the Menu." *Business Week*, June 11.

Hironaka, Ann. 2005. *Neverending Wars.* Cambridge, MA: Harvard University Press.

Hirschman, Albert O. 1958. *The Strategy of Economic Development.* New Haven, CT: Yale University Press.

———. 1997. *The Passions and the Interests: Political Arguments for Capitalism before Its Triumph.* Princeton, NJ: Princeton University Press.

Hitchner, R. Bruce. 2008. "Globalization Avant la Lettre: Globalization and the History of the Roman Empire." *New Global Studies* 2 (2): article 2.

Hoeting, Jennifer A., David Madigan, Adrian E. Raftery, and Chris T. Volinsky. 1999. "Bayesian Model Averaging: A Tutorial." *Statistical Science* 14 (4): 382–417.

Hoff, Karla, Avishay Braverman, and Joseph E. Stiglitz, eds. 1993. *The Economics of Rural Organization: Theory, Practice, and Policy.* New York: Oxford University Press.

Holzmann, Robert, and Joseph E. Stiglitz, eds. 2001. *New Ideas about Old Age Security.* Washington, DC: World Bank.

Howells, Jeremy. 2006. "Intermediation and the Role of Intermediaries in Innovation." *Research Policy* 35 (5): 715–28.

Hoynes, Hilary, Marianne Page, and Ann Stevens. 2005. "Poverty in America: Trends and Explanations." NBER Working Paper 11681, National Bureau of Economic Research, Cambridge, MA.

Hsiao, Frank S., and Mei-Chu W. Hsiao. 2003. "'Miracle Growth' in the Twentieth Century—International Comparisons of East Asian Development." *World Development* 31 (2): 227–57.

Hudson, Valerie M., and Andrea M. den Boer. 2004. *Bare Branches: Security Implications of Asia's Surplus Male Population.* Cambridge, MA, and London: MIT Press.

Hummels, David. 2001. "Time as a Trade Barrier." Global Trade Analysis Project Working Paper 1152, Center for Global Trade Analysis, Department of Agricultural Economics, Purdue University, West Lafayette, IN.

Huntington, Samuel P. 1993. *The Third Wave: Democratization in the Late Twentieth Century.* Norman, OK: University of Oklahoma Press.

ILO (International Labour Office). 1976. *Employment, Growth, and Basic Needs: A One-World Problem.* Geneva: International Labour Office.

"India: Democracy Is Embedded, Despite Flawed Outcomes." 2008. *Oxford Analytica*, July 18.

"Indonesia: Power Problems Affect Economy, Politics." 2008. *Oxford Analytica*, July 15.

"Infectious Disease Threat Remains." 2006. *Oxford Analytica*, June 30.

"International: Asian Infrastructure Presents Challenges." 2008. *Oxford Analytica*, May 23.

IPCC (Intergovernmental Panel on Climate Change). 2007. *Fourth Assessment Report: Climate Change 2007*. Geneva: IPCC.

Iqbal, Kazi, and Anwar Shah. 2008. "How Do Worldwide Governance Indicators Measure Up?" World Bank, Washington, DC.

Ito, Takatoshi. 1995. "Comment on William Easterly, 'Explaining Miracles: Growth Regressions Meet the Gang of Four.'" In *Growth Theories in Light of the East Asian Experiences*, NBER East Asia Seminar on Economics, vol. 4, ed. Takatoshi Ito and Anne O. Krueger, 291–98. Chicago: University of Chicago Press.

———. 1998 "What Can Developing Countries Learn from East Asian Economic Growth?" In *Proceedings of the World Bank Annual Conference on Development Economics 1997*, vol. 1, ed. Boris Pleskovic and Joseph E. Stiglitz, 183–200. Washington, DC: World Bank.

———. 2000. "Perspectives on Asian Economic Growth: Neoclassical Growth vs. Flying Geese Growth." In *East Asian Economic Growth with Structural Change: Neoclassical Growth Theory vs. Flying Geese Pattern*, ed. Takatoshi Ito, Tesushi Sonobe, A. Shibata, and K. Fukao, 1–33. Tokyo: Economic Research Institute, Economic Planning Agency.

Ito, Takatoshi, and Anne O. Krueger, eds. 2004. *Governance, Regulation, and Privatization in the Asia-Pacific Region*. Chicago: University of Chicago Press.

Jacks, David S., and Krishna Pendakur. 2008. "Global Trade and the Maritime Transport Revolution." NBER Working Paper 14139, National Bureau of Economic Research, Cambridge, MA.

Jalilian, Hossein, Colin Kirkpatrick, and David Parker. 2007. "The Impact of Regulation on Economic Growth in Developing Countries: A Cross-Country Analysis." *World Development* 35 (1): 87–103.

Johnson, Simon, Kalpana Kochhar, Todd Mitton, and Natalia Tamirisa. 2006. "Malaysian Capital Controls: Macroeconomics and Institutions." IMF Working Paper 51, International Monetary Fund, Washington, DC.

Johnson, Simon, and Todd Mitton. 2001. "Cronyism and Capital Controls: Evidence from Malaysia." NBER Working Paper 8521, National Bureau of Economic Research, Cambridge, MA.

Jones, Benjamin F., and Benjamin A. Olken. 2005. "The Anatomy of Start-Stop Growth." NBER Working Paper 11528, National Bureau of Economic Research, Cambridge, MA.

Jones, Charles I. 2007. "The Weak Link Theory of Economic Development." HKIMR Working Paper 4/2007, Hong Kong Institute for Monetary Research, Hong Kong, China.

————. 2008. "Intermediate Goods, Weak Links, and Superstars: A Theory of Economic Development." NBER Working Paper 13834, National Bureau of Economic Research, Cambridge, MA.

Judt, Tony. 1996. *A Grand Illusion?* New York: Hill & Wang.

Kagan, Robert. 2008. *The Return of History and the End of Dreams.* New York: Alfred A. Knopf.

Kahneman, Daniel, Paul Slovic, and Amos Tversky, eds. 1982. *Judgment under Uncertainty: Heuristics and Biases.* New York: Cambridge University Press.

Kanbur, Ravi. 2000. "Income Distribution and Development." In *Handbook of Income Distribution,* ed. Anthony B. Atkinson and François Bourguignon, 791–841. Amsterdam: Elsevier.

————. 2005. "The Development of Development Thinking." Cornell University, Ithaca, NY.

Kanbur, Ravi, and David Vines. 2000. "The World Bank and Poverty Reduction: Past, Present, and Future." In *The World Bank: Structure and Policies,* ed. Christopher L. Gilbert and David Vines, 87–107. Cambridge, U.K.: Cambridge University Press.

Kapur, Devesh, John P. Lewis, and Richard Webb. 1997. *The World Bank: Its First Half Century.* Washington, DC: Brookings Institution Press.

Kareiva, Peter, Sean Watts, Robert McDonald, and Tim Boucher. 2007. "Domesticated Nature: Shaping Landscapes and Ecosystems for Human Welfare." *Science* 316 (5833): 1866–69.

Kaufmann, Daniel, and Aart Kraay. 2008. "Governance Indicators: Where Are We, Where Should We Be Going?" *World Bank Research Observer* 23 (1): 1–30.

Kay, John. 2002. "The Balance Sheet." *Prospect Magazine* 76 (July): 22–28.

Kendrick, David Andrew. 1981. *Stochastic Control for Economic Models.* New York: McGraw Hill.

————. 2003. "Themes from GAMS in Computational Economics." Paper presented at the GAMS Workshop on Optimization, Modeling, and Applications, Washington, DC, September 19.

Kendrick, David Andrew, and Ardy Stoutjesdijk. 1978. *The Planning of Industrial Programs: A Methodology.* Baltimore, MD: Johns Hopkins University Press.

Khan, Mohsin S., and Abdelhak S. Senhadji. 2001. "Threshold Effects in the Relationship between Inflation and Growth." *IMF Staff Papers* 48 (1): 1–21.

Kintisch, Eli. 2008. "Roads, Ports, Rails Aren't Ready for Changing Climate, Says Report." *Science* 319 (5871): 1744–45.

Klein, Michael W. 2003. "Capital Account Openness and the Varieties of Growth Experience." NBER Working Paper 9500, National Bureau of Economic Research, Cambridge, MA.

Klinenberg, Eric. 2003. *Heat Wave: A Social Autopsy of Disaster in Chicago.* Chicago: University of Chicago Press.

Kneller, Richard, C. W. Morgan, and Sunti Kanchanahatakij. 2008. "Trade Liberalisation and Economic Growth." *World Economy* 31 (6): 701–19.

Kohli, Atul. 2004. *State-Directed Development.* Cambridge, U.K.: Cambridge University Press.

Köthenbürger, Marko, Hans-Werner Sinn, and John Whalley, eds. 2006. *Privatization Experiences in the European Union.* Cambridge, MA: MIT Press.

Kozul-Wright, Richard, and Paul Rayment. 2008. *The Resistible Rise of Market Fundamentalism: Rethinking Development Policy in an Unbalanced World.* London: Zed Books and Third World Network.

Kremer, Michael. 1993. "O-Ring Theory of Economic Development." *Quarterly Journal of Economics* 108 (3): 551–75.

Krueger, Anne O. 1993. "Virtuous and Vicious Circles in Economic Development." *American Economic Review* 83 (2): 351–55.

Krugman, Paul. 1994. "The Myth of Asia's Miracle." *Foreign Affairs* 73 (6): 62–78.

Kuijs, Louis. 2006. "How Will China's Saving-Investment Balance Evolve?" Policy Research Working Paper 3958, World Bank, Washington, DC.

Kuziemko, Ilyana, and Eric Werker. 2006. "How Much Is a Seat on the Security Council Worth? Foreign Aid and Bribery at the United Nations." *Journal of Political Economy* 114 (5): 905–30.

Kuznets, Simon. 1966. *Modern Economic Growth: Rate, Structure, and Spread.* New Haven, CT: Yale University Press.

Landes, David S. 1999. *The Wealth and Poverty of Nations: Why Some Are So Rich and Some So Poor.* New York: W. W. Norton.

Lange, Fabian, and Robert H. Topel. 2006. "The Social Value of Education and Human Capital." In *Handbook of the Economics of Education*, ed. Eric A. Hanushek and Finis Welch, 459–509. Amsterdam: North-Holland.

La Porta, Rafael, Florencio López-de-Silanes, and Andrei Schleifer. 2007. "The Economic Consequences of Legal Origins." NBER Working Paper 13608, National Bureau of Economic Research, Cambridge, MA.

Leibenstein, Harvey. 1957. *Economic Backwardness and Economic Growth.* New York and London: John Wiley and Chapman & Hall.

Levine, Ross. 2004. "Finance and Growth: Theory and Evidence." NBER Working Paper 10766, National Bureau of Economic Research, Cambridge, MA.

Levine, Ross, and David Renelt. 1992. "A Sensitivity Analysis of Cross-Country Growth Regressions." *American Economic Review* 82 (4): 942–63.

Lewis, W. Arthur. 2003. *The Principles of Economic Planning.* New York: Routledge.

Lin, Justin Y. 1992. "Rural Reforms and Agricultural Growth in China." *American Economic Review* 82 (1): 34–51.

Lindauer, David, and Lant Pritchett. 2002. "What's the Big Idea? The Third Generation of Policies for Economic Growth." *Economía* 3 (1): 1–39.

Lipsey, Richard G., and Kenneth I. Carlaw. 2004. "Total Factor Productivity and the Measurement of Technological Change." *Canadian Journal of Economics* 37 (4): 1118–50.

Little, Ian, Tibor Scitovsky, and Maurice Scott. 1970. *Industry and Trade in Some Developing Countries.* London and New York: Oxford University Press.

López, Ricardo A. 2005. "Trade and Growth: Reconciling the Macroeconomic and Microeconomic Evidence." *Journal of Economic Surveys* 19 (4): 623–48.

Low, Donald A. 1993. *Eclipse of Empire.* Cambridge, U.K.: Cambridge University Press.

Lucas, Robert. 1988. "On the Mechanics of Economic Development." *Journal of Monetary Economics* 22 (1): 3–42.

Lucas Jr., Robert E. 2003. Comment on "British Imperialism Revisited: The Costs and Benefits of 'Anglobalization,'" by Niall Ferguson. http://home.uchicago.edu/~sogrodow/homepage/Niall_Ferguson.pdf.

———. 2004. *The Industrial Revolution: Past and Future.* 2003 Annual Report Essay. Minneapolis: Federal Reserve Bank of Minneapolis.

Lutz, Wolfgang, Jesús Crespo Cuaresma, and Warren Sanderson. 2008. "The Demography of Educational Attainment and Economic Growth." *Science* 319 (5866): 1047–48.

MacKenzie, Debora. 2008a. "Are We Doomed?" *New Scientist* 197 (2650): 32.

———. 2008b. "The End of Civilisation." *New Scientist* 197 (2650): 28.

Maddison, Angus. 2007. "Statistics on World Population, GDP, and Per Capita GDP, 1–2003 AD." http://www.ggdc.net/maddison.

Mahbubani, Kishore. 2008. *The New Asian Hemisphere: The Irresistible Shift of Global Power to the East.* New York: Public Affairs.

Mangum, Garth L., Stephen L. Mangum, and Andrew M. Sum. 2003. *The Persistence of Poverty in the United States.* Baltimore, MD: Johns Hopkins Press.

Mankiw, N. Gregory, David Romer, and David N. Weil. 1992. "A Contribution to the Empirics of Economic Growth." *Quarterly Journal of Economics* 107 (2): 407–37.

Mansuri, Ghazala, and Vijayendra Rao. 2004. "Community-Based and -Driven Development: A Critical Review." *World Bank Research Observer* 19 (1): 1–39.

Marcus, Edward. 2002. "The History of the World Bank." *Economic Journal* 112 (17): F119–35.

Marglin, Stephen A. 1992. "Lessons of the Golden Age: An Overview." In *The Golden Age of Capitalism: Reinterpreting the Postwar Experience*, ed. Stephen A. Marglin and Juliet B. Schor, 1–38. Oxford, U.K.: Clarendon Press.

Mathews, John A. 2005. "The Intellectual Roots of Latecomer Industrial Development." *International Journal of Technology and Globalization* 1 (3–4): 433–50.

Mayda, Anna Maria, and Dani Rodrik. 2001. "Why Are Some People (and Countries) More Protectionist Than Others?" NBER Working Paper 8461, National Bureau of Economic Research, Cambridge, MA.

Mckenna, Phil. 2006. "The Waste at the Heart of the Web." *New Scientist* 192 (2582): 24–34.

McNamara, Robert S. 1973. "Address to the Board of Governors." Speech presented at the Annual Meeting of the World Bank, Nairobi, Kenya, September 24. Report 42031, World Bank, Washington, DC.

Meadows, Donella H, Dennis L. Meadows, and Jorgen Randers. 1993. *Beyond the Limits: Confronting Global Collapse, Envisioning a Sustainable Future.* White River Junction, Vermont: Chelsea Green Publishing.

Meadows, Donella H., Dennis L. Meadows, Jorgen Randers, and William W. Behrens III. 1972. *The Limits to Growth.* New York: Universe Books.

Meadows, Donella H., Jorgen Randers, and Dennis L. Meadows. 2004. *Limits to Growth: The 30-Year Update.* White River Junction, Vermont: Chelsea Green Publishing.

Meier, Gerald M. 2005. *Biography of a Subject: An Evolution of Development Economics.* New York: Oxford University Press.

Michaely, Michael, Demetris Papageorgiou, and Armeane M. Choksi. 1991. *Liberalizing Foreign Trade: Lessons of Experience in the Developing World.* Oxford, U.K.: Blackwell.

Ming, Ruan. 1994. *Deng Xiaoping: Chronicle of an Empire.* Boulder, CO: Westview Press.

Mitchener, Kris James, and Marc Weidenmier. 2008. "Trade and Empire." NBER Working Paper 13765, National Bureau of Economic Research, Cambridge, MA.

Mlodinow, Leonard. 2008. *The Drunkard's Walk: The Story of Randomness and Its Role in Our Lives.* New York: Pantheon Books.

Montgomery, Mark R. 2008. "The Urban Transformation of the Developing World." *Science* 319 (5864): 761–64.

Mookherjee, Dilip. 2005. "Is There Too Little Theory in Development Economics?" *Economic and Political Weekly* 40 (40): 4328–32.

Morris, Charles R. 2008. *The Trillion Dollar Meltdown.* New York: Public Affairs.

Moss, Todd, Gunilla Pettersson, and Nicolas van de Walle. 2008. "An Aid-Institutions Paradox? A Review Essay on Aid Dependency and State Building in Sub-Saharan Africa." In *Reinventing Foreign Aid*, ed. William Easterly, 255–82. Cambridge, MA: MIT.

Mullainathan, Sendhil. 2005. "Development Economics through the Lens of Psychology." In *Annual Bank Conference on Development Economics 2005: Lessons of Experience*, ed. François Bourguignon and Boris Pleskovic, 45–70. Washington, DC: World Bank.

Murphy, Kevin M., Andrei Schleifer, and Robert W. Vishny. 1989. "Increasing Returns, Durables, and Economic Fluctuations." NBER Working Paper 3014, National Bureau of Economic Research, Cambridge, MA.

Myrdal, Gunnar. 1968. *Asian Drama: An Inquiry into the Poverty of Nations.* New York: Twentieth Century Fund.

Narayan, Deepa, Robert Chambers, Meera Kaul Shah, and Patti Petesch. 2000. *Voices of the Poor: Crying Out for Change.* New York: Oxford University Press.

Narayan, Deepa, with Raj Patel, Kai Schafft, Anne Rademacher, and Sarah Koch-Schulte. 1999. *Voices of the Poor: Can Anyone Hear Us?* New York: Oxford University Press.

Narayan, Deepa, and Patti Petesch. 2002. *Voices of the Poor: From Many Lands.* New York: Oxford University Press.

Nelson, Richard R. 1956. "A Theory of the Low-Level Equilibrium Trap in Underdeveloped Economies." *American Economic Review* 46 (5): 894–908.

"The Next Green Revolution." 2008. *Economist* 386 (8568): 67.

Nicholas, Howard. 2005. "Introduction: Putting Industrialization Back into Development." *Development and Change* 36 (6): 1031–33.

Nicita, Alessandro. 2008. "Avian Influenza and the Poultry Trade." Policy Research Working Paper 4551, World Bank, Washington, DC.

Nordhaus, William D. 2008. "Baumol's Diseases: A Macroeconomic Perspective." *B. E. Journal of Macroeconomics* 8 (1): 1–37.

North, Douglass C., and Robert Paul Thomas. 1976. *The Rise of the Western World: A New Economic History.* New York: Cambridge University Press.

Nozick, Robert. 1974. *Anarchy, State, and Utopia.* New York: Basic Books.

Nunn, Nathan. 2008. "The Long-Term Effects of Africa's Slave Trades." *Quarterly Journal of Economics* 123 (1): 139–76.

Nurkse, Ragner. 1959. "Notes on 'Unbalanced Growth.'" *Oxford Economic Papers* 11 (3): 295–97.

Olson, Mancur. 2000. *Power and Prosperity: Outgrowing Communist and Capitalist Dictatorships.* Oxford, U.K.: Oxford University Press.

Orlove, Ben, Ellen Wiegandt, and Brian Luckman, eds. 2008. *Darkening Peaks: Glacier Retreat, Science, and Society.* Berkeley, CA: University of California Press.

Orszag, Peter, and Joseph E. Stiglitz. 2001. "Rethinking Pension Reform: Ten Myths about Social Security Systems." In *New Ideas about Old Age Security,* ed. Robert Holzmann and Joseph E. Stiglitz, 17–56. Washington, DC: World Bank.

O'Rourke, Kevin H., and Jeffrey G. Williamson. 2001. *Globalization and History.* Cambridge, MA: MIT Press.

Osterhammel, Jürgen, and Niels P. Petersson. 2005. *Globalization: A Short History.* Princeton, NJ: Princeton University Press.

Paarlberg, Robert. 2008. *Starved for Science*. Cambridge, MA: Harvard University Press.

Paldam, Martin, and Erich Gundlach. 2008. "Two Views on Institutions and Development: The Grand Transition vs. the Primacy of Institutions." *Kyklos* 61 (1): 65–100.

Pardey, Philip G., Vincent H. Smith, eds. 2004. *What's Economics Worth? Valuing Policy Research*. Baltimore: Johns Hopkins University Press.

Pearce, Fred. 2006. "Earth: The Parched Planet." *New Scientist*, February 25, 32–36.

Phelps, Edmund S. 1966. *Golden Rules of Economic Growth*. New York: W. W. Norton.

Phillips, Fred. 2008. "Change in Socio-technical Systems: Researching the Multis, the Biggers, and the More Connecteds." *Technological Forecasting and Social Change* 75 (5): 721–34.

Portugal-Pérez, Alberto, and John S. Wilson. 2008. "Trade Costs in Africa: Barriers and Opportunities for Reform." Policy Research Working Paper 4619, World Bank, Washington, DC.

Posner, Richard A. 2007. "Thinking about Catastrophe." In *Blindside: How to Anticipate Forcing Events and Wild Cards in Global Politics*, ed. Francis Fukuyama. Washington, DC: American Interest and Brookings Institution Press.

Prasad, Eswar S., and Raghuram G. Rajan. 2007. "Practical Approaches to Capital Account Liberalization." Working paper, University of Chicago, Chicago.

Prasad, Eswar S., Raghuram G. Rajan, and Arvind Subramanian. 2007. "Foreign Capital and Economic Growth." *Brookings Papers on Economic Activity* 38 (1): 153–230.

Prasad, Eswar, Kenneth Rogoff, Shang-Jin Wei, and M. Ayhan Kose. 2003. "Effects of Financial Globalization on Developing Countries: Some Empirical Evidence." IMF Occasional Paper 220. International Monetary Fund, Washington, DC.

Prebisch, Raul. 1962. "The Economic Development of Latin America and Its Principle Problems." *Economic Bulletin for Latin America* 7 (1): 1–22.

Preston, Samuel H., Ronald Lee, and G. Greene. 1986. *Population Growth and Economic Development: Policy Questions*. Washington, DC: National Academy of Sciences.

Pritchett, Lant. 2001. "Where Has All the Education Gone?" *World Bank Economic Review* 15 (3): 367–91.

———. 2006. "Does Learning to Add Up Add Up? The Returns to Schooling in Aggregate Data." In *Handbook of the Economics of Education*, ed. Eric A. Hanushek and Finis Welch, 635–95. Amsterdam: North-Holland.

Psacharopoulos, George. 2006. "The Value of Investment in Education: Theory, Evidence, and Policy." *Journal of Education Finance* 32 (2): 113–36.

Psacharopoulos, George, and Harry Patrinos. 2002. "Returns to Investment in Education: A Further Update." Policy Research Working Paper 2881, World Bank, Washington, DC.

Putnam, Robert D. 2000. *Bowling Alone: The Collapse and Revival of American Community*. New York: Simon & Schuster.

———. 2007. "*E Pluribus Unum*: Diversity and Community in the Twenty-First Century—The 2006 Johan Skytte Prize Lecture." *Scandinavian Political Studies* 30 (2): 137–74.

Quah, Danny T. 1999. "The Weightless Economy in Growth." *Business Economist* 30 (1): 40–53.

Quibria, M. G. 2006. "Does Governance Matter? Yes, No, or Maybe: Some Evidence from Developing Asia." *Kyklos* 59 (1): 99–114.

Ranis, Gustav. 2004a. "Arthur Lewis' Contribution to Development Thinking and Policy." Discussion Paper 891, Economic Growth Center, Yale University, New Haven, CT.

———. 2004b. "The Evolution of Development Thinking: Theory and Policy." Paper prepared for the Annual World Bank Conference on Development Economics, Washington, DC, May 3–4. World Bank, Washington, DC.

Ravallion, Martin. 2001. "Growth, Inequality, and Poverty: Looking Beyond the Averages." *World Development* 29 (11): 1803–15.

———. 2004. "Defining Pro-Poor Growth: A Response to Kakwani." *One Pager* November 2004 (4): 1.

———. 2008. "Should the Randomistas Rule?" World Bank, Washington, DC.

Ravallion, Martin, and Shaohua Chen. 2007. "China's (Uneven) Progress against Poverty." *Journal of Development Economics* 82 (1): 1–42.

Ravallion, Martin, and Gaurav Dutt. 2002. "Why Has Economic Growth Been More Pro-Poor in Some States of India Than Others?" *Journal of Development Economics* 68 (2): 381–400.

Reinhart, Carmen M., and Kenneth Rogoff. 2008. "The Time Is Different: A Panoramic View of Eight Centuries of Financial Crises." NBER Working Paper 13882, National Bureau of Economic Research, Cambridge, MA.

Ritzer, George. 2007. *The Blackwell Companion to Globalization*. Malden, MA: Blackwell Publishing.

Robinson, James A., and Ragnar Torvik. 2002. "White Elephants." CEPR Discussion Paper 3459, Centre for Economic Policy Research, London.

Rodrik, Dani. 2004. "Industrial Policy for the Twenty-First Century." CEPR Discussion Paper 4767, Centre for Economic Policy Research, London.

———. 2006. "Goodbye Washington Consensus, Hello Washington Confusion? A Review of the World Bank's Economic Growth in the 1990s: Learning from a Decade of Reform." *Journal of Economic Literature* 44 (4): 973–87.

———. 2007. *One Economics, Many Recipes*. Princeton, NJ: Princeton University Press.

———. 2008. "Second-Best Institutions." CEPR Discussion Paper 6764, Centre for Economic Policy Research, London.

Rogers, Peter. 2008. "Facing the Freshwater Crisis." *Scientific American* 299 (2): 46–53.

Romer, Paul M. 1989. "Human Capital and Growth: Theory and Evidence." NBER Working Paper 3173, National Bureau of Economic Research, Cambridge, MA.

———. 1993. "Ideas Gaps and Object Gaps in Economic Development." *Journal of Monetary Economics* 32 (3): 543–73.

———. 2000. "Should the Government Subsidize Supply or Demand in the Market for Scientist and Engineers?" NBER Working Paper 7723, National Bureau of Economic Research, Cambridge, MA.

Roodman, David. 2007. "The Anarchy of Numbers: Aid, Development, and Cross-Country Empirics." *World Bank Economic Review* 21 (2): 255–77.

Root, Hilton L. 2008. *Alliance Curse*. Washington, DC: Brookings Institution.

Rose, John. 2008. "Britain Needs an Industrial Route Map." *Financial Times*, April 22.

Rosenberg, Nathan, and L. E. Birdzell. 1986. *How the West Grew Rich: The Economic Transformation of the Industrial World*. New York: Basic Books.

Rosenfield, Allan, and Karyn Schwartz. 2005. "Population and Development-Shifting Paradigms, Setting Goals." *New England Journal of Medicine* 352 (7): 647–49.

Rosenstein-Rodan, P. N. 1943. "Problems of Industrialisation of Eastern and South-Eastern Europe." *Economic Journal* 53 (210–11): 202–11.

Rosenzweig, Philip. 2007. *The Halo Effect...and the Eight Other Business Delusions That Deceive Managers*. New York: Free Press.

Rousseau, Peter L. 2002. "Historical Perspectives on Financial Development and Economic Growth." NBER Working Paper 9333, National Bureau of Economic Research, Cambridge, MA.

Rozelle, Scott, and Johan F. M. Swinnen. 2007. "Why Did the Communist Party Reform in China, but Not in the Soviet Union? The Political Economy of Agricultural Transition." University of California–Davis, Stanford University, World Bank, and University of Leuven, Washington, DC.

Rozenzweig, Mark. 1988. "Labor Markets in Low Income Countries." In *Handbook of Development Economics*, ed. Hollis Chenery and T. N. Srinivasan, 713–62. Amsterdam: Elsevier.

Rubio, María del Mar. 2006. "Protectionist but Globalised? Latin American Custom Duties and Trade during the Pre-1914 Belle Époque." Economics Working Paper 967, Department of Economics and Business, Universitat Pompeu Fabra, Barcelona.

"Running Dry." 2008. *Economist*. http://www.economist.com/business/display story.cfm?story_id=11966993.

Sachs, Jeffrey D. 2003. "Institutions Don't Rule: Direct Effects of Geography on Per Capita Income." NBER Working Paper 9490, National Bureau of Economic Research, Cambridge, MA.

———. 2005. *The End of Poverty: Economic Possibilities for Our Time*. New York: Penguin Press.

———. 2008. *Common Wealth: Economics for a Crowded Planet*. New York: Penguin Press.

Sala-i-Martin, Xavier. 1997. "I Just Ran Two Million Regressions." *American Economic Review* 87 (2): 178–83.

———. 2002. "15 Years of New Growth Economics: What Have We Learnt?" Discussion Paper 0102-47, Department of Economics, Columbia University, New York.

Sala-i-Martin, Xavier, Gernot Doppelhofer, and Ronald I. Miller. 2004. "Determinants of Long-Term Growth: A Bayesian Averaging of Classical Estimates (BACE) Approach." *American Economic Review* 94 (4): 813–35.

Schroeder, Susan K. 2008. "The Underpinnings of Country Risk Assessment." *Journal of Economic Surveys* 22 (3): 498–535.

"Science/Technology: Construction Allows Energy Saving." 2008. *Oxford Analytica*, July 11.

"Science/Technology: How Likely Is Internet Collapse?" 2008. *Oxford Analytica*, May 15.

Sen, Amartya. 1979. "Equality of What?" Speech presented at the Tanner Lecture on Human Values, Stanford University, Stanford, CA, May 22.

Shaikh, Nermeen. 2007. *The Present as History: Critical Perspectives on Global Power*. New York: Columbia University Press.

Sheffi, Yossi. 2005. *The Resilient Enterprise: Overcoming Vulnerability for Competitive Advantage*. Cambridge, MA: MIT Press.

Shihata, Ibrahim F. I., Franziska Tschofen, and Antonio R. Parra. 1991. *The World Bank in a Changing World: Selected Essays*. Dordrecht, Netherlands: Kluwer.

Shiller, Robert J. 2005. *Irrational Exuberance*. 2nd ed. Princeton, NJ: Princeton University Press.

Singer, H. W. 1950. "The Distribution of Gains between Investing and Borrowing Countries." *American Economic Review* 40 (2): 473–85.

Smil, Vaclav. 2005. "The Next 50 Years: Fatal Discontinuities." *Population and Development Review* 31 (2): 201–36.

———. 2008a. *Energy in Nature and Society: General Energetics of Complex Systems*. Cambridge, MA, and London: MIT Press.

———. 2008b. *Global Catastrophes and Trends: The Next Fifty Years*. Cambridge, MA: MIT Press.

———. 2008c. "Water News: Bad, Good, and Virtual." *American Scientist* 96 (5): 399–407.

Smith, Donald E. 1959. *Nehru and Democracy*. New York: Longmans, Green & Co.

Solow, Robert M. 1956. "A Contribution to the Theory of Economic Growth." *Quarterly Journal of Economics* 70 (1): 65–94.

———. 2007. "The Last 50 Years in Growth Theory and the Next 10." *Oxford Review of Economic Policy* 23 (1): 3–14.

Son, Hyun H., and Nanak Kakwani. 2008. "Global Estimates of Pro-poor Growth." *World Development* 36 (6): 1048–66.

"Special Report: Privatisation in Europe." 2002. *Economist* 363 (8279): 71–74.

Spence Commission (World Bank Commission on Growth and Development). 2008. *The Growth Report: Strategies for Sustained Growth and Inclusive Development*. Washington, DC: World Bank.

Stein, Herbert. 1969. *The Fiscal Revolution in America*. Chicago, IL: University of Chicago Press.

Stern, Nicholas. 2007. *The Economics of Climate Change: The Stern Review*. Cambridge, U.K.: Cambridge University Press.

Stern, Nicholas, and Francisco Ferreira. 1997. "The World Bank as 'Intellectual Actor.'" In *The World Bank: Its First Half Century*, ed. Kapur Devesh, John P. Lewis, and Richard Webb, 523–609. Washington, DC: Brookings Institution Press.

Stiglitz, Joseph E. 1986. *Economics of the Public Sector*. New York: W.W. Norton.

———. 1990. "Peer Monitoring and Credit Markets." *World Bank Economic Review* 4 (3): 351–66.

———. 1991. "The Invisible Hand and Modern Welfare Economics." In *Information Strategy and Public Policy*, ed. David Vines and Andrew Stevenson, 12–50. Oxford, U.K.: Basil Blackwell.

———. 1997a. "The Role of Government in Economic Development (Keynote Address)." In *Annual World Bank Conference on Development Economics 1996*, ed. Michael Bruno and Boris Pleskovic, 11–23. Washington, DC: World Bank.

———. 1997b. "The Role of Government in the Economies of Developing Countries." In *Development Strategy and Management of the Market Economy*, ed. Edmond Malinvaud and Amartya K. Sen, 61–109. Oxford, U.K.: Clarendon Press.

———. 1998a. "An Agenda for Development in the Twenty-First Century." In *Annual World Bank Conference on Development Economics 1997*, ed. Joseph E. Stiglitz and Boris Pleskovic, 17–31. Washington, DC: World Bank.

———. 1998b. "Towards a New Paradigm for Development: Strategies, Policies, and Processes." Ninth Raul Prebisch Lecture, United Nations Conference on

Trade and Development, delivered at the Palais des Nations, Geneva, October 19. (Published in *The Rebel Within*, ed. Ha-Joon Chang, 57–93. London: Wimbledon, 2001.)

———. 1999. "Knowledge for Development: Economic Science, Economic Policy, and Economic Advice." In *Annual World Bank Conference on Development Economics 1998*, ed. Boris Pleskovic and Joseph E. Stiglitz, 9–58. Washington, DC: World Bank.

———. 2000. "Introduction." In *The World Bank: Structure and Policies*, ed. Christopher L. Gilbert and David Vines, 1–9. Cambridge, U.K.: Cambridge University Press.

———. 2003a. "Banks versus Markets as Mechanisms for Allocating and Coordinating Investment." In *The Economics of Cooperation: East Asian Development and the Case for Pro-Market Intervention*, ed. James A. Roumasset and Susan Barr, 15–38. Boulder, CO: Westview Press. (Presented at Investment Coordination in the Pacific Century: Lessons from Theory and Practice Conference, given at the University of Hawaii, January 1990.)

———. 2003b. *Roaring Nineties*. New York: W. W. Norton.

———. 2004a. "Capital-Market Liberalization, Globalization, and the IMF." *Oxford Review of Economic Policy* 20 (1): 57–71.

———. 2004b. "Towards a Pro-development and Balanced Intellectual Property Regime." Keynote address at the World Intellectual Property Organization meeting, Seoul, Republic of Korea, October 25.

———. 2006. *Making Globalization Work*. New York: W. W. Norton.

———. 2007. "The Economic Foundations of Intellectual Property." Sixth Annual Frey Lecture in Intellectual Property, Duke University, Durham, NC, February 16. (Published in *Duke Law Journal* 57 (6) (2008): 1693–724.)

Stiglitz, Joseph E., William Easterly, and Roumeen Islam. 2001. "Shaken and Stirred: Volatility and Macroeconomic Paradigms for Rich and Poor Countries." In *Advances in Macroeconomic Theory*, IEA Conference Volume 133, ed. Jacques Drèze, 353–72. Houndsmill, U.K.: Palgrave. (Speech given for Michael Bruno Memorial Lecture, 12th World Congress of IEA, Buenos Aires, August 27, 1999.)

Stiglitz, Joseph E., and José Antonio Ocampo, eds. 2008. *Capital Market Liberalization: Risks without Rewards?* New York: Oxford University Press.

Stiglitz, Joseph E., José Antonio Ocampo, Shari Spiegel, Richard Ffrench-Davis, and Deepak. Nayyar. 2006. *Stability with Growth: Macroeconomics, Liberalization, and Development*. Oxford, U.K.: Oxford University Press.

Stiglitz, Joseph E., with Patrick Rey. 1993 [rev. 1996]. "Moral Hazard and Unemployment in Competitive Equilibrium." Université de Toulouse, Toulouse, France.

Streeten, Paul, Shahid Javed Burki, Mahbub ul Haq, Norman Hicks, and Frances Stewart. 1982. *First Things First: Meeting Basic Human Needs in the*

Developing Countries. New York and Washington, DC: Oxford University Press and World Bank.

Summers, Lawrence H., and Richard J. Zeckhauser. 2008. "Policymaking for Posterity." NBER Working Paper 14359, National Bureau of Economic Research, Cambridge, MA.

Sutton, John. 2000. "Rich Trades, Scarce Capabilities: Industrial Development Revisited." Paper presented at the British Academy Keynes Lecture, London School of Economics, October 26, London.

Tabellini, Guido. 2004. "The Role of the State in Economic Development." IGI-ER Working Paper 265, Innocenzo Gasparini Institute for Economic Research, Bocconi University, Milan.

Temple, Jonathan. 2000. "Inflation and Growth: Stories Short and Tall." *Journal of Economic Surveys* 14 (4): 395–426.

Tignor, Robert L. 2006. *W. Arthur Lewis and the Birth of Development Economics.* Princeton, NJ: Princeton University Press.

Topel, Robert H. 1999. "Labor Markets and Economic Growth." In *Handbook of Labor Economics,* ed. Orley C. Ashenfelter and David Card, 2943–84. Amsterdam: Elsevier.

UNDP (United Nations Development Programme). 1990. *Human Development Report 1990.* New York: Oxford University Press.

———. 2007. *Human Development Report 2007/2008.* New York: Oxford University Press.

Van Ark, Bart, Mary O'Mahony, and Marcel P. Timmer. 2008. "The Productivity Gap between Europe and the United States: Trends and Causes." *Journal of Economic Perspectives* 22 (1): 25–44.

Warsh, David. 2006. *Knowledge and the Wealth of Nations.* New York: W. W. Norton.

Wilkinson, Paul, Kirk R. Smith, Sean Beevers, Cathryn Tonne, and Tadj Oreszczyn. 2007. "Energy and Health 4: Energy, Energy Efficiency, and the Built Environment." *Lancet* 370 (9592): 1175–87.

Wilkinson, Paul, Kirk R. Smith, Michael Joffe, and Andrew Haines. 2007. "Energy and Health 1: A Global Perspective on Energy: Health Effects and Injuries." *Lancet* 370 (9592): 965–78.

Williamson, Jeffrey G. 2008. "Globalization and the Great Divergence: Terms of Trade Booms and Volatility in the Poor Periphery, 1782–1913." NBER Working Paper 13841, National Bureau of Economic Research, Cambridge, MA.

Williamson, John. 2003. "From Reform Agenda to Damaged Brand Name." *Finance and Development* 40 (3): 10–13.

Winters, L. Alan. 2004. "Trade Liberalisation and Economic Performance: An Overview." *Economic Journal* 114 (493): F4–21.

Wolpert, Stanley. 2006. *Shameful Flight.* Oxford, U.K.: Oxford University Press.

Woodcock, James, David Banister, Phil Edwards, Andrew M. Prentice, and Ian Roberts. 2007. "Energy and Health 3: Energy and Transport." *Lancet* 370 (9592): 1078–88.

World Bank. 1978. *World Development Report 1978*. Washington, DC: World Bank.

———. 1984. *World Development Report 1984*. New York: Oxford University Press.

———. 1992. *Governance and Development*. Washington, DC: World Bank.

———. 1993. *The East Asian Miracle: Economic Growth and Public Policy*. World Bank Policy Research Report. New York: Oxford University Press.

———. 1993. *World Development Report 1993: Investing in Health*. New York: Oxford University Press.

———. 1997. *Helping Countries Combat Corruption: The Role of the World Bank*. Washington, DC: World Bank.

———. 2005. *World Development Report 2006: Equity and Development*. New York: Oxford University Press.

———. 2006. *World Development Report 2007: Development and the Next Generation*. New York: Oxford University Press.

———. 2007. *World Development Report 2008: Agriculture for Development*. New York: Oxford University Press.

———. 2008a. *Public Sector Reform: What Works and Why?* Washington, DC: World Bank.

———. 2008b. *Unleashing Prosperity: Productivity Growth in Eastern Europe and the Former Soviet Union*. Washington, DC: World Bank.

Yusuf, Shahid. 2008. "Intermediating Knowledge Exchange between Universities and Businesses." *Research Policy* 37 (8): 1167–74.

Yusuf, Shahid, Kaoru Nabeshima, and Dwight H. Perkins. 2005. *Under New Ownership: Privatizing China's State-Owned Enterprises*. Stanford, CA: Stanford University Press.

Zakaria, Fareed. 2008. "The Future of American Power: How America Can Survive the Rise of the Rest." *Foreign Affairs* 87 (3): 18–43.

Zysman, John, and Eileen Doherty. 1995. "The Evolving Role of the State in Asian Industrialization." BRIE Working Paper 84, Berkeley Roundtable on the International Economy, Berkeley, CA.

INDEX

A

adjustments, 27, 28–29, 71. *See also* structural adjustments
Africa, lack of understanding for poor growth in, 52
African decolonization, 4n
agricultural innovation system, 43
agricultural technology, 97n
agriculture, 19, 44, 46–47
   exports to cut financing gap, 30–31
   productivity, 21–22, 42
aid effectiveness, 79, 81–83, 82n, 84
antibiotics, 101n

B

banking crises and capital mobility, 70n
basic needs approach, 22, 22n
Big Push, 8, 8n, 83
Brazil, 58n
British economy, historical, 56n
British Empire, dismantling of, 4n
business barriers, 61–62

C

capital, 9, 53, 54
   as growth determinant, 7
   banking crises impact, 70n
   dismantling of controls, 70
capital investment rate, reaching minimum, 85
capital transfer, 83
capitalism, validation of, 32
child health, 78n
China, 7n, 59, 59n
cities, 98–99, 100n
climate change, 43, 95–98, 100n
   impacts on urban environment, 98–100
coaxed, 57n
commodity price increase, 97n
communist regimes, 3
community involvement, 42, 42n, 77
competition, 38, 40
conditional cash transfer programs, 77, 77n
construction, green, 99
corruption, 40n, 58n, 82n
country comparison, 41n

D

data collection, for measuring poverty, 75
debt relief, 82, 82n
decolonization, 4–6, 4n
democracy impacts on growth, 55n
denationalization, 72
development, 35, 69
   and politics, 102–104

environmental spillovers, 41–44
frustration with progress, 24n
internal and external financing, 31
knowledge-based, 64–65
poverty objective, 20–21
pro-poor approach, 52, 76
state-directed to market-led, 45
development economics, 6–9, 58
development publications, 1–2, 1n
development technology, progress
variations, 90
disability-adjusted life year (DALY), 48n
disease, 48n, 101
doing business, 40, 41n, 61–62
domestic savings, 9, 23n
donors, recipient selectivity, 80–81

E
East Asia
institution impacts, 59–60
policies leading to "miracle"
performance, 73–74
support of unprofitable industries, 74n
tiger economies, 27–28, 28n
econometric bias, reducing, 86–87
economic depression, 3, 3n
economic engineering, microlevel, 29
economic focus, macro to micro, 45,
45n–46n
economic goals of new countries, 5–6
economic health, measured by GDP, 21n
economic power and politics, 102–104
economic slowdown, 13–15
economic stimulation, 8n
economics, integration with social and
other disciplines, 103–104
economy, 15n, 25, 65n
climate change, 95–96
history of, 89–90
education, 37, 38
social returns to, 63, 64n, 65n
student and teacher absenteeism,
36n–37n
energy demand, meeting, 54
energy requirements due to urban
expansion, 98–99, 98n

environment, impacts of development,
41–44
ethnic conflict, 15n
exchange rate flexibility, 27n
Expanded Program on Immunization, 78n

F
Fabian socialism, 5n
failure, recognizing, 81
farming, sky, 97–98
financial crises of 2007–8, 12n, 70n,
71, 71n
financial innovations, 12n
financial institutions, government
involvement, 55
financial mismanagement, 26
financial reform, 27
financial repression policies, 69
financial sector, contribution to growth, 31n
financing gaps, 30–31
firms, barriers to entry, 40
fiscal health, 33
food prices, 43
foreign direct investment (FDI), 68f, 68t
free trade, 27–28
freight rates, 53n

G
general equilibrium models, stochastic, 12n
global integration, 3n–4n, 32
global power structure change, 103n
global warming. *See* climate change
governance, 40n, 58n, 69, 92
government, 33n, 39, 103n
financial mismanagement, 26
interventions and failure, 57n
market regulation, 71–72
role of, 32–34, 72–74, 92
shrinking of, 85–86
spending effects on growth, 55
Great Depression, 3, 3n
Great Divergence, 5n
Great Spurt, 8
green technology, 99
gross domestic product (GDP), as a
measure of economic well-being, 21n

growth, 56n, 59n, 65
    aid effectiveness, 82–83, 82n, 84
    and policy making, 48
    capital investment minimum
        requirement, 85
    competition to increase, 38
    countries catching up, 10
    democracy and other constraining
        factors, 55n
    due to natural resource–based products,
        68
    early links to agriculture sector, 19
    education, 64n
    ethnic conflicts, 15n
    financial sector effects, 31n
    foundations to increase speed of, 74
    golden age of industrialization, 12
    government spending, 55
    human capital as determinant, 23n
    in fastest-growing economies, 53
    in the 1970s, 13–15
    in the 1990s, 29
    increased trade, 70n
    inequality, 75
    lack of policy effect, 90, 92
    lack of understanding for poorness
        of, 52
    leadership, 92
    link to investment rates, 53n
    physical capital important source of,
        66–67
    policy reform, 59
    poverty reduction, 78–79
    pro-poor strategies, 35–36
    resource transfers, 80
    social policy support, 76
    stimulation through Big Push, 8
    sustaining, 56–59, 92
    TFP main driver, 56
    United States and Korea, 91f
growth economics, 52n, 63
growth rates, 10f, 14f, 85t
    by country, 11f, 13f
    China and India, 59
growth spells, pro-poor determination,
    78n

H
Harrod-Domar model, 7
health, 64n, 78, 101n
    intervention savings, 48n
    of children, 78n
heatwaves, 95n
heavily indebted poor countries initiative,
    82n
herding, 83
household data, 75
human capital, 7n, 36, 85
    and knowledge development, 63–65
    growth determinant, 23n
    poverty reduction efforts, 76
Human Development Index, 75
Human Development Report, 22n

I
I-O models, 11, 11n
immunization, 78n
import-substituting industrialization (ISI),
    25n
income distribution, 39
independence, 4
India, 4n, 5, 5n, 42n
    growth rate, 59, 85t
industrialization, 5n, 6, 66, 74n
    as a development approach, 9n
    golden age, 12
    growth rates by country, 13f
    policies, 73
industry, support of nonprofitable, 74n
inequality, 75, 86
inflation, 27n
information technology (IT) services
    growth, 65
infrastructure, 54, 102n
    and urban sprawl, 98–99
innovation, 43, 95
institutions, 32–34, 58n
    aid effectiveness, 82
    creating and roles of, 60–62
    efficiency to speed growth, 74
    fostering privatization, 26n
    markets, 39
    sustaining growth, 56–59

international integration, 32
Internet, and vulnerability of, 102n
investment, 54, 62
investment climate, 54–55
    assessment, 40
    research, 40n–41n
    surveys and variables, 41n
investment rate, 53n, 67n, 85t

J
judicial access, 58n

K
knowledge, 63–65, 85
    and productivity gap, 63n
    transfer, 83
    using, 94–95
Korea, 28n, 74n, 91f

L
Laffer curve, 26n
land distribution, by country, 43t
Latin America, 6n, 9n, 25n, 59
leadership impacts on growth, 92
Living Standards Measurement Study, 21n
local participation experiment, 42n
logistics costs, 53n
Los Angeles, California, 98n

M
manufacturing sector, 8, 65n
market economy, shifting to, 25, 45, 72
market logic, 60
markets, 28, 30, 39
    and validation of capitalism, 32
    efficiency of, 25n
    growth and government role, 33
    regulation and monitoring, 71–72
Mekong Delta, 100n
microeconomic engineering, 29
microeconomic focus, 45, 45n–46n
migration, 100
modeling, relevance of, 12
models, stochastic general equilibrium, 12n
monitoring, 77

N
natural resource balances, 67–69
natural resources, cause of instability, 15n
Nehru, Jawaharlal, 5n
New Deal, 3n
night watchman state, 33n
nongovernmental organizations (NGOs),
    83n

O
official development assistance (ODA), 79,
    80–81, 83–84

P
per capita income, 21n
physical capital, 23n, 66–67, 66n
policy logic, 60
policy making, 47–48, 93–94
    and institutions, 58
    financial repression, 69
    inefficient, 55n
    influence of aid, 82
    lack of effect for developing countries,
        90, 92
    progress, 87
    shifting away from industrialization, 73
    strategies, 51–53
politics, 102–104, 104n
poor, people and defining levels of, 79, 79n
population growth, slowing, 23, 23n
poverty, 15, 38, 79
    aid effectiveness, 81–82
    raising awareness of, 84–85
poverty reduction, 75–79, 84–85, 97n
    and policy making, 48
    migration, 100
    moving away from trickle down
        approach, 21–23
    ODA, 79
    prime development objective, 20–21
    pro-poor growth strategies, 35–36
    progress, 77
    rural efforts, 19
    social capital to accelerate, 38
power structure, changing of, 103n

prices, commodities and food, 97n
private sector involvement, 35
privatization, 25, 26, 72n
  and denationalization, 72
  importance of institutional environment,
    26n
  problems with, 73
  pros and cons, 69
pro-poor development strategy, 76
pro-poor growth spells, 78n
pro-poor strategies, 51, 76
product discovery, 57n
productivity gap due to knowledge
    development, 63n
productivity, services, 65
progress, frustration with, 24n
property rights, 59n
protectionism, 6, 6n, 28n
public health services, 78
public sector reform, 26, 82n

R
random experimentation, 87n
regulation, markets, 39
regulatory organizations, 58n
resource imbalances, 26, 67–69
resource transfers, 80

S
safety nets, 77, 78
savings, domestic, 9, 23n
service delivery, 36, 38–39
  local participation, 42n
  to complement human capital, 85
services sector, productivity growth, 65
services, financing of, 38
shocks, 30, 101–102
simulation, relevance of, 12
sky farming, 97–98
social accounting, 11n
social capital, 38
social policy, to support growth, 76
social returns to education, 63, 64n, 65n
social turbulence, 101n
socialism, Fabian, 5n

societal development, 100–102
South Asia, 68f, 68t, 85t
stabilization policies, 29
state. *See* government
structural adjustment, 24, 28–29, 28n, 30
student absenteeism, 36n–37n
Sub-Saharan Africa, 68f, 68n, 68t

T
take-off events, 83n
tax reform, 26
teacher absenteeism, 36n–37n
teacher quality, 37
technology, 83, 90, 94, 97n
total factor productivity (TFP), 56, 63, 85
trade, 6, 6n, 27n, 67
  liberalization, 27–28, 70, 70n
transaction costs, 53n, 62
two-gap model, 9, 9n

U
United States, 71n, 79n, 91f
urbanization, 47, 98, 100
user charges, 38

W
Washington Consensus, 32, 69
water scarcity, 96–97, 96n
weather, 95n, 102n
white elephant, 12n
World Bank, 16–17, 17n, 96, 104
  absence of discussion on politics, 103,
    104n
  capital and knowledge transfer
    assistance, 83
  development areas of interest, 44–47
  poverty awareness and elimination,
    84–85
  poverty data to raise awareness and
    focus, 21
  poverty elimination and measuring, 75
  privatization, 72
  public perception of and protesters, 34
  recipient selectivity, 80–81
  recognition of failure, 81

shift from macro- to microeconomic
    concerns, 24
World Development Indicators, 46
World Development Reports (WDRs), 1,
    16, 42
  audience for, 93–94
  citations per year, 48n
  comparison of issues, 46
  contents and innovations of, 20–21

evolution of, 18, 44–47
government role in development, 32–34
policy scorecard, 84–87
poverty, 31, 38
validity of, 47–48, 80
World War II recovery, 3

Y
youth needs, 37, 64n